The Benedictine Handbook

The
Benedictine Handbook

CANTERBURY
PRESS
Norwich

© the Contributors 2003

The Rule of St Benedict © Ampleforth Abbey Trustees 1997

First published in 2003 by the Canterbury Press Norwich
(a publishing imprint of Hymns Ancient & Modern Limited,
a registered charity)
St Mary's Works, St Mary's Plain,
Norwich, Norfolk, NR3 3BH

Third impression 2005

www.scm-canterburypress.co.uk

British Library Cataloguing in Publication Data

A catalogue record for this book is available
from the British Library

ISBN 1-85311-499-5

Typeset by Rowland Phototypesetting Ltd,
Bury St Edmunds, Suffolk
Printed and bound in Great Britain by
William Clowes Ltd, Beccles, Suffolk

Contents

Contents

Part Four: Living The Rule

Part Five: The Benedictine Family

Part Six: A Glossary of Benedictine Terms

Introduction

When St Benedict of Nursia put down his pen some time in the sixth century, he had completed one of the most remarkable and long-lasting achievements of his and any other century. Since his time, there have been men and women committed to the search for God that he describes, a search that has always been shared with oblates, friends, pilgrims and visitors who have come to Benedict's monasteries since the beginning. This handbook is one expression of that ongoing sharing.

Most people coming to a monastery for the first time have one question at the back of their minds: 'What do you, the monks or nuns, actually do?' This is not a bad question with which to approach the heart of the Benedictine life – let me give an example.

In 1309, two rather dishevelled monks were summoned to answer exactly this question. It was not, at the beginning, a friendly encounter.

On the one side were three busy officials of the King of England, Edward I. They had been sent to the last remaining fragments of the King's regions in France, and specifically to the island of Jersey, to enquire into the state of Royal property. Facing them were two monks, by birth loyal to the King of France, by monastic vow attached to a Norman monastery and by chance of appointment abandoned on a remote outcrop of rock between Jersey and the Cherbourg peninsula. Their rock was truly tiny – at high tide little more than a break in the waves – but the King of England was nevertheless interested in who owned it, and, more particularly, in what its only two residents did. Their answer is recorded in the plain style of a legal document:

> 'He who is called Prior and his companion . . . dwelling in the chapel throughout the whole year maintain a light burning in that chapel so that the sailors crossing the sea by that light may avoid the peril of the reef . . . where the greatest danger exists of being wrecked. These two always perform the divine office.'

To me, this simple answer reveals much about the nature of the Benedictine vocation. In so many different ways throughout its history, and in so many different places throughout the world today, Benedictine women and men have engaged in precisely that same task of bearing a light that shines not for their own glory but for the good of the church and the world. So the aim of this Benedictine handbook is very simple – to be a support to those many people who come into contact with monasteries today and who want to deepen their experience of the monastic way in their own lives. You may live under the shadow of some mighty monastery, or you may be a visitor who has always wondered whether such places still exist. You may be an oblate or supporter of a new foundation, or you may live a long way from a monastery such that you want to take a part of it with you. If you belong to any one of these groups, then this handbook is for you.

Our aim is to create a lifelong companion for you, the friends of monasteries, you want to seek God with the sons and daughters of St Benedict. This handbook is not written for monks and nuns themselves, but rather for those who belong, in whatever sense, to the wider family of the Benedictines. It is not meant to be read all at once – we hope that you will dip in and out of it, sometimes for information but more often for support in prayer and for deepening your own sense of belonging.

The handbook starts, in Part One, with Benedict's own Rule, the foundation charter for the ongoing experience of monasticism in the Latin churches. Though enriched over the centuries by commentaries and interpretations of every sort, the Rule must always stand alone, for it is to St Benedict's timeless wisdom that all those who take his name must return. It is the basis for everything else that follows, and all the later sections will, we hope, lead you back to Benedict, and through him to the Gospel of Christ which is Benedict's inspiration. It is a short document, and a mixture of the spiritual and the practical, just as our lives are called to become.

Part Two explores the tools of monastic life, the particular activities which shape the son or daughter of St Benedict and his or her relation to the world.

From these tools, in Part Three we go on to explore their goal, which Benedict describes in his Prologue in these words:

'Let us open our eyes to the light that comes from God and our ears to the voice that every day calls out.'

In this part, you will find a simple structure of daily prayer, which might be of value to anyone who wishes to share in an uncomplicated way in the rhythm of monastic prayer. This is followed by brief explorations of other aspects of holiness, the treasury of Benedictine prayers, the lives of some of Benedict's disciples and the tradition of Benedictine holy places.

It is the breadth of the Benedictine search for God that takes us forward to Part Four of the handbook, which focuses on living the Rule. We look at life in community, then in solitude, and then in the life of oblates. Finally, we examine what it might mean to live the Benedictine life in the world.

Part Five focuses on the Benedictine family throughout the world, both past and present. This part, along with Part Six, a glossary of Benedictine terms, might enable you to understand more of why particular monasteries live the way they do, and of how so many different interpretations of Benedict's words are, each in their own way, faithful to his vision.

Wherever you are within the Benedictine world, it is the aim of this handbook that you might feel that you belong there. It is the prayer of all of those who have been involved with this handbook that, with its help, you may continue 'to prefer nothing whatever to Christ'.

Fr Anthony Marett-Crosby OSB
Ampleforth Abbey

About the Contributors

Robert Atwell is an Anglican priest working in the Diocese of London. After six years as Chaplain of Trinity College, Cambridge, where he taught Patristics, he became a Benedictine monk, spending the next ten years in a monastery in the Cotswolds. He is currently Vicar of St Mary's, Primrose Hill, in north London. His collections of daily spiritual readings, *Celebrating the Saints* and *Celebrating the Seasons*, are published by the Canterbury Press.

Patrick Barry OSB was born in England in 1917. He became a monk of Ampleforth Abbey in 1936 and was ordained priest in 1945. He was Headmaster of Ampleforth College for fifteen years and Abbot of the Abbey from 1984 to 1997.

Maria Boulding OSB is a nun of Stanbrook Abbey, Worcestershire. She is the author of the spiritual classic *The Coming of God*. published by the CP.

Michael Casey OCSO is a monk of Tarrawarra Abbey, Australia. He is involved in the formation of his own community and other monastic communities internationally. He is the author of several books on monastic spirituality.

Demetrius R. Dumm OSB is a monk of St Vincent Archabbey, Latrobe, Pennsylvania, a professor of the New Testament in St Vincent Seminary, and the author of several books, including *Cherish Christ Above All: The Bible in the Rule of St Benedict.*

Mary Forman OSB is a member of the Monastery of St Gertrude, Cottonwood, Idaho. She teaches monastic studies at the School of Theology Seminary, St John's University, Collegeville, Minnesota.

Kym Harris OSB is a nun of the Monastery of Transfiguration at Yeppoon in Central Queensland, Australia. She has worked in various areas in her monastic life, primarily in crafts like pottery, leather work and candle decoration. She was editor of *Tjurunga: The Australasian Benedictine Review* for five years. In 1996 she received a Master's Degree from the Melbourne College of Divinity for a thesis on the spirituality of the medieval monastic women. She is a keen gardener.

Terrence Kardong OSB is a monk of Assumption Abbey, Richardton, North Dakota, and the editor of *The American Benedictine Review*.

Nivard Kinsella OCSO was born in Dublin, Ireland. On leaving school, he entered Mount St Joseph Abbey, Rosciea, County Tipperary. He spent a couple of years on the foundation of Tarrawarra Abbey in Australia. Later he studied in Rome, taking an STD at the Angelicum University. He has held various offices in the Community of Rosciea and is now Guestmaster.

Dwight Longenecker grew up in America, moving to England in the early 1980s, where he studied theology and was ordained an Anglican priest. With his family he was received into the Catholic Church in 1995. He now works as a freelance writer, broadcaster and lecturer on Benedictine and Thérèsian spirituality. His books include *Listen My Son – St Benedict For Fathers* and *St Benedict and St Thérèse – The Little Rule and the Little Way*.

Anthony Marett-Crosby OSB was educated at University College, Oxford, where he read history. He became a Benedictine monk in 1990 and was solemnly professed at Ampleforth Abbey,

North Yorkshire, in 1995. From 1994–98 he read theology at Oxford and gained his doctorate in 2000. He is the author of several books on monastic spirituality and history.

Oswald McBride OSB is a monk of Ampleforth Abbey. He trained in anatomy and medicine at Edinburgh, graduating in 1990. Having worked as a doctor, he joined the Ampleforth community in 1991, pursuing further studies in theology at Oxford and in liturgy at the Pontifical Liturgical Institute, S. Anselmo, Rome. Ordained priest in 1999, he is at present Director of Liturgy at Ampleforth.

Laurence McTaggart grew up in Nottingham where his parents were doctors. In 1991 he became a monk of Ampleforth Abbey where he enjoys teaching in the monastic school, giving retreats, playing the organ and picking apples.

Dominic Milroy OSB is a monk of Ampleforth Abbey. After studying modern languages at Oxford, he taught at Ampleforth for a number of years and was a housemaster. For five years he was Prior of the International Benedictine College at S. Anselmo in Rome, after which he became Headmaster of Ampleforth College.

Jill Maria Murdy of West Bend, Wisconsin, is experienced in monastic spirituality and pastoral ministry.

Kathleen Norris is the author of four memoirs, *Dakota: A Spiritual Geography*, *The Cloister Walk*, *Amazing Grace: A Vocabulary of Faith*, and *The Virgin of Bennington*, and several volumes of poetry. She has been an oblate of Assumption Abbey, Richardton, North Dakota, since 1986.

Colmán Ó Clabaigh OSB is a monk of Glenstal Abbey in Ireland. A medieval historian, he is also monastery librarian.

Joel Rippinger OSB is a monk of Marmion Abbey, Aurora,

Illinois, where he serves as formation director, instructor at Marmion Academy, and the abbey archivist.

Columba Stewart OSB teaches monastic history and spirituality at St John's University, Collegeville, Minnesota, and has served as formation director at St John's Abbey.

Richard Yeo OSB is Abbot of Downside and Abbot President of the English Benedictine Congregation. Born in 1948, he became a monk of Downside in 1970. Studies in Rome included work on the structure and content of the monastic profession. Before becoming Abbot, he worked in the Vatican office dealing with religious orders.

Esther de Waal is the author of a number of classic texts on Benedictine spirituality including *Seeking God: The Way of St Benedict* and *Living with Contradiction: Reflections on the Rule of St Benedict*. She has also written many books on Celtic spirituality. A very popular speaker and retreat guide, she lives near Hereford.

Part One

Saint Benedict's Rule

A Short Introduction

It may seem extravagant today to suggest that not only monks and nuns but also ordinary laymen and laywomen of the twenty-first century can learn something invaluable about themselves and about how to live their lives on this earth by reading what St Benedict wrote in the sixth century and by taking it to heart. Yet in considering that strange proposition we might start by looking at the actual use of the Rule throughout the ages, and reflecting that it has been alive and active through all the centuries that have elapsed since it was written. During all that time it has provided spiritual inspiration to countless monks and nuns in their desire to dedicate their whole being to God. During all that time it has also stretched out beyond the walls of the monasteries. It has given spiritual inspiration and encouragement to many of the laity who have been associated as oblates with Benedictine abbeys throughout the world. And now in this present age it has gone even further than that.

Since the Second Vatican Council the Rule has acquired a new lease of life among the laity. There have been young lay movements in the Church that have adopted St Benedict's Rule to provide them with structure and guidance in their way of life. There have been lay groups at parochial and national level who have found in it much of the spiritual inspiration that they seek in their desire to lead lay lives in more faithful service of Christ and of their fellow men and women. There have been groups in other Churches, Anglican, Episcopalian, Protestant, who have recognized in the Rule a seminal document from the days before the schisms and sad divisions of Christianity and find in it a source of spirituality untainted by the rancour of division. There are Buddhists in open, peaceful dialogue with Christianity who have found in the Rule of St Benedict echoes, affirmations and analogies which correspond with something in their own search for self-understanding, for community, for harmony and for ultimate meaning in their journey of life. All this evidence of a new life for the Rule among the laity is no dream but solid fact of what has actually already happened. It raises the deep and interesting question about what it is in the Rule that can span the centuries in this way and still provide spiritual inspiration for the future.

The Rule was written by St Benedict for his monks to guide them in their search for God through their life of dedication. Whatever the sources and influences that went into its creation, it has a simplicity and directness of appeal which is still power-ful. It is without pretension and is written in the rough, common Latin of the time, which is far from the polished sonority of classical Latin but which has a deeply attractive rhythm of its own. St Benedict had an ear for the music of words. He also had an insight into the hearts of human beings in their search for self-knowledge and truth and meaning in life. There are parts of the Rule which are simply regulations, so necessary to make community life harmonious and possible. There are parts which are disciplinary, which are there – in Benedict's own words – because they are 'demanded reasonably for the correction of vice and the preservation of love'.[1] Yet, even when he is dealing with the control of real wickedness, it is never stern regulations that matter to him but the ultimate supremacy of prayer and love. Thus he recommends that, when all other means have failed to correct wrongdoing, the abbot should turn to some-thing 'which is still more powerful' than any disciplinary measures, 'namely the personal prayer of the superior and of all the community that the Lord, who can do all things, may himself bring healing to the delinquent'.[2]

The real heart of the Rule, however, and the power which has kept it alive and relevant to Christian life today is not the regulations and practical directions for community living, valuable though they are. The heart of the Rule is in the chapters of spiritual guidance which are so full of the timeless wisdom of scripture. Outstanding among these are the Prologue, Chapter 4 on guidelines for Christian living, Chapter 7 on humility, the chapters of guidance for the abbot in the exercise of authority and Chapter 72, which in a few short sentences summarizes the whole spirit of the Rule. In these chapters and in many other passages which could be quoted, St Benedict writes as though speaking in intimate dialogue with a young aspirant who is seeking his advice. His manner, and his very words, are couched in this vein so that he seems even to be offering himself more as a spiritual companion than as a masterful leader in the journey of life. He achieves this through reflections of great depth on our relationships with our creator, our redeemer, on our use of the world we live in, on our interaction with each other, on our considered assessment of ourselves and our place in the universe, on freedom from vice and egomania, on our search for a peace and a fulfilment which is free from arrogance, greed, anger and all that disturbs the inner tranquility of 'that love of God which in its fullness casts out all fear'.[3]

There is one other point to be made and it is perhaps the most important of all. St Benedict does not speak on his own authority. He is personally formed on the word of God in scripture and his language is shot through with scriptural phrases and concepts. Even when he is not actually quoting scripture there is usually a scriptural echo in his words. The whole power of the Rule, then, comes from the word of scripture and that is what makes its message timeless, participating, as it does, in the richness of the word of scripture which is ever old and ever new.

A Note on the Text

In the Latin text of the Rule the sentences in each chapter have been numbered. This may sometimes be a help to scholarly study. This translation, however, is intended to be read holistically as an experience of sacred reading which is close to prayer or meditation. References can nevertheless be made to it by chapter and paragraph. Where references to the text have been made in this book they have followed that pattern.

Patrick Barry OSB

Notes

1 See Prologue, last paragraph.
2 See Chapter 28.
3 See Chapter 7, last paragraph.

Saint Benedict's Rule

A New Translation for Today

Patrick Barry OSB

CONTENTS

Prologue to The Rule

LISTEN, CHILD OF GOD, TO THE GUIDANCE OF YOUR
teacher. Attend to the message you hear and make sure that
it pierces to your heart, so that you may accept with willing
freedom and fulfil by the way you live the directions that
come from your loving Father. It is not easy to accept and
persevere in obedience, but it is the way to return to Christ,
when you have strayed through the laxity and carelessness
of disobedience. My words are addressed to you especially,
whoever you may be, whatever your circumstances, who
turn from the pursuit of your own self-will and ask to
enlist under Christ, who is Lord of all, by following him
through taking to yourself that strong and blessed armour
of obedience which he made his own on coming into our
world.

This, then, is the beginning of my advice: make prayer the
first step in anything worthwhile that you attempt.
Persevere and do not weaken in that prayer. Pray with
confidence, because God, in his love and forgiveness, has
counted us as his own sons and daughters. Surely we
should not by our evil acts heartlessly reject that love.
At every moment of our lives, as we use the good things
he has given us, we can respond to his love only by
seeking to obey his will for us. If we should refuse, what
wonder to find ourselves disinherited! What wonder if he,
confronted and repelled by the evil in us, should abandon
us like malicious and rebellious subjects to the never-

ending pain of separation since we refused to follow Him to glory.

However late, then, it may seem, let us rouse ourselves from lethargy. That is what scripture urges on us when it says: the time has come for us to rouse ourselves from sleep.[1] Let us open our eyes to the light that can change us into the likeness of God. Let our ears be alert to the stirring call of his voice crying to us every day: today, if you should hear his voice, do not harden your hearts.[2] And again: let anyone with ears to hear listen to what the Spirit says to the churches.[3] And this is what the Spirit says: Come my children, hear me, and I shall teach you the fear of the Lord.[4] Run, while you have the light of life, before the darkness of death overtakes you.[5]

It is to find workers in his cause that God calls out like that to all peoples. He calls to us in another way in the psalm when he says: Who is there with a love of true life and a longing for days of real fulfilment?[6] If you should hear that call and answer: 'I', this is the answer you will receive from God: If you wish to have that true life that lasts for ever, then keep your tongue from evil; let your lips speak no deceit; turn away from wrongdoing; seek out peace and pursue it.[7] If you do that, he says, I shall look on you with such love and my ears will be so alert to your prayer that, before you so much as call on me, I shall say to you: here I am.[8] What gentler encouragement could we have, my dear brothers and sisters, than that word from the Lord calling us to himself in such a way! We can see with what loving concern the Lord points out to us the path of life.

And so to prepare ourselves for the journey before us let us renew our faith and set ourselves high standards by which to lead our lives. The gospel should be our guide in following the way of Christ to prepare ourselves for his presence in the kingdom to which he has called us. If we want to make our lasting home in his holy kingdom, the only way is to set aright the course of our lives in doing what is good. We should make our own the psalmist's question: Lord, who will dwell in your kingdom or who will find rest on your holy mountain?[9] In reply we may hear from the same psalmist the Lord's answer to show us the way that leads to his kingdom: anyone who leads a life without guile, who does what is right, who speaks truth from the heart, on whose tongue there is no deceit, who never harms a neighbour nor believes evil reports about another,[10] who at once rejects outright from the heart the devil's temptations to sin, destroying them utterly at the first onset by casting them before Christ himself.[11] Such a follower of Christ lives in reverence of him and does not take the credit for a good life but, believing that all the good we do comes from the Lord, gives him the credit and thanksgiving for what his gift brings about in our hearts. In that spirit our prayer from the psalm should be: not to us, O Lord, not to us give the glory but to your own name.[12] That is St Paul's example, for he took no credit to himself for his preaching when he said: it is by God's grace that I am what I am.[13] And again he says: Let anyone who wants to boast, boast in the Lord.[14]

The Lord himself in the gospel teaches us the same when he says: I shall liken anyone who hears my words and carries them out in deed to one who is wise enough to build on a rock; then the floods came and the winds blew and struck that house, but it did not fall because it was built on a rock.[15] It is in the light of that teaching that the Lord waits for us every day to see if we will respond by our deeds, as we should, to his holy guidance. For that very reason also, so that we may mend our evil ways, the days of our mortal lives are allowed us as a sort of truce for improvement. So St Paul says: Do you not know that God is patient with us so as to lead us to repentance?[16] The Lord himself says in

his gentle care for us: I do not want the death of a sinner;
let all sinners rather turn away from sin and live.[17]

Well then, brothers and sisters, we have questioned the Lord
about who can dwell with him in his holy place and we
have heard the demands he makes on such a one; we can
be united with him there, only if we fulfil those demands.
We must, therefore, prepare our hearts and bodies to serve
him under the guidance of holy obedience. Conscious in
this undertaking of our own weakness let us ask the Lord
to give us through his grace the help we need. If we want
to avoid the pain of self-destruction in hell and come to
eternal life, then, while we still have the time in this mortal
life and the opportunity to fulfil what God asks of us
through a life guided by his light, we must hurry forward
and act in a way that will bring us blessings in eternal life.

With all this in mind what we mean to establish is a school
for the Lord's service. In the guidance we lay down to achieve
this we hope to impose nothing harsh or burdensome. If,
however, you find in it anything which seems rather strict,
but which is demanded reasonably for the correction of vice
or the preservation of love, do not let that frighten you into
fleeing from the way of salvation; it is a way which is bound
to seem narrow to start with. But, as we progress in this
monastic way of life and in faith, our hearts will warm to its
vision and with eager love and delight that defies expression
we shall go forward on the way of God's commandments.
Then we shall never think of deserting his guidance; we shall
persevere in fidelity to his teaching in the monastery until
death so that through our patience we may be granted some
part in Christ's own passion and thus in the end receive a
share in his kingdom. Amen.

CHAPTER 1

Four approaches to monastic life

WE CAN ALL RECOGNIZE THE DISTINCTION BETWEEN the four different kinds of monk. First of all there are the cenobites. These are the ones who are based in a monastery and fulfil their service of the Lord under a rule and an abbot or abbess.

Anchorites, who are also known as hermits, are the second kind. Their vocation is not the result of the first fervour so often experienced by those who give themselves to a monastic way of life. On the contrary they have learnt well from everyday experience with the support of many others in a community how to fight against the devil. Thus they are well trained in the ranks of their brothers or sisters before they have the confidence to do without that support and venture into single combat in the desert relying only on their own arms and the help of God in their battle against the evil temptations of body and mind.

Sarabaites are the third kind of monk and the example they give of monasticism is appalling. They have been through no period of trial under a rule with the experienced guidance of a teacher, which might have proved them as gold is proved in a furnace. On the contrary they are as malleable as lead and their standards are still those of the secular world, so that it is clear to everyone that their tonsure is a lie before God himself. They go around in twos or threes, or even singly, resting in sheepfolds which are not those of the Lord, but which they make to suit themselves. For a rule of life they have only the satisfaction of their own desires. Any precept they think up for themselves and then decide to adopt they do not hesitate to call holy. Anything they dislike they consider inadmissible.

Finally those called gyrovagues are the fourth kind of monk. They spend their whole life going round one province after another enjoying the hospitality for three or four days at a time at any sort of monastic cell or community. They are always on the move; they never settle to put down the roots of stability; it is their own wills that they serve as they seek the satisfaction of their own gross appetites. They are in every way worse than the sarabaites.

About the wretched way of life that all these so-called monks pursue it is better to keep silence than to speak. Let us leave them to themselves and turn to the strongest kind, the cenobites, so that with the Lord's help we may consider the regulation of their way of life.

‹‹‹

CHAPTER 2

Gifts needed by an abbot or abbess

ANYONE WHO ASPIRES AS ABBOT OR ABBESS TO BE superior of a monastery should always remember what is really meant by the title and fulfil in their monastic life all that is required in one holding the office of monastic superior. For it is the place of Christ that the superior is understood to hold in the monastery by having a name which belongs to Christ, as St Paul suggests when he writes: You have received the spirit of adopted children whereby we cry *abba*, Father.[1] That means that the abbot or abbess should never teach anything nor make any arrangement nor give any order which is against the teaching of the Lord. Far from it, everything he or she commands or teaches should be like a leaven of the holiness that comes from God infused into the minds of their disciples. In fact they should remember that they will have to account in the awesome judgement of God both for their own teaching and also for the obedience of their disciples. They should be well aware that the shepherd will have to bear the blame for any deficiency that God, as the Father of the whole human family, finds in his sheep. However, it is also true that, if the flock has been unruly and disobedient and the superiors have done everything possible as shepherds to cure their vicious ways, then they will be absolved in the judgement of God and may say with the psalmist: I have not hidden your teaching in my heart; I have proclaimed your truth and the salvation you offer, but they despised and rejected me.[2]

Any, then, who accept the name of abbot or abbess should give a lead to their disciples by two distinct methods of teaching – by the example of the lives they lead (and that is the most important way) and by the words they use in their teaching. To disciples who can understand they may teach the way of the Lord with words; but to the less receptive and uneducated they should teach what the Lord commands us by example. Of course, whenever they teach a disciple that something is wrong they should themselves show by the practical example they give that it must not be done. If they fail in this they themselves, although they have preached well to others, may be rejected and God may respond to their sinfulness by saying: Why do you repeat my teaching and take the words of my covenant on your lips, while you yourself have rejected my guidance and cast my words away?[3] And again: You noticed the speck of dust in your brother's eye but failed to see the beam in your own.[4]

They should not select for special treatment any individual
in the monastery. They should not love one more than
another unless it is for good observance of the Rule and
obedience. One who is free-born should not, for that
reason, be advanced before one coming to monastic life
from a condition of slavery, unless there is some other good
reason for it. If such a reason is seen by the abbot or
abbess to be justified they can decide on a change for any
member of the community. Otherwise all must keep their
proper place in the community order, because whether slave
or free we are all one in Christ and we owe an equal service in
the army of one Lord, who shows no special favour to one
rather than another.[5] The only grounds on which in Christ's
eyes one is to be preferred to another is by excelling in good
works and humility. The abbot or abbess, then, should show
equal love to all and apply the same standards of discipline to
all according to what they deserve.

They should make their own the different ways of teaching
which the Apostle Paul recommended to Timothy when he
told him to make use of criticism, of entreaty and of
rebuke.[6] Thus in adapting to changing circumstances they
should use now the encouragement of a loving parent and
now the threats of a harsh disciplinarian. This means that
they should criticize more sternly those who are
undisciplined and unruly; they should entreat those who are
obedient, docile and patient so as to encourage their
progress; but they should rebuke and punish those who
take a feckless attitude or show contempt for what they are
taught.

A monastic superior should never show tolerance of
wrongdoing, but as soon as it begins to grow should
root it out completely to avoid the dangerous error of Eli,
the priest of Shiloh.[7] Any who are reliable and able to
understand should be admonished by words on the first
and second occasion; but those who are defiant and

resistant in the pride of their disobedience will need to be corrected by corporal punishment at the very beginning of their evil course. It should be remembered that scripture says: a fool cannot be corrected by words alone;[8] and again: strike your child with a rod whose soul will by this means be saved from death.[9]

Reflection on their own high status in the monastery and the meaning of their title should be ever present to the abbot or abbess. This will make them aware of what is meant by the saying that more is demanded of those to whom more is entrusted.[10] They should reflect on what a difficult and demanding task they have accepted, namely that of guiding souls and serving the needs of so many different characters; gentle encouragement will be needed for one, strong rebukes for another, rational persuasion for another, according to the character and intelligence of each. It is the task of the superiors to adapt with sympathetic understanding to the needs of each so that they may not only avoid any loss but even have the joy of increasing the number of good sheep in the flock committed to them.

It is above all important that monastic superiors should not underrate or think lightly of the salvation of the souls committed to them by giving too much attention to transient affairs of this world which have no lasting value. They should remember always that the responsibility they have undertaken is that of guiding souls and that they will have to render an account of the guidance they have given. If resources are slender for the monastery they should remember this saying from scripture: seek first the kingdom of God and his righteousness and all these things will be given to you also;[11] then also there is the text: nothing is lacking for those who fear him.[12]

It should be very clear to superiors that all who undertake the guidance of souls must in the end prepare themselves to give an account of that guidance. However many the souls for whom they are responsible all superiors may be sure that they will be called to account before the Lord for each one of them and after that for their own souls as well. Frequent reverent reflection on that future reckoning before the Good Shepherd who has committed his sheep to them will, through their concern for others, inspire them to greater care of their own souls. By encouraging through their faithful ministry better standards for those in their care, they will develop higher ideals in their own lives as well.

⁂

CHAPTER 3

Calling the community together for consultation

WHEN ANY BUSINESS OF IMPORTANCE IS TO BE considered in the monastery, the abbot or abbess should summon the whole community together and personally explain to them the agenda that lies before them. After hearing the advice of the community, the superior should consider it carefully in private and only then make a judgement about what is the best decision. We have insisted that all the community should be summoned for such consultation, because it often happens that the Lord makes the best course clear to one of the youngest. The community themselves should be careful to offer their advice with due deference and respect, avoiding an obstinate defence of their own convictions. It is for the abbot or abbess in the end to make the decision and everyone else should obey what the superior judges to be best. To get the balance right it should be remembered that, whereas it is right for subordinates to obey their superior, it is just as important for the superior to be far-sighted and fair in administration.

Such an ideal can be achieved only if everyone duly conforms to the authority of the Rule and no one gives way to self-will by deviating from it. In a monastery no one should follow the prompting of what are merely personal desires nor should any monk or nun take it on themselves to oppose the abbot or abbess defiantly, especially in a public forum outside the monastery. Anyone who is rash enough to act in such a way should be disciplined in accordance with the Rule. However the superior should in everything personally keep the fear of God clearly in view and take care to act in accordance with the requirements of the Rule, while also remembering the future account of all such decisions to be rendered before the supremely just tribunal of the Lord.

What has been said about consultation so far, applies to matters of weight and importance. When questions of lesser concern arise in the monastery and call for a decision, the abbot or abbess should consult with seniors alone. Such is the appropriate way to conform to that precept of scripture: If you act always after hearing the counsel of others, you will avoid the need to repent of your decision afterwards.[1]

CHAPTER 4

Guidelines for Christian and monastic good practice

THE FIRST OF ALL THINGS TO AIM AT IS TO LOVE THE
Lord God with your whole heart and soul and strength and
then to love your neighbour as much as you do yourself.
The other commandments flow from these two: not to kill,
not to commit adultery, not to steal, not to indulge our
base desires, not to give false evidence against another, to
give due honour to all and not to inflict on someone else
what you would resent if it were done to yourself.

Renounce your own desires and ambitions so as to be free to
follow Christ. Control your body with self-discipline; don't
give yourself to unrestrained pleasure; learn to value the
self-restraint of fasting. Give help and support to the poor;
clothe the naked, visit the sick and bury the dead. Console
and counsel those who suffer in time of grief and bring
comfort to those in sorrow.

Don't get too involved in purely worldly affairs and count
nothing more important than the love you should cherish
for Christ. Don't let your actions be governed by anger nor
nurse your anger against a future opportunity of indulging
it. Don't harbour in your heart any trace of deceit nor
pretend to be at peace with another when you are not;
don't abandon the true standards of charity. Don't use
oaths to make your point for fear of perjury, but speak
the truth with integrity of heart and tongue.

If you are harmed by anyone, never repay it by returning the
harm. In fact you should never inflict any injury on another
but bear patiently whatever you have to suffer. Love your
enemies, then; refrain from speaking evil but rather call a

blessing on those who speak evil of you; if you are
persecuted for favouring a just cause, then bear it patiently.

Avoid all pride and self-importance. Don't drink to excess nor
over-eat. Don't be lazy nor give way to excessive sleep.
Don't be a murmurer* and never in speaking take away the
good name of another.

Your hope of fulfilment should be centred in God alone.
When you see any good in yourself, then, don't take it to
be your very own, but acknowledge it as a gift from God.
On the other hand you may be sure that any evil you do is
always your own and you may safely acknowledge your
responsibility.

You should recognize that there will be a day of reckoning
and judgement for all of us, which should make us afraid
of how we stand between good and evil. But, while you
should have a just fear of the loss of everything in hell, you
should above all cultivate a longing for eternal life with a
desire of great spiritual intensity. Keep the reality of death
always before your eyes, have a care about how you act
every hour of your life and be sure that God is present
everywhere and that he certainly sees and understands what
you are about.

If ever evil thoughts occur to your mind and invade your
heart cast them down at the feet of Christ and talk about
them frankly to your spiritual father or mother. Take care
to avoid any speech that is evil and degenerate. It is also
well to avoid empty talk that has no purpose except to
raise a laugh. As for laughter that is unrestrained and
raucous, it is not good to be attracted to that sort of
thing.

* See note in Chapter 5.

You should take delight in listening to sacred reading and in often turning generously to prayer. You should also in that prayer daily confess to God with real repentance any evil you have done in the past and for the future have the firm purpose to put right any wrong you may have done.

Don't act out the sensuous desires that occur to you naturally[1] and turn away from the pursuit of your own will. Rather you should follow in obedience the directions your abbot or abbess gives you, even if they, which God forbid, should contradict their own teaching by the way they live. In such a case just remember the Lord's advice about the example of the Pharisees: accept and follow their teaching but on no account imitate their actions.[2]

No one should aspire to gain a reputation for holiness. First of all we must actually become holy; then there would be some truth in having a reputation for it. The way to become holy is faithfully to fulfil God's commandments every day by loving chastity, by hating no one, by avoiding envy and hostile rivalry, by not becoming full of self but showing due respect for our elders and love for those who are younger, by praying in the love of Christ for those who are hostile to us, by seeking reconciliation and peace before the sun goes down whenever we have a quarrel with another,[3] and finally by never despairing of the mercy of God.

These, then, are the guidelines to lead us along the way of spiritual achievement. If we follow them day and night and never on any account give up, so that on judgement day we can give an account of our fidelity to them, that reward will be granted us by the Lord which he himself promised in the scriptures: what no eye has seen nor ear heard God has prepared for those who love him.[4]

The workshop in which we are called to work along these
lines with steady perseverance is the enclosure of the
monastery and stability in community life.

🕸

CHAPTER 5

Monastic obedience

THE FIRST STEP ON THE WAY TO HUMILITY IS TO OBEY
an order without delaying for a moment. That is a response
which comes easily to those who hold nothing dearer than
Christ himself. And so, because of the holy service monks
and nuns have accepted in their monastic profession or
because they fear the self-destruction of hell or value so
much the glory of eternal life, as soon as a superior gives
them an order it is as though it came from God himself and
they cannot endure any delay in carrying out what they
have been told to do. Of such servants of his the Lord says
that they obeyed him as soon as they heard him.[1] We
should remember also that he said to the teachers: whoever
listens to you, listens to me.[2]

The obedience of such people leads them to leave aside their
own concerns and forsake their own will. They abandon
what they have in hand and leave it unfinished. With a
ready step inspired by obedience they respond by their
action to the voice that summons them. It is, in fact, almost
in one single moment that a command is uttered by the
superior and the task carried to completion by the disciple,
showing how much more quickly both acts are
accomplished together because of their reverence for God.

Those who are possessed by a real desire to find their way to eternal life don't hesitate to choose the narrow way to which our Lord referred when he said: Narrow is the way that leads to life.[3] They live not to serve their own will nor to give way to their own desires and pleasures, but they submit in their way of life to the decisions and instructions of another, living in a monastery and willingly accepting an abbot or abbess as their superior. No one can doubt that they have as their model that saying of the Lord: I came not to do my own will but the will of him who sent me.[4]

We should remember, however, that such obedience will be acceptable to God and rewarding to us, if we carry out the orders given us in a way that is not fearful, nor slow, nor half-hearted, nor marred by murmuring or the sort of compliance that betrays resentment. Anything like that would be quite wrong because obedience to superiors is obedience to God, as the Lord himself made clear when he said: He who listens to you, listens to me.[5] Indeed, obedience must be given with genuine good will, because God loves a cheerful giver.[6] If obedience is given with a bad will and with murmuring not only in words but even in bitterness of heart, then even though the command may be externally fulfilled it will not be accepted by God, for he can see the resistance in the heart of a murmurer.* One

---

* Note on 'murmuring' in the Rule. The Latin word 'murmuratio' is vital for St Benedict's teaching on life in community but it defies translation into everyday English. The scriptural source is the murmuring of the Israelites against Moses in the desert (Numbers 14:2). The framework of monastic life is obedience. As presented in Chapter 5 it is more than a juridical concept because external conformity is not enough and inner assent is called for. Other texts in the Rule (especially in the Prologue and Chapter 72) make it clear that the motive of inner assent to obedience must be love – ultimately it is that love of God which Christ proclaimed as mediated through the love of brothers and sisters. In monastic life obedience and love are so intimately bound together that each becomes an expression of the other. Nothing is so corrosive of that ideal as the sort of constant complaining St Benedict has in mind when he writes about 'murmuring' and 'murmurers' in a Benedictine community. The damage is done not by the fact that there is a complaint. There are always procedures for legitimate complaints, which are healthy in a monastic

who behaves in such a way not only fails to receive the reward of grace but actually incurs the punishment deserved by murmurers. Only repentance and reparation can save such a one from this punishment.

❦

CHAPTER 6

Cherishing silence in the monastery

IN A MONASTERY WE OUGHT TO FOLLOW THE ADVICE of the psalm which says: I have resolved to keep watch over my ways so that I may not sin with my tongue. I am guarded about the way I speak and have accepted silence in humility refraining even from words that are good.[1] In this verse the psalmist shows that, because of the value of silence, there are times when it is best not to speak even though what we have in mind is good. How much more important it is to refrain from evil speech, remembering what such sins bring down on us in punishment. In fact so important is it to cultivate silence, even about matters concerning sacred values and spiritual instruction, that permission to speak should be granted only rarely to monks

community provided they are not destructive and are honestly brought forward in a spirit which is open and ready to accept a decision. Murmuring is not like that; it is underhand and quickly becomes part of the 'underlife' of a community. Thus it destroys confidence and is incompatible with the monastic ideals of Chapter 5 and of the Prologue and Chapter 72. In a community it is impossible for the superior to deal with it; it affects others; in the end it affects the spirit of a whole community. For individuals it becomes increasingly addictive and they develop a corresponding blindness to the harm they are doing to themselves and to others. That is the ground for St Benedict's exceptionally severe treatment of it. Murmuring is a technical monastic concept; it is best to retain the word, recognizing its unique meaning.

and nuns although they may themselves have achieved a high standard of monastic observance. After all, it is written in scripture that one who never stops talking cannot avoid falling into sin.[2] Another text in the same book reminds us that the tongue holds the key to death and life.[3] We should remember that speaking and instructing belong to the teacher; the disciple's role is to be silent and listen.

If any, then, have requests to make of the superior they should make them with deference and respect. As for vulgarity and idle gossip repeated for the sake of a laugh, such talk is forbidden at all times and in all places; we should never allow a disciple to utter words like that.

CHAPTER 7

The value of humility

THE WORD OF GOD IN SCRIPTURE TEACHES US IN clear and resounding terms that anyone who lays claim to a high position will be brought low and anyone who is modest in self-appraisal will be lifted up. This is Christ's teaching about the guest who took the first place at the king's banquet: all who exalt themselves, he said, will be humbled and all who humble themselves will be exalted.[1] He taught us by these words that whenever one of us is raised to a position of prominence there is always an element of pride involved. The psalmist shows his concern to avoid this when he says: there is no pride in my heart, O Lord, nor arrogance in the look of my eyes; I have not aspired to a role too great for me nor the glamour of

pretensions that are beyond me.[2] We should be wary of
such pride. And why does he say this? It is because lack
of humility calls for correction and so the psalm goes on:
If I failed to keep a modest spirit and raised my ambitions
too high, then your correction would come down on me as
though I were nothing but a newly weaned child on its
mother's lap.[3]

If the peak of our endeavour, then, is to achieve profound
humility, if we are eager to be raised to that heavenly
height, to which we can climb only through humility during
our present life, then let us make for ourselves a ladder like
the one which Jacob saw in his dream.[4] On that ladder angels
of God were shown to him going up and down in a constant
exchange between heaven and earth. It is just such an
exchange that we need to establish in our own lives, but with
this difference for us: our proud attempts at upward climbing
will really bring us down, whereas to step downwards in
humility is the way to lift our spirit up towards God.

This ladder, then, will symbolize for each of us our life in this
world during which we aspire to be lifted up to heaven by
the Lord, if only we can learn humility in our hearts. We
can imagine that he has placed the steps of the ladder, held
in place by the sides which signify our living body and soul,
to invite us to climb on them. Paradoxically, to climb
upwards will take us down to earth but stepping down will
lift us towards heaven. The steps themselves, then, mark the
decisions we are called to make in the exercise of humility
and self-discipline.

The first step of humility is to cherish at all times the sense
of awe with which we should turn to God. It should drive
forgetfulness away; it should keep our minds alive to all
God's commandments; it should make us reflect in our
hearts again and again that those who despise God and
reject his love prepare for themselves that irreversible

spiritual death which is meant by hell, just as life in eternity is prepared for those who fear God.

One who follows that way finds protection at all times from sin and vice of thought, of tongue, of hand, of foot, of self-will and of disordered sensual desire, so as to lead a life that is completely open before the scrutiny of God and of his angels who watch over us from hour to hour. This is made clear by the psalmist who shows that God is always present to our very thoughts when he says: God searches the hearts and thoughts of men and women,[5] and again: the Lord knows the thoughts of all,[6] and: from afar you know my thoughts,[7] and again: the thoughts of men and women shall give you praise.[8] Thus it may help one concerned about thoughts that are perverse to repeat the psalmist's heartfelt saying: I shall be blameless in his sight only if I guard myself from my own wickedness.[9]

As to pursuing our own will we are warned against that when scripture says to us: turn away from your own desires;[10] and in the Lord's prayer itself we pray that his will may be brought to fulfilment in us. It will be clear that we have learnt well the lesson against fulfilling our own will if we respond to that warning in scripture: there are ways which seem right to human eyes, but their end plunges down into the depths of hell.[11] Another good sign is to be afraid of what scripture says of those who reject such advice: they are corrupt and have become depraved in their pleasure seeking.[12]

As to sensual desires we should believe that they are not hidden from God, for the psalmist says to the Lord: all my desires are known to you.[13] We must indeed be on our guard against evil desires because spiritual death is not far from the gateway to wrongful pleasure, so that scripture gives us this clear direction: do not pursue your lusts.[14] And so, if the eyes of the Lord are watching the good and the wicked, and if at all times the Lord looks down from heaven on the sons and daughters of men to see if any show understanding in seeking God,[15] and if the angels assigned to care for us report our deeds to the Lord day and night, we must be on our guard every hour or else, as the psalmist says, the time may come when God will observe us falling into evil and so made worthless. He may spare us for a while during this life, because he is a loving father who waits and longs for us to do better, but in the end his rebuke may come upon us with the words: You were guilty of these crimes and I was silent.[16]

The second step of humility is not to love having our own way nor to delight in our own desires. Instead we should take as our model for imitation the Lord himself when he says: I have come not to indulge my own desires but to do the will of him who sent me.[17] Again remember that scripture says: self-indulgence brings down on us its own penalty, but there is a crown of victory for submitting to the demands of others.[18]

The third step of humility is to submit oneself out of love of God to whatever obedience under a superior may require of us; it is the example of the Lord himself that we follow in this way, as we know from St Paul's words: he was made obedient even unto death.[19]

The fourth step of humility is to go even further than this by readily accepting in patient and silent endurance, without thought of giving up or avoiding the issue, any hard and demanding things that may come our way in the course of that obedience, even if they include harsh impositions which are unjust. We are encouraged to such patience by the words of scripture: whoever perseveres to the very end will be saved.[20] And again there is the saying of the psalm: be steadfast in your heart and trust in the Lord.[21] Then again there is that verse from another psalm: it is for you we face death all the day long and are counted as sheep for the slaughter.[22]

Those who follow in that way have a sure hope of reward from God and they are joyful with St Paul's words on their lips: in all these things we are more than conquerors through him who loved us.[23] They remember also the psalm: you, O God, have tested us and have tried us as silver is tried; you led us, God, into the snare; you laid a heavy burden on our backs.[24] Then this is added in the psalm: you placed leaders over us[25] to show how we should be under a superior. In this way they fulfil the Lord's command through patience in spite of adversity and in spite of any wrongs they may suffer; struck on one cheek they offer the other; when robbed of their coat they let their cloak go also; pressed to go one mile they willingly go two;[26] with the Apostle Paul they put up with false brethren and shower blessings on those who curse them.[27]

The fifth step of humility is that we should not cover up but humbly confess to our superior or spiritual guide whatever evil thoughts come into our minds and the evil deeds we have done in secret. That is what scripture urges on us when it says: make known to the Lord the way you have taken and trust in him.[28] Then again it says: confess to the Lord, for he is good, for his mercy endures for ever.[29] And again: I have made known to you my sin and have not covered over my wrongdoing. I have said: against myself I shall proclaim my own faults to the Lord and you have forgiven the wickedness of my heart.[30]

The sixth step of humility for monks or nuns is to accept without complaint really wretched and inadequate conditions so that when faced with a task of any kind they would think of themselves as poor workers not worthy of consideration and repeat to God the verse of the psalm: I am of no account and lack understanding, no better than a beast in your sight. Yet I am always in your presence.[31]

The seventh step of humility is that we should be ready to speak of ourselves as of less importance and less worthy than others, not as a mere phrase on our lips but we should really believe it in our hearts. Thus in a spirit of humility we make the psalmist's words our own: I am no more than a worm with no claim to be a human person for I am despised by others and cast out by my own people.[32] I was raised up high in honour, but then I was humbled and overwhelmed with confusion.[33] In the end we may learn to say: it was good for me, Lord, that you humbled me so that I might learn your precepts.[34]

The eighth step of humility teaches us to do nothing which goes beyond what is approved and encouraged by the common rule of the monastery and the example of our seniors.

The ninth step of humility leads us to refrain from unnecessary speech and to guard our silence by not speaking until we are addressed. That is what scripture recommends with these sayings: anyone who is forever chattering will not escape sin[35] and there is another saying from a psalm: one who never stops talking loses the right way in life.[36]

The tenth step of humility teaches that we should not be given to empty laughter on every least occasion because: a fool's voice is for ever raised in laughter.[37]

The eleventh step of humility is concerned with the manner of speech appropriate in a monastery. We should speak gently and seriously with words that are weighty and restrained. We should be brief and reasonable in whatever we have to say and not raise our voices to insist on our own opinions.

The wise, we should remember, are to be recognized in words that are few.

The twelfth step of humility is concerned with the external impression conveyed by those dedicated to monastic life. The humility of their hearts should be apparent by their bodily movements to all who see them. Whether they are at the work of God, at prayer in the oratory, walking about the monastery, in the garden, on a journey or in the fields, wherever they may be, whether sitting, walking or standing they should be free of any hint of arrogance or pride in their manner or the way they look about them. They should guard their eyes and look down. They should remember their sins and their guilt before the judgement of God, with the words of the publican in the gospel for ever on their lips as he stood with his eyes cast down saying: Lord, I am not worthy, sinner that I am, to lift my eyes to the heavens.[38] Or the words of the psalmist might fit just as well: I am bowed down and utterly humbled.[39]

Any monk or nun who has climbed all these steps of humility will come quickly to that love of God which in its fullness casts out all fear. Carried forward by that love, such a one will begin to observe without effort as though they were natural all those precepts which in earlier days were kept at least partly through fear. A new motive will have taken over, not fear of hell but the love of Christ. Good habit and delight in virtue will carry us along. This happy state the Lord will bring about through the Holy Spirit in his servant whom he has cleansed of vice and sin and taught to be a true and faithful worker in the Kingdom.

CHAPTER 8

The Divine Office at night

IT SEEMS REASONABLE THAT DURING WINTERTIME, that is from the first of November until Easter all should arise at the eighth hour of the night. By that time, having rested until a little after midnight, they may rise with their food well digested. Any time which is left after Vigils should be devoted to study of the psalter or lessons by those who are behind hand in these tasks. From Easter until the first of November the times should be arranged so that there is a very short break after Vigils for the needs of nature. Lauds can then follow at the first light of daybreak.

CHAPTER 9

The number of psalms at the night office

DURING THIS WINTER SEASON THE OFFICE OF VIGILS begins with this verse recited three times; Lord, open my lips and my mouth will declare your praise.[1] To this should be added the third psalm and the *Gloria*. Then will come the ninety fourth psalm chanted with its antiphon and after that an Ambrosian hymn, followed by six psalms with their antiphons.

On the completion of these psalms there is a versicle and a blessing from the abbot or abbess. Then all sit on benches while three lessons are read out from the lectern by members of the choir, taking it in turns. Responsories are sung after each but the *Gloria Patri* comes only after the third and as soon as the cantor intones it all rise from their seats out of reverence for the Holy Trinity. The readings at Vigils are to be taken from the inspired books of the Old and New Testaments with commentaries on them by recognized and orthodox catholic Fathers.

After these three lessons with their responsories there follow six psalms which are to be sung with the *alleluia*. A reading from the Apostle recited by heart should follow with a verse and the petition from the litany, that is: Lord, have mercy. That brings the night Vigils to a conclusion.

CHAPTER 10

The night office in summertime

FROM EASTER UNTIL THE FIRST DAY OF NOVEMBER the same number of psalms should be said as we have established for winter, but because the nights are shorter, instead of reading three lessons from the book on the lectern only one should be recited by heart from the Old Testament with a brief responsory to follow. Apart from that the arrangements for winter are followed exactly so that never less than twelve psalms should be recited at Vigils, not counting the third and ninety fourth psalms.

CHAPTER 11

Vigils or night office on Sunday

ALL SHOULD RISE EARLIER FOR THE NIGHT-TIME
vigils on Sunday. In these Vigils the arrangement should be
that six psalms and a verse should be chanted, as described
above, and then, when everyone has sat down in an orderly
way on the benches, four lessons should be read from the
book on the lectern with their responsories. The *Gloria* is
added only to the fourth lesson and when the cantor begins to
sing it, all rise out of reverence. The other six psalms follow
these lessons in due order with their responsories and a
versicle, as described above. After that, four more lessons
should be read in the same way with their responsories. Then
three canticles from the prophets, chosen by the superior, are
chanted with the *alleluia*. Then after a versicle and blessing
from the abbot or abbess, four further lessons should be read
from the New Testament, as described above. After the
fourth, the superior intones the *Te Deum laudamus* and at
the end of that reads the gospel while all in the choir stand as
a sign of profound reverence. At the end of the gospel all
respond with *Amen* and the superior intones the *Te decet laus*
and after the blessing Lauds begins.

This arrangement for Vigils is followed in the same way on
every Sunday both in summer and winter, unless – which
God forbid – the community gets up late, in which case the
lessons or responsories should to some extent be shortened.
Care, however, should be taken to avoid this. If it should
happen, whoever is responsible must express fitting
repentance to God in the oratory.

CHAPTER 12

The celebration of solemn Lauds

FOR LAUDS ON SUNDAY THE SIXTY SIXTH PSALM should be said first of all straight through without an antiphon. After that comes the fiftieth psalm with its *alleluia*. Then come the hundred and seventeenth psalm and the sixty second followed by the *Benedicite* and *Laudate* psalms, a reading from the book of the Apocalypse recited by heart, the responsory, an Ambrosian hymn, a versicle, the *Benedictus*, litany and conclusion.

CHAPTER 13

Lauds on ordinary days

ON ORDINARY DAYS LAUDS SHOULD BE CELEBRATED like this: the sixty sixth psalm should be said with its antiphon but rather slowly, as on Sunday, to make sure that all are present for the fiftieth psalm which is said with its antiphon. Two other psalms are said after that according to the usual arrangement, namely: on Monday the fifth and thirty fifth; on Tuesday the forty second and fifty sixth; on Wednesday the sixty third and sixty fourth; on Thursday the eighty seventh and eighty ninth; on Friday the seventy fifth and ninety first; on Saturday the one hundred and forty second and the canticle from Deuteronomy divided into two sections with the *Gloria* following each section. On the other days a canticle is

37

recited from the prophets on the days allotted by the Roman Church. Then come the *Laudate* psalms of praise, a reading from the apostle recited by heart, a responsory, an Ambrosian hymn, a versicle, the *Benedictus*, the litany and the conclusion.

It is important that the celebration of Lauds and Vespers should never be concluded without the recitation by the superior of the whole of the Lord's prayer so that all may hear and attend to it. This is because of the harm that is often done in a community by the thorns of conflict which can arise. Bound by the very words of that prayer 'forgive us as we also forgive' they will be cleansed from the stain of such evil. At the other offices only the ending of the Lord's prayer is said aloud so that all may respond: 'but deliver us from evil'.[1]

CHAPTER 14

The celebration of Vigils on feasts of saints

ON THE FEASTS OF SAINTS AND ON ALL OTHER solemnities Vigils should follow the order laid down for the celebration of Sunday except that the psalms, antiphons and readings that are appropriate to the day should be recited; the order of the liturgy itself remains the same as that described for Sunday.

CHAPTER 15

When the Alleluia should be said

FROM THE HOLY FEAST OF EASTER UNTIL PENTECOST the *Alleluia* must always be said in the psalms and the responsories. From Pentecost until the beginning of Lent it is said only with the last six psalms in the night office. On every Sunday outside Lent, however, the *alleluia* is included in Lauds, Prime, Terce, Sext and None, but at Vespers an antiphon is intoned instead. The *alleluia* is never added to the responsories except from Easter to Pentecost.

CHAPTER 16

The hours of the work of God during the day

THE WORDS OF THE PSALM ARE: I HAVE UTTERED your praises seven times during the day.[1] We shall fulfil that sacred number of seven if at the times of Lauds, Prime, Terce, Sext, None, Vespers and Compline we perform the duty of our service to God, because it was of these day hours that the psalm said: I have uttered your praise seven times during the day. About the night Vigil that same psalm says: In the middle of the night I arose to praise you.[2] And so at these times let us offer praise to our Creator because of his justice revealed in his judgements[3] – that is at Lauds, Prime, Terce, Sext, None, Vespers and Compline and in the night let us arise to praise him.

CHAPTER 17

The number of psalms to be sung at the hours

WE HAVE ALREADY SET OUT THE ORDER OF THE
psalms for Vigils and for Lauds. Now let us look at the
order of the psalms for the rest of the Hours. At Prime
three psalms should be recited separately and not under one
Gloria and a hymn appropriate to each hour should be said
after the *Deus in adiutorium* before the psalms are begun.
After the three psalms there should be one lesson and the
Hour is concluded with a versicle and 'Lord have mercy'
and the concluding prayers.

At Terce, Sext and None the same order of prayer obtains,
that is, after the opening verse and the hymn for each Hour
there are three psalms, a reading, versicle, 'Lord have
mercy' and the conclusion. If the community is a large one
they have antiphons as well but, if it is small, they sing the
psalms alone.

For the office of Vespers the number of psalms should be
limited to four with their antiphons. After the psalms a
lesson is repeated, then a responsory, an Ambrosian hymn,
a versicle, the *Magnificat*, litany and the Hour is concluded
with the Lord's prayer.

Compline will consist in the recitation of three psalms on
their own without antiphons. Then comes the hymn for
Compline, one lesson, a versicle, 'Lord have mercy' and the
Office is concluded with a blessing.

CHAPTER 18

The order for reciting the psalms

EACH HOUR BEGINS WITH THE FOLLOWING VERSE: O God come to my assistance, O Lord make haste to help me. The *Gloria* and the hymn for each Hour then follow.

At Prime on Sunday four sections of psalm one hundred and eighteen are said and at the other Hours, that is at Terce, Sext and None, three sections of the same psalm are said. At Prime on Monday there are three psalms, namely the first, second and sixth and so on for each day at Prime until Sunday when three psalms are said in order up to the nineteenth psalm, but the ninth and seventeenth are divided into two. This will mean that Vigils on Sunday always begin with the twentieth psalm.

Then at Terce, Sext and None on Monday the nine sections left over from the one hundred and eighteenth psalm are recited – three at each of these hours. That psalm is completed, then, in two days, namely Sunday and Monday, and on Tuesday at Terce, Sext and None three psalms are sung at each Hour starting from the one hundred and nineteenth and going on to the one hundred and twenty seventh, that is nine psalms. These same psalms are repeated daily until Sunday and the identical arrangement of hymns, lessons and verses is retained every day. That means, of course, that the series always starts again on Sunday with the one hundred and eighteenth psalm.

Vespers each day has four psalms to be sung. These psalms should start with the one hundred and ninth going through to the one hundred and forty seventh, omitting those which are taken from that series for other Hours, that is the one

hundred and seventeenth to the one hundred and twenty
seventh and the one hundred and thirty third and the one
hundred and forty second; with these exceptions all the
others are sung at Vespers. But since that leaves us short
of three psalms the longer psalms in this series should be
divided in two, that is the one hundred and thirty eighth,
the one hundred and forty third and the one hundred and
forty fourth. The one hundred and sixteenth psalm,
however, because it is very short should be joined to the
one hundred and fifteenth. With the order of psalmody
thus arranged for Vespers the rest of the office, that is the
lesson, response, hymn, versicle and *Magnificat* should
follow the principles which are set out above. At Compline
the same psalms are recited daily, that is the fourth,
ninetieth and one hundred and thirty third.

After we have arranged the psalms for the day Hours in this
way all the other psalms which are left over should be
divided equally between the Vigils on the seven nights of
the week, which can be done by dividing the longer psalms
and allotting twelve psalms or divisions to each night.

We have no hesitation in urging that, if any are dissatisfied
with this distribution of psalms they should re-arrange them
in whatever way seems better, provided that one principle
is preserved, namely that the whole psalter of one hundred
and fifty psalms should be recited each week and that the
series should start again on Sunday at Vigils. Any monastic
community which chants less than the full psalter with the
usual canticles each week shows clearly that it is too
indolent in the devotion of its service of God. After all, we
read that our holy Fathers had the energy to fulfil in one
single day what we in our lukewarm devotion only aspire
to complete in a whole week.

CHAPTER 19

Our approach to prayer

GOD IS PRESENT EVERYWHERE – PRESENT TO THE good and to the evil as well, so that nothing anyone does escapes his notice; that is the firm conviction of our faith. Let us be very sure, however, without a moment's doubt that his presence to us is never so strong as while we are celebrating the work of God in the oratory. And so we should always recall at such times the words of the psalm: serve the Lord with awe and reverence,[1] and: sing the Lord's praises with skill and relish,[2] and: I shall sing your praise in the presence of the angels.[3] All of us, then, should reflect seriously on how to appear before the majesty of God in the presence of his angels. That will lead us to make sure that, when we sing in choir, there is complete harmony between the thoughts in our mind and the meaning of the words we sing.

CHAPTER 20

The ideal of true reverence in prayer

IF IN ORDINARY LIFE WE HAVE A FAVOUR TO ASK OF someone who has power and authority, we naturally approach that person with due deference and respect. When we come, then, with our requests in prayer before the Lord, who is God of all creation, is it not all the more important that we should approach him in a spirit of real humility and a devotion that is open to him alone and free from distracting thoughts? We really must be quite clear that our prayer will be heard, not because of the eloquence and length of all we have to say, but because of the heartfelt repentance and openness of our hearts to the Lord whom we approach. Our prayer should, therefore, be free from all other preoccupations and it should normally be short, although we may well on occasions be inspired to stay longer in prayer through the gift of God's grace working within us. Our prayer together in community, on the other hand, should always be moderate in length and when the sign is given by the superior all should rise together.

⁊⳽

CHAPTER 21

The deans of the monastery

DEANS SHOULD BE CHOSEN FROM AMONG THE community, if that is justified by its size. They should be chosen for their good reputation and high monastic standards of life. Their office will be to take care of all the needs of the groups of ten placed under them and to do so in all respects in accordance with God's commandments and the instructions of their superior. They must be selected for their suitability in character and gifts so that the abbot or abbess may, without anxiety, share some responsibilities with them. For that reason they should not be chosen simply because of their order in the community but because of their upright lives and the wisdom of their teaching.

If any of the deans are affected by some breath of pride which lays them open to adverse criticism, they should be corrected once or twice or even three times. After that, if any are unwilling to change for the better, they should be deposed from their position of responsibility so that another who is more worthy of the office may be brought in. In the case of the prior or prioress we propose the same course of action.

CHAPTER 22

Sleeping arrangements for the community

THE MEMBERS OF THE COMMUNITY SHOULD EACH have beds for themselves and they should all receive from the superior bedding which is suitable to monastic life. If possible they should all sleep in one room, but if the community is too large for that they should sleep in groups of ten or twenty with senior members among them to care for them. A lamp should be kept alight in the dormitories until the morning.

They should sleep in their normal clothes wearing a belt or cord round their waists; but they should not keep knives in their belts for fear of cutting themselves accidentally while asleep. All should be prepared to rise immediately without any delay as soon as the signal to get up is given; then they should hurry to see who can get first to the oratory for the work of God, but of course they should do this with due dignity and restraint. The young should not have their beds next to each other but they should be placed among those of the seniors. In the morning, as they are getting up for the work of God, they should quietly give encouragement

to those who are sleepy and given to making excuses for
being late.

᠅

CHAPTER 23

Faults which deserve excommunication

IF AN INDIVIDUAL IN THE COMMUNITY IS DEFIANT,
disobedient, proud or given to murmuring or in any other
way set in opposition to the holy Rule and contemptuous
of traditions of the seniors, then we should follow the
precept of our Lord. Such a one should be warned once
and then twice in private by seniors. If there is no
improvement, the warning should be followed by a severe
public rebuke before the whole community. If even this
does not bring reform then excommunication should be
the next penalty, provided that the meaning of such a
punishment is really understood. In a case of real defiance,
corporal punishment may be the only cure.

᠅

CHAPTER 24

Different degrees of severity in punishment

THE SEVERITY OF EXCOMMUNICATION OR ANY OTHER
punishment should correspond to the gravity of the fault
committed, and it is for the superior to decide about the

seriousness of faults. Anyone found guilty of faults which are not too serious should be excluded from taking part in community meals at the common table. This exclusion from the common table also means that in the oratory the guilty person will not be allowed to lead a psalm or antiphon nor to recite a reading until satisfaction has been made. Meals should be provided for such a one to take alone after the community meal at, for instance, the ninth hour, if the community eats at the sixth or after Vespers, if the community eats at the ninth hour. That regime should continue until fitting satisfaction has been made and pardon granted.

CHAPTER 25

Punishment for more serious faults

ANYONE WITH THE INFECTION OF A REALLY SERIOUS offence is to be excluded not only from the common table but from common prayer in the oratory as well. None of the community should associate with or talk to the guilty person, who is to persevere alone in sorrow and penance in whatever work has been allotted, remembering St Paul's fearful judgement when he wrote to the Corinthians that: such a one should be handed over for the destruction of the flesh so that the spirit may be saved on the day of the Lord.[1] As for meals, they are to be provided in solitude and the abbot or abbess must decide the amounts and the times that are appropriate. No one should offer a blessing in passing the guilty person nor should the food provided be blessed.

CHAPTER 26

Unlawful association with the excommunicated

IF ANY MEMBER OF THE COMMUNITY PRESUMES
without the permission of the abbot or abbess to associate
in any way with or speak to or give instructions to one
who has been excommunicated then that person should
receive exactly the same punishment of excommunication.

᛭

CHAPTER 27

The superior's care for the excommunicated

EVERY POSSIBLE CARE AND CONCERN SHOULD BE
shown for those who have been excommunicated by the
abbot or abbess, who are themselves also to remember that
it is not the healthy who need a physician but the sick.[1]
Therefore the superior should use every curative skill as a
wise doctor does, for instance by sending in *senpectae*, that
is, mature and wise senior members of the community who
may discreetly bring counsel to one who is in a state of
uncertainty and confusion; their task will be to show the
sinner the way to humble reconciliation and also to bring
consolation, as St Paul also urges,[2] to one in danger of
being overwhelmed by excessive sorrow and in need of the
reaffirmation of love which everyone in the community
must achieve through their prayer.

As for the abbot or abbess, they must show the greatest possible concern with great wisdom and perseverance to avoid losing any one of the sheep committed to their care. They should be well aware that they have undertaken an office which is more like the care of the sick than the exercise of power over the healthy. They should be anxious to avoid the Lord's rebuke to the shepherds through the Prophet Ezekiel: you made your own those you saw to be fat and healthy and cast out those who were weak.[3] They should follow the loving example of the Good Shepherd who left ninety-nine of his flock on the mountains and went off to look for the one sheep who had strayed. So great was his compassion for the weakness of that one erring sheep that he actually lifted it onto his sacred shoulders and so carried it back to the rest of the flock.

CHAPTER 28

The treatment of those who relapse

IF THERE SHOULD BE ANY WHO HAVE BEEN frequently reproved for some fault and have not reformed, even after excommunication, there is a sharper correction to be applied; that is to subject such a one to the punishment of the rod. But if even this does not bring reform and if – may God forbid it – the guilty one is puffed up with pride to the point of wanting to defend wrongful actions, then the superior must follow the practice of an experienced doctor. After applying dressings and the ointment of exhortation and the medicine of divine scripture and proceeding to the extreme resource of cauterization by excommunication and strokes of the rod, and if even then the superior sees that no such efforts are of any avail, yet another remedy must be brought to bear which is still more powerful, namely the personal prayer of the superior and of all the community that the Lord, who can do all things, may himself bring healing to the delinquent. If even such prayer does not bring healing, the superior must turn to the knife of amputation, following the guidance of St Paul, who told the Corinthians to banish the evil from their midst,[1] and again he said: if the unfaithful one wishes to go, let him go, lest one diseased sheep corrupt the whole flock.[2]

ᚬ

CHAPTER 29

The readmission of any who leave the monastery

ANYONE WHO IS GUILTY OF SERIOUS WRONG BY THE personal decision to leave the monastery but then asks to be received back again must first of all promise full reparation for leaving the monastery. That will be enough for restoration into the community, but it must be in the lowest place as a test of humility. If the same monk or nun departs again, they may be received back until the third time, but after that all must understand that any question of return to the community is to be refused.

ᚬ

CHAPTER 30

The correction of young children

THERE IS A PROPER WAY OF DEALING WITH EVERY
age and every degree of understanding, and we should find
the right way of dealing with the young. Thus children and
adolescents or others who are unable to appreciate the
seriousness of excommunication need some other mode of
correction, when they go astray. If they are guilty of bad
behaviour, then they should be subjected to severe fasting
or sharp strokes of the rod to bring them to a better
disposition.

CHAPTER 31

The qualities required by the cellarer

THE CELLARER OF THE MONASTERY SHOULD BE
chosen from among the community. To qualify for this
choice a candidate should be wise and mature in behaviour,
sober and not an excessive eater, not proud nor apt to give
offence nor inclined to cause trouble, not unpunctual, nor
wasteful but living in the fear of God and ready to show
the community all the love a father or mother would show
to their family. The cellarer will be responsible for the care
of all the monastery's goods but must do nothing without
the authority of the superior, being content to look after
what is committed to the cellarer's care without causing
annoyance to the community. If one of the community

comes with an unreasonable request, the cellarer should, in refusing what is asked, be careful not to give the impression of personal rejection and so hurt the petitioner's feelings. Such a refusal of an ill-judged request should be measured and given with due deference towards the person involved. As an incentive to personal spiritual progress the cellarer might remember St Paul's saying that those who give good service to others earn a good reputation.[1] The cellarer should show special concern and practical care for the sick and the young, for guests and for the poor, and never forget the account to be rendered for all these responsibilities on the day of judgement. All the utensils of the monastery and in fact everything that belongs to the monastery should be cared for as though they were the sacred vessels of the altar. There must be no negligence on the part of the cellarer nor any tendency to avarice nor to prodigality nor extravagance with the goods of the monastery. The administration should be carried out in all respects with moderation and in accordance with the instructions of the abbot or abbess.

Among the most important qualities the cellarer needs to cultivate is humility and the ability to give a pleasant answer even when a request must be refused. Remember how scripture says that a kindly word is of greater value than a gift, however precious.[2] Although the cellarer's responsibility embraces all that is delegated by the superior there must be no attempt to include what the superior has forbidden. The community should receive their allotted food without any self-important fuss or delay on the part of the cellarer which might provoke them to resentment. The cellarer should remember what is deserved, according to the Lord's saying, by those who provoke to sin one of his little ones.[3]

If the community is large, the cellarer must receive the assistance of helpers whose support will make the burden of this office tolerable. There will, of course, be appropriate times for the cellarer to hand out what is needed and for requests for goods or services to be made; these times should be observed by all so that failure to respect them may not cause any disturbance or unhappiness in the house of God.

⚜

CHAPTER 32

The tools and property of the monastery

THE SUPERIOR SHOULD ENTRUST THE PROPERTY OF the monastery consisting in tools, clothing or any other items to various members of the community whose character and reliability inspire confidence. Their job will be to take care of the various articles, assigned to their care individually, and to issue them for use and collect them again afterwards. The superior should keep a list with the details of what has been issued to them so that, when one member of the community succeeds another in any responsibility, there may be no doubt about what items have been entrusted to each individual and what they have returned at the end.

Anyone who is negligent in dealing with the monastery property or allows it to deteriorate must be corrected with a view to improvement. If there is no improvement the one responsible should be subjected to the appropriate discipline of the Rule.

⚜

CHAPTER 33

Personal possessions in the monastery

IT IS VITALLY IMPORTANT TO CUT OUT BY THE ROOTS
from the monastery the bad practice of anyone in the
community giving away anything or accepting any gift for
themselves, as though it were their own personal property,
without the permission of the superior. Those in monastic
vows should not claim any property as their own exclusive
possession – absolutely nothing at all, not even books and
writing materials. After all they cannot count even their
bodies and their wills as their own, consecrated, as they
are, to the Lord. They may expect that everything they
need in their lives will be supplied by the superior of the
community without whose permission they may not retain
for themselves anything at all. Following the practice of the
early church described in Acts, everything in the monastery
should be held in common and no one should think of
claiming personal ownership of anything.[1] If any in the
community are found to be addicted to this wicked
practice, they must be warned on the first and second
occasion and then, if there is no improvement, subjected
to punishment.

CHAPTER 34

Fair provision for the needs of all

THIS PRINCIPLE FROM SCRIPTURE SHOULD BE established in the monastery, namely that distribution was made to each in accordance with their needs.[1] This, however, should not be taken to mean that favouritism of individuals can be tolerated; far from it. It should simply be a way of showing proper consideration for needs arising from individual weakness. Those who do not need as much as some others should thank God for the strength they have been given and not be sorry for themselves. Those who need more should be humble about their weakness and not become self-important in enjoying the indulgence granted them. In that way all in the community will be at peace with each other. Above all the evil of murmuring* must not for any reason at all be shown by any word or gesture. Anyone found indulging in such a fault must be subjected to really severe discipline.

CHAPTER 35

Weekly servers in the kitchen and at table

EVERYONE IN THE COMMUNITY SHOULD TAKE TURNS serving in the kitchen and at table. None should be exonerated from kitchen duty except in the case of sickness

* See note in Chapter 5.

or the call of some important business for the monastery, because serving each other in this way has the great merit of fostering charity. Nevertheless those who are not very strong should be given assistance to make sure that they will not be distressed by the demands of this work. In fact all should receive the assistance they need because of the regime under which they may be living and the conditions of the locality. In a large community the cellarer should be excused from kitchen service and that should apply also, as we have said, to those engaged in the more demanding business of the monastery. All others in the community must take their turn in serving in a spirit of charity.

On Saturday those who have completed their service should do the washing. This should include the towels which are used by the community when they wash their hands and feet. The feet of all should be washed by the one beginning a week of service as well as the one completing it. All the vessels used in their service should be returned to the cellarer in a clean and sound condition. The cellarer can then pass them on to those taking up these duties with a reliable record of what has been returned and what has been issued again.

One hour before the time of a meal those serving in the kitchen and at table should each receive a drink and some bread in addition to their regular portion. This will help them to serve the community at mealtime without stress and without murmuring* about their lot. On days, however, when there is the solemn celebration of a feast they should wait until after Mass.

On Sundays after the celebration of Lauds the weekly servers should bow low before all the community asking for their prayers. The server who has completed a week intones

* See note in Chapter 5.

three times the verse: 'Blessed are you, Lord God, because you have helped me and given me consolation'[1] and then receives a blessing. The one beginning the week follows on three times with the verse: 'O God, come to my assistance, Lord, make haste to help me'[2] and after the verse has been repeated by everyone receives a blessing and begins a week of service.

❧

CHAPTER 36

The care of the sick in the monastery

THE CARE OF THOSE WHO ARE SICK IN THE community is an absolute priority, which must rank before every other requirement, so that there may be no doubt that it is Christ who is truly served in them. After all Christ himself said: I was sick and you came to visit me, and also: what you did to one of these my least brethren you did to me.[1] The sick themselves, on the other hand, should reflect that the care and attention they receive is offered them to show honour to God and so they must be careful not to distress by selfish and unreasonable demands those attending to their needs. Still such behaviour in the sick should be tolerated by those attending them, who will receive a richer reward for such patience. The abbot or abbess should certainly make very sure that the sick suffer no neglect.

Separate infirmary accommodation should be provided for the sick with a member of the community in charge who has true reverence for God and can be relied on to meet the needs of the patients with sensitive care. The sick may be offered baths whenever it will help, although those in good health and especially the young should not be given this permission so easily. The sick who are really failing may be allowed to eat meat to restore their strength, but when they get better they should all abstain from meat as usual.

The abbot or abbess should keep a careful eye on the sick to make sure that they suffer no neglect through the forgetfulness of the cellarer or infirmary staff, because the responsibility for the shortcomings of their disciples rests on them.

⚜

CHAPTER 37

Care for the elderly and the young

HUMAN NATURE ITSELF IS DRAWN TO TENDER concern for those in the two extremes of age and youth, but the authority of the Rule should reinforce this natural instinct. Their frailty should always be given consideration so that they should not be strictly bound to the provisions of the Rule in matters of diet. They should receive loving consideration and be allowed to anticipate the regular hours laid down for food and drink.

⚜

CHAPTER 38

The weekly reader

THERE SHOULD ALWAYS BE READING FOR THE
community during meal times. The reader, however, should
not be one who has taken up the book casually to read
without preparation, but whoever reads should do so for a
whole week beginning on Sunday. Then after Mass and
Communion the reader should ask for the assistance of the
prayers of all the community to ward off the spirit of pride
in the performance of this task. So before God in the
oratory this verse should be intoned three times by all after
the incoming reader has begun the chant: 'O Lord, open
my lips and my mouth shall proclaim your praise'.[1] With
the blessing that will follow the reader can safely begin the
week of reading in public.

During meals there should be complete silence disturbed by
no whispering nor should anyone's voice be heard except
the reader's. Everyone in the community should be attentive
to the needs of their neighbours as they eat and drink so
that there should be no need for anyone to ask for what
they require. However, if such a need should arise there
should be agreed signs for such requests so as to avoid the
sound of voices. No one should venture to ask a question
about the reading during meal times nor about anything
else for fear of giving opportunities which would destroy
the spirit of silence. The only exception is that the superior
might wish to make some comment for the instruction of
all.

The weekly reader can eat afterwards with the cooks and
servers for the week but should also be given a drink of
watered wine just before starting to read because of Holy

Communion and also to relieve the burden of a long fast. The choice of readers should be determined by their ability to read intelligibly to others and not by their order in the community.

❧

CHAPTER 39

The amount of food to be made available

WHETHER THE MAIN MEAL EACH DAY IS AT NOON OR in mid-afternoon, two cooked dishes on every table should be enough to allow for differences of taste so that those who feel unable to eat from one may be satisfied with the other. Two dishes, then, should be enough for the needs of all, but if there is a supply of fruit and fresh vegetables available a third may be added. A full pound of bread every day for each member of the community should be enough both on days when there is only one meal and on those when there is a supper as well as dinner. If the community is to have supper the cellarer must retain a third of each one's bread ration to give them at supper.

If, however, the workload of the community is especially heavy it will be for the abbot or abbess at the time to decide whether it is right to make some addition to the amount of food made available. We must always be careful, however, to avoid excessive eating which might also cause indigestion. Nothing is so opposed to Christian values as overeating, as we can see from the words of our Lord: take care that your hearts are not weighed down by overeating.[1]

The same quantities should not be served to young children as to adults. They should receive less which will preserve in this, as in all monastic practice, the principle of frugality. Everyone should abstain completely from eating the flesh of four-footed animals except, of course, the sick whose strength needs building up.

※

CHAPTER 40

The proper amount of drink to be provided

St paul says that each of us has a special gift from God, one kind for one of us and quite a different one for another.[1] That reflection makes me reluctant to decide on the measure of food and drink for others. However, having due regard for the weakness of those whose health is not robust, perhaps a half-measure of wine every day should suffice for each member of the community. As for those to whom God has given the self-control that enables them to abstain from strong drink, they should be encouraged by the knowledge that the Lord will also give them a fitting reward.

Of course, the local conditions or the nature of the community's work or the heat of summer may suggest that a more liberal allowance of drink is needed by the community. In that case it lies with the superior to decide what is needed to meet these conditions while at the same time guarding against the subtle danger of excessive drinking leading to drunkenness. We do, indeed, read that wine is entirely unsuitable as a drink for monks and nuns but, since in our day they cannot all be brought to accept this, let us at least agree that we should drink in moderation and not till we are full. The words of scripture should warn us: wine makes even the wise turn away from the truth.[2]

It may be that local circumstances may make it impossible to provide the amount of wine we have suggested above so that there may be much less available or even none at all. Those who live in such a locality should praise God and avoid any murmuring.* Above all else I urge that there should be no murmuring in the community.

CHAPTER 41

The times for community meals

FROM EASTER TO PENTECOST THE COMMUNITY should have dinner at noon and supper in the evening. From Pentecost throughout the whole summer on Wednesday and Friday they should normally fast until mid-afternoon, provided that they are not working out in the fields or exposed to an excessively hot summer. On other days dinner should be at noon, but it is for the superior to decide whether noon should be the time for dinner every day, if they have work to do in the fields and the summer heat is too much. The principle is that the superior should manage everything so prudently that the saving work of grace may be accomplished in the community and whatever duties the community undertakes they may be carried out without any excuse for murmuring.

* See note in Chapter 5.

From the thirteenth of September until the beginning of Lent dinner will always be in mid-afternoon. Then from the beginning of Lent until Easter they eat after Vespers which should be timed so that lamps are not needed during the meal and everything can be completed by the light of day. That should always be the principle to determine the time of supper or the fast-day meal, namely that all should be done while it is still light.

CHAPTER 42

The great silence after Compline

SILENCE SHOULD BE SOUGHT AT ALL TIMES BY MONKS and nuns and this is especially important for them at night time. The final community act, then, before the great silence throughout the year both on fast days and on ordinary days should be the same. On ordinary days as soon as the community rises from supper they should go and sit down together while one of them reads from the Conferences of Cassian or the Lives of the Fathers or from some other text which will be inspiring at that time. However, the Heptateuch or the Book of Kings should not be chosen because these texts might prove disturbing to those of rather delicate feelings so late in the evening; they should be read at other times.

On fast days there should be a short interval after Vespers and then all should assemble for the reading of the *Conferences* as we have already described. Four or five pages should be read or as many as time permits so that everyone can gather together during this period of reading in case anyone has been assigned to a task and is detained by it. As soon as everyone is present they celebrate Compline together. It is after that, when they leave the oratory at the end of Compline, that there must be no further permission for anyone to speak at all. Any infringement of this rule of silence which comes to light must incur severe punishment. There may be an exception if some need of the guests requires attention or if the superior has occasion to give someone an order. If something like that cannot be avoided, it should be performed with great tact and the restraint which good manners require.

⁂

CHAPTER 43

Late-comers for the work of God or in the refectory

WHEN THE TIME COMES FOR ONE OF THE DIVINE offices to begin, as soon as the signal is heard, everyone must set aside whatever they may have in hand and hurry as fast as possible to the oratory, but of course they should do so in a dignified way which avoids giving rise to any boisterous behaviour. The essential point is that nothing should be accounted more important than the work of God.

Vigils start with Psalm 94 and we want this to be recited at a slow and meditative pace to give time for all to gather. Then, if anyone arrives after the *Gloria* of that psalm, they may not join the choir in their proper order but must take a place apart, which the superior has established at the end of the choir order for any who fail in this way. That will

mean that as offenders they will be in full view of the
superior and all the community until they purge their
offence by public penance at the end of the office. The
reason for deciding that they should stand in the last
place and apart from everyone else is so that shame itself
may teach them to do better. If they were excluded and
made to stay outside the oratory, there might be some
who would actually go back to bed for further sleep,
or they might sit outside and gossip with each other so
that an opportunity would be given to the devil to lead
them astray. They should go inside just as I have
described which will bring them to better standards and
not abandon them to the worst consequences of their
fault.

During the day hours any who arrive at the work of God
after the introduction and the *Gloria* of the first psalm
which follows it must stand in the last place, as explained
above. They must not presume to join the rest of the choir
without doing penance, unless the superior permits it as an
exception; even in that case the one who is at fault should
apologize.

In the refectory all must come to table together so as to offer
their grace together as one community. Any, therefore, who
through carelessness or some other personal fault do not
arrive in the refectory in time for grace should simply be
corrected until after the second occurrence of this failure. If
there is no improvement after that they should not be
allowed a place at the common table but should eat
separately out of contact with the rest of the community
and be deprived of their portion of wine until they have
made due apology and reformed their behaviour. Anyone
failing to be present at grace after meals should be treated
in the same way.

None may take it on themselves to eat or drink before or after the established times for community meals. In fact, if any are offered something to eat or drink by the superior and refuse it but then later begin to feel a desire for what they formerly refused or for anything else, they should receive nothing at all until they have made due apology.

⁂

CHAPTER 44

The reconciliation of those excommunicated

ANY MEMBERS OF THE COMMUNITY WHO HAVE BEEN excommunicated from the oratory and the refectory for faults which are really serious must prostrate themselves at the entrance to the oratory at the time when the celebration of the work of God comes to an end. They should in complete silence simply lay their heads on the ground before the feet of all the community coming out of the oratory and stay there until the superior judges that they have done enough in reparation. When called they should rise and prostrate themselves first of all at the feet of the superior and then of all the community to beg their prayers. After that they should be received back into the choir in whatever order the superior decides. However they should not venture to take the lead in reciting psalms or in reading or in any other choir duty until they are again permitted to do so. Indeed at the end of every office they should prostrate themselves again on the ground in their place in choir and thus continue their reparation until permission is given by the superior to give up this penitential act.

Anyone who is excommunicated from the refectory only for a less serious fault should perform the same act of reparation in the oratory until permitted to cease; the superior brings this penance to an end by giving a blessing and saying 'that is enough'.

❦

CHAPTER 45

Mistakes in the Oratory

ANYONE WHO MAKES A MISTAKE IN A PSALM, responsory, antiphon or reading must have the humility to make immediate reparation there before all the community in the oratory. A failure to do that so clearly shows lack of the humility to put right a fault which was due to carelessness that it must incur a more severe punishment. Children, however, should be smacked for such faults of careless inattention.

❦

CHAPTER 46

Faults committed elsewhere

ANY MEMBER OF THE COMMUNITY WHO IN THE course of some work in the kitchen, in the stores, while fulfilling a service to others or in the bakery, the garden or the workshops or anywhere else does something wrong or happens to break or lose something or to be guilty of some other wrongdoing, must as soon as possible appear before the superior and the community with a voluntary admission of the failure and willing reparation for it. If any are guilty of such faults and fail to make such amends immediately and the truth comes out in another way then the guilty should be punished more severely.

It is, however, important that, if the cause of wrongdoing lies in a sinful secret of conscience, it should be revealed only to the superior or one of those in the community with recognized spiritual experience and understanding, who will know the way to the healing of their own wounds and those of others without exposing them in public.

CHAPTER 47

Signalling the times for the work of God

THE SUPERIOR IS PERSONALLY RESPONSIBLE FOR making sure that the time for the work of God, both at night and during the daytime, is clearly made known to all. This may, of course, be done by delegating the duty to a responsible member of the community, who can be relied on to make sure that everything is done at the proper time.

The superior, followed by other authorized members of the community in their due order, should give a lead by intoning psalms and antiphons for the choir. Only those, however, should come forward to sing and read who have the ability to fulfil this role in a way which is helpful to others. All must play their part under the directions of

the superior with humility and restraint and out of
reverence to God.

☙

CHAPTER 48

Daily manual labour

IDLENESS IS THE ENEMY OF THE SOUL. THEREFORE
all the community must be occupied at definite times in
manual labour and at other times in *lectio divina*.* We
propose the following arrangements, then, to cater for both
these needs.

From Easter to the first of October they will go out in the
morning from after Prime until the fourth hour and work
at whatever needs to be done. The period from the fourth

---

* *Lectio divina* for St Benedict meant careful and attentive reading of the
scriptures and of other sacred writings especially the monastic Fathers. It was
done with a conscious openness of heart to the Holy Spirit who was perceived
to be speaking to the individual through the sacred text; it was thus closely
linked to prayer and became a primary source of spiritual growth. *Lectio* also
involved learning by heart the psalms and other passages of scripture. It was
this discipline of *lectio* that gave rise in the dark times that were to come to
the emergence of Benedictine monasteries as centres of literacy and of learning
in scripture and theology. That learning was thorough but never exclusively
intellectual, because openness of mind and heart were integral to the discipline
of *lectio* which was always faithfully cherished in the monasteries. It led them
in due course to go beyond St Benedict's immediate perspective and to embrace
the riches of classical literature and learning which they, together with the Irish
monasteries in Europe, did so much to preserve from oblivion through monastic
scriptoria. Justice cannot be done to all this in a brief note. It is enough to say
here that the *lectio divina* to which St Benedict refers in this chapter became
the basis and source of all Benedictine education, both religious and secular,
and is still perhaps its most precious inspiration in an age so threatened by the
barriers of narrow specialization in everything.

hour until about the sixth hour should be given to *lectio divina*. After Sext when they have finished their meal they should rest in complete silence on their beds. If anyone wants to read at that time it should be done so quietly that it does not disturb anyone. The office of None could then be a little early coming half way through the eighth hour after which any work which is necessary should be attended to until Vespers. It may be, of course, that because of local conditions or the poverty of the monastery the community may themselves have to do the harvest work. If that happens it should not discourage anyone because they will really be in the best monastic tradition if the community is supported by the work of their own hands. It is just what our fathers did and the apostles themselves. Nevertheless there must always be moderation in whatever such demands are made on the community to protect those who have not a strong constitution.

From the first of October to the beginning of Lent they should devote themselves to *lectio divina* until the end of the second hour, at which time they gather for Terce and then they work at the tasks assigned to them until the ninth hour.* At the first signal for the ninth hour they must all put aside their work so as to be ready for the second signal. Then after the community meal they will spend their time in reading or learning the psalms.

There will be a different arrangement for the time of Lent. The morning will be given to reading until the end of the third hour and then until the end of the tenth hour they

---

* Note on 'hours' in the Rule. For the Romans, each day (from dawn to dusk) and each night (from dusk to dawn) was divided into twelve 'hours'. The actual length of these 'hours' varied according to the season; in summer they were longer during the day and shorter at night, but in winter they were shorter during the day and longer at night. Only at the two equinoxes did the actual length of the hours even out. Timekeeping, therefore, called for a special expertise and flexibility.

will work at their assigned tasks. As a special provision during these days of Lent each member of the community is to be given a book from the library to read thoroughly each day in a regular and conscientious way. These books should be handed out at the beginning of Lent.

It is very important that one or two seniors should be assigned to the task of doing the rounds of the monastery during any of the periods when the community is engaged in reading. They should make sure that there is no one overcome by idle boredom and wasting time in gossip instead of concentrating on the reading before them. Such a one is also a distraction to others. Any of the community who are discovered – which God forbid – to be guilty of such behaviour should be corrected on the first and second occasion. If there is no improvement then they should be given a punishment, in accordance with the Rule, which will act as a deterrent to others. Of course, it is always wrong for members of the community to associate with each other at times when this is not appropriate.

Sunday is the day on which all should be occupied in *lectio divina*, except for those who are assigned to particular duties. If there are any who are so feckless and lazy that they have become unwilling or unable any longer to study or read seriously then they must be given suitable work which is within their powers so that they may not sink into idleness.

As for those who are sick or too frail for demanding work, they should be given the sort of work or craft which will save them from idleness but not burden them with physical work that is beyond their strength. The superior should show understanding concern for their limitations.

CHAPTER 49

How Lent should be observed in the monastery

THERE CAN BE NO DOUBT THAT MONASTIC LIFE
should always have a Lenten character about it, but there
are not many today who have the strength for that.
Therefore we urge that all in the monastery during these
holy days of Lent should look carefully at the integrity of
their lives and get rid in this holy season of any thoughtless
compromises which may have crept in at other times. We
can achieve this as we should if we restrain ourselves from
bad habits of every kind and at the same time turn
wholeheartedly to the prayer of sincere contrition, to *lectio
divina*, to heartfelt repentance and to self-denial. So during
Lent let us take on some addition to the demands of our
accustomed service of the Lord such as special prayers and
some sacrifice of food and drink. Thus each one of us may
have something beyond the normal obligations of monastic
life to offer freely to the Lord with the joy of the Holy
Spirit[1] by denying our appetites through giving up
something from our food or drink or sleep or from
excessive talking and loose behaviour so as to increase the
joy of spiritual longing with which we should look forward
to the holy time of Easter.

Everyone should, of course, submit the details of these
personal offerings for Lent to the superior for approval and
a blessing. This is important; any individual obligation
undertaken in the monastery without the permission of the
superior will be accounted the result of presumption and
vainglory so that no reward can be expected for it.
Everything undertaken in the monastery must have the
approval of the superior.

CHAPTER 50

Those whose work takes them away from the monastery

THOSE WHOSE WORK TAKES THEM SOME DISTANCE from the monastery so that they cannot manage to get to the oratory at the right times for prayer must kneel with profound reverence for the Lord and perform the work of God at their place of work. It is for the superior to make the decision that this is necessary and appropriate.

In the same way those sent on a journey must be careful not to omit the hours of prayer which are prescribed for the whole community. They must observe them in the best way they can so as not to neglect the service they owe the Lord by their profession.

CHAPTER 51

Those on local errands or work

ANY WHO ARE SENT ON AN ERRAND WHICH WILL allow them to return to the monastery on the same day must not eat outside, in spite of pressing invitations whatever their source, unless the superior has approved this. The penalty for infringement of this principle will be excommunication.

CHAPTER 52

The oratory of the monastery

THE ORATORY MUST BE SIMPLY A PLACE OF PRAYER,
as the name itself implies, and it must not be used for any
other activities at all nor as a place for storage of any kind.
At the completion of the work of God all must depart in
absolute silence which will maintain a spirit of reverence
towards the Lord so that anyone wishing to pray alone in
private may not be prevented by the irreverent behaviour of
another. Then also anyone who at some other time wants
to pray privately may very simply go into the oratory and
pray secretly, not in a loud voice but with tears of devotion
that come from the heart. That is why, as I have said, those
who do not share this purpose are not permitted to stay in
the oratory after the end of any Office for fear of
interfering with the prayers of others.

CHAPTER 53

The reception of guests

ANY GUEST WHO HAPPENS TO ARRIVE AT THE
monastery should be received just as we would receive
Christ himself, because he promised that on the last day he
will say: I was a stranger and you welcomed me.[1] Proper
respect should be shown to everyone while a special
welcome is reserved for those who are of the household of
our Christian faith[2] and for pilgrims.

As soon as the arrival of a guest is announced, the superior and
members of the community should hurry to offer a welcome
with warm-hearted courtesy. First of all, they should pray
together so as to seal their encounter in the peace of Christ.
Prayer should come first and then the kiss of peace, so to
evade any delusions which the devil may contrive.

Guests should always be treated with respectful deference.
Those attending them both on arrival and departure should
show this by a bow of the head or even a full prostration
on the ground which will leave no doubt that it is indeed
Christ who is received and venerated in them. Once guests
have been received they should be invited to pray and then to
sit down with the superior or whoever is assigned to this
duty. Then some sacred scripture should be read for the
spiritual encouragement it brings us, and after that every
mark of kindness should be shown the guests. The rules of a
fast day may be broken by the superior to entertain guests,
unless it is a special day on which the fast cannot be broken,
but the rest of the community should observe all the fasts as
usual. The superior pours water for the guests to wash their
hands and then washes their feet with the whole community
involved in the ceremony. Then all recite this verse: Lord we
have received your mercy in the very temple that is yours.

The greatest care should be taken to give a warm reception to
the poor and to pilgrims, because it is in them above all
others that Christ is welcomed. As for the rich, they have a
way of exacting respect through the very fear inspired by
the power they wield.

The kitchen to serve the superior together with the guests
should be quite separate, so that guests, who are never
lacking in a monastery, may not unsettle the community by
arriving, as they do, at all times of the day. Two competent
members of the community should serve in this kitchen for

a year at a time. They should be given assistants whenever
they need it, so as to have no cause for murmuring* in
their service. When the pressure from guests dies down the
assistants can then be moved to other work assigned them.
Of course, it is not only for those serving in the kitchen for
superior and guests that this principle should obtain. It
should be a guideline for all the duties in the monastery
that relief should be made available when it is needed and
then, when the need is over, the assistants should
obediently move to whatever other work is assigned them.

The accommodation for the guests should be furnished with
suitable beds and bedding and one God-fearing member of
the community should also be assigned to look after them.
The monastery is a house of God and should always be
wisely administered by those who are wise themselves. No
member of the community should associate in any way or
have speech with guests without permission. If they should
meet guests or see them it would be right to greet them
with deep respect, as we have said; then after asking a
blessing they should move on explaining that they may not
enter into conversation with guests.

CHAPTER 54

The reception of letters and gifts in the monastery

NO ONE IN A MONASTIC COMMUNITY MAY RECEIVE
or send to others letters, gifts of piety or any little tokens
without the permission of the superior, whether it is their

* See note in Chapter 5.

parents who are concerned or anyone else at all or another member of the community. Even if their parents send them a present they must not decide for themselves to accept without first referring the matter to the superior. Then it will be for the superior, after agreeing to the reception of the gift, to decide who in the community should receive the gift and, if it is not the one to whom it was sent, that should not give rise to recriminations lest the devil be given an opportunity.[1] Anyone who infringes these principles must be corrected by the discipline of the Rule.

CHAPTER 55

Clothing and footwear for the community

THE LOCAL CONDITIONS AND CLIMATE SHOULD BE the deciding factors in questions about the clothing of the community, because obviously in a cold climate more clothing is needed and less where it is warm. The superior must give careful thought to these questions. However my suggestion for temperate regions is that each member of the community should receive a cowl and tunic, a scapular to wear at work and both sandals and shoes as footwear. The cowl should be thick and warm in winter but of thinner or well-worn material in summer. The community must not be too sensitive about the colour and quality of this clothing; they should be content with what is available in the locality at a reasonable cost. However the superior should see to it that the garments are not short and ill-fitting but appropriate to the size and build of those who wear them.

When new clothing is issued, the old should be immediately returned to be put in store for distribution to the poor. Two tunics and cowls should be enough for each member of the community to provide for night-wear and for laundering. Anything more than that would be excessive and this must be avoided. Sandals also and other articles which are worn out should be handed in when new ones are issued. Underclothing for those going on a journey should be provided from the community wardrobe which, on their return, should be washed and handed in again. Then there should be cowls and tunics available of slightly better quality than usual, which may be issued to travellers from the wardrobe and restored there on their return.

For bedding a mat, a woollen blanket, a coverlet and a pillow should be enough. The superior ought to inspect the beds at regular intervals to see that private possessions are not being hoarded there. If anyone is found with something for which no permission has been given by the superior, this fault must be punished with real severity. In order to root out completely this vice of hoarding personal possessions, the superior must provide all members of the community with whatever they really need, that is: cowl, tunic, sandals, shoes, belt, knife, stylus, needle, handkerchief and writing tablets. Every excuse about what individuals need will thus be removed.

There is one saying, however, from the Acts of the Apostles which the superior must always bear in mind, namely that proper provision was made according to the needs of each.[1] It is on these grounds that the superior should take into account what is truly necessary for those who suffer from an individual weakness, while ignoring the ill will of the envious, and in every decision remembering that an account must be given of it in the future judgement of God.

CHAPTER 56

The table for the superior and community guests

THE SUPERIOR'S TABLE SHOULD ALWAYS BE WITH
the guests and pilgrims. In the absence of guests members
of the community, invited by the superior, may take their
place but one or two seniors should always be left with the
community to keep an eye on standards of behaviour.

❧

CHAPTER 57

Members of the community with creative gifts

IF THERE ARE ANY IN THE COMMUNITY WITH
creative gifts, they should use them in their workshops with
proper humility, provided that they have the permission of
the superior. If any of them conceive an exaggerated idea of
their competence in this sort of work, imagining that the
value of their work puts the monastery in their debt, they
should be forbidden further exercise of their skills and not
allowed to return to their workshops unless they respond
with humility to this rebuke and the superior permits them
to resume their work.

If any product of the workshops is to be sold, those
responsible for the sale must be careful to avoid any
dishonest practice. They should remember Ananias[1] and
Sapphira who suffered bodily death for their sin, whereas
any who are guilty of fraud in the administration of the

monastery's affairs will suffer death of the soul. In fixing the prices for these products care should be taken to avoid any taint of avarice. What is asked by the monastery should be somewhat lower than the price demanded by secular workshops so that God may be glorified in everything.[2]

ॐ

CHAPTER 58

The reception of candidates for the community

THE ENTRY OF POSTULANTS INTO THE MONASTIC LIFE should not be made too easy, but we should follow St John's precept to make trial of the spirits to see if they are from God.[1] If, then, a newcomer goes on knocking at the door and after four or five days has given sufficient evidence of patient perseverance and does not waver from the request for entry but accepts the rebuffs and difficulties put in the way, then let a postulant with that strength of purpose be received and given accommodation in the guest quarters for a few days. Then later the new recruit can be received among the novices in the quarters where they study, eat and sleep.

A senior who is skilled at guiding souls should be chosen to look after the novices and to do so with close attention to their spiritual development. The first concern for novices should be to see whether it is God himself that they truly seek, whether they have a real love for the work of God combined with a willing acceptance of obedience and of any demands on their humility and patience that monastic life may make on them. They should not be shielded from

any of the trials of monastic life which can appear to us to
be hard and even harsh as they lead us on our way to God.

If novices after two months show promise of remaining
faithful in stability, they should have the whole of this Rule
read to them and then be faced with this challenge at the
end: that is the law under which you ask to serve; if you
can be faithful to it, enter; if you cannot, then freely depart.
Those who still remain firm in their intention should be led
back to the novitiate so that their patience may be further
tested. After another six months the Rule should again be
read to them so as to remove all doubt about what they
propose to undertake. If they still remain firm, then after
four more months the same Rule should again be read to
them. By that stage they have had plenty of time to think it
all over and, if they promise to observe everything and to
be faithful to anything that obedience may demand they
should be received into the community. Of course, they
must by now be fully aware that from that day forward
there can be no question of their leaving the monastery nor
of shaking off the yoke of the Rule, which in all that time
of careful deliberation they were quite free to turn away
from or to accept as their way of life.

When the decision is made that novices are to be accepted,
then they come before the whole community in the oratory
to make solemn promise of stability, fidelity to monastic life
and obedience. The promise is made before God and the
saints and the candidates must reflect that, if they ever by
their actions deny what they have promised, they will be
condemned by the God they have betrayed. Novices must
record their promises in a document in the name of the
saints whose relics are there in the oratory and also in
the name of their abbot or abbess in whose presence the
promise is made. Each must write the document in his or
her own hand or, if unable to write, ask another to write it
instead; then, after adding a personal signature or mark to

the document, each must place it individually on the altar.
As the record lies on the altar they intone this verse:
'Receive me, O Lord, in accordance with your word and I
shall live, and do not disappoint me in the hope that you
have given me.'[2] The whole community will repeat this
verse three times and add at the end the *Gloria Patri*.
Each novice then prostrates before every member of the
community asking their prayers and from that day is
counted as a full member of the community.

Before making their profession novices should give any
possessions they may have either to the poor or to the
monastery in a formal document keeping back for themselves
nothing at all in the full knowledge that from that day they
retain no power over anything – not even over their own
bodies. As a sign of this the newly professed in the oratory
immediately after the promises discard their own clothing
and are clothed in habits belonging to the monastery. Their
lay clothes are kept safely in case – which God forbid – any
should listen to the enticements of the devil and leave the
monastery discarding the monastic habit as they are dismissed
from the community. The record of their profession, however,
which the superior took from the altar should not be returned
but should be preserved in the monastery.

CHAPTER 59

Children offered by nobles or by the poor

IF PARENTS WHO ARE FROM THE NOBILITY WANT TO
offer to God in the monastery one of their children, who is
too young to take personal responsibility, they should draw

up a document like that described above and, as they make the offering, wrap the document with the child's hand in the altar cloth.

As to questions of property, they should add a promise to the document under oath that they will not themselves, nor through any other person, give the child anything at any time, nor yet contrive any opportunity whereby the child might be able in the future to acquire possessions. If they are unwilling to do this and insist on making a gift to the monastery and so merit a reward from God, they should draw up a form of donation transferring the property in question to the monastery keeping, if they wish, the revenue for themselves. Everything concerned with this property should be negotiated in such a way that not the slightest hint of personal expectations can be entertained by the child in a way which could lead through deception to ruin. Experience has shown how this can happen.

Poor people may make the offering of a child in the same way. If they have no property at all, they simply write and offer the child with the document in the presence of witnesses.

CHAPTER 60

The admission of priests into the monastery

An ordained priest who asks to be received into the monastery should not be accepted too quickly. If, however, he shows real perseverance in his request, he must understand that, if accepted, he will be bound to observe the full discipline of the Rule and may expect no relaxations. He will have to face up to the scriptural question: friend what have you come here for?[1] He should be allowed, however, to take his place after the abbot and exercise his ministry in giving blessings and offering Mass, provided that the abbot allows it.

He must understand that he is subject to the requirements of the Rule. He must not make any special demands but rather give everyone else an example of humility. If any question of rank arises in the community on the score of ordination or any other matter, he must take the place determined by the date of his entry into the community not by any concession granted through reverence for his priesthood. If anyone in one of the orders of clerics asks to join the monastery, the right place will be somewhere about the middle of the community, but they too are required to make the promises about observing the Rule and monastic stability.

❧

CHAPTER 61

Monastic pilgrims from far away

MONKS OR NUNS ON A PILGRIMAGE FROM FAR AWAY, who come to the monastery asking to be received as guests, should be received for as long as they wish to stay, provided that they are content with the local style of life they encounter and cause no disturbance in the monastery by any excess in personal behaviour. It may happen, of course, that one of them may find something to point out in criticism about the customs of the monastery, using sound arguments in a spirit of charitable deference. In that case the superior should consider the whole question with care and prudence in case it was for this very purpose that the pilgrim was sent by the Lord. Then, if later such a pilgrim wishes to embrace stability in the monastery, the request should not meet with automatic refusal, especially since it will have been possible to discern the qualities of the new postulant while still a guest.

If, on the other hand, such a pilgrim monk or nun has been revealed as a guest to be overbearing and full of bad habits then not only should all further association with the community be refused but such a guest should quite openly be requested to depart for fear that such a wretched example might lead others astray. But if no such negative signs are apparent it may be right to go further and not wait for a request to be accepted in the community. It may even be right to persuade such a one to stay so that others may benefit and learn from such example. After all, in all the world there is only one Lord and one King in whose service we are all engaged to fight. The superior may even perceive qualities in such a pilgrim to suggest that it would be right to grant a somewhat higher position in the community order than would be justified merely by the date of entry. The same principle would apply also to a postulant from the orders of priests and clerics, who have been mentioned above. The superior may decide to place one of them in a position higher than that dictated by the date of their entry, if he sees that their monastic observance is worthy of it.

The abbot or abbess, however, must be careful not to accept to stay as a guest any monk or nun from another known monastery without the consent of the appropriate superior and a letter of commendation. They must bear in mind the warning of scripture: do not do to another what you would not wish to suffer yourself.[1]

CHAPTER 62

The priests of the monastery

IF AN ABBOT WISHES TO HAVE A MONK ORDAINED
priest or deacon he must select one from his community
who has the gifts needed for the priesthood. When
ordained a monk must be careful to avoid a spirit of
self-importance or pride and he must avoid taking on
himself any duties to which the abbot has not assigned him.
He must be amenable to the discipline of the Rule, all the
more because of his priesthood. His ordination to the
priesthood should be no occasion for him to be forgetful of
obedience and the obligations of the Rule, but he must
more and more direct the growth of his spiritual life
towards the Lord. He must keep his place in community
order according to the date of his coming to the monastery
except in his priestly duties at the altar and unless by the
will of the community and with the approval of the abbot
he is promoted because of the good example of his
monastic observance.

He must in any case be faithful to the principles laid down
for the deans and the prior of the monastery. If he should
be headstrong enough to behave in any other way, he will
be accounted not a priest but a rebel and treated
accordingly. If he ignores repeated warnings and does not
reform, the evidence of this must be brought before the
Bishop. If even that brings no improvement and his
offences become notorious, he will have to be dismissed
from the monastery, but that must be avoided unless he is
so arrogant that he refuses to submit and obey.

CHAPTER 63

Community order

THE THREE CRITERIA FOR THE ORDER OF
precedence in the community are first of all the date of
entry, then monastic observance and the decision of the
abbot or abbess. But they must not cause unrest in the
flocks committed to them by acting unjustly and as though
with arbitrary authority but must remember at all times
that an account will have to be given of all their decisions
and works in this world. Well then, whenever the
community gets into order for the kiss of peace, or for
Holy Communion or for intoning the psalms or taking
their place in choir or in any other circumstances they
must be guided by the superior's directions or the order
established by the date of their entry. Age must never be
the deciding factor in community order just as it was that
Samuel and Daniel judged their elders when they were still
only boys.[1] So, apart from those whom the superior has
promoted for a more cogent reason or demoted for specific
faults, all the others retain the order of their conversion
to monastic life so exactly that one who arrived at the
monastery door at the second hour must accept a place
junior to another who came an hour earlier, whatever their
age or former rank may have been. Children, of course,
must be kept in their subordinate place by everyone on all
occasions.

Juniors in the community should show due respect for their
seniors, and seniors should love and care for their juniors.
When they address each other it should not be simply by
name, but senior monks call their juniors 'brother' and the
juniors address their seniors as 'nonnus' or 'reverend
father'. The abbot is understood to hold the place of Christ

in the monastery and for this reason is called 'lord' or 'abbot', not because he demands it for himself but out of reverence and love of Christ;* it is a point on which he should often reflect to help him to live up to so great an honour.

When members of a monastic community meet each other, the junior asks a blessing of the senior. As a senior passes by, the junior rises and yields a place for the senior to sit down and will never sit without the senior's permission. In that way they will conform to scripture which says they should try to be the first to show respect for each other.[2] Small children and adolescents must keep their places in the oratory and the refectory in a disciplined way. Anywhere else, and especially outside the monastery, they must be under supervision and control until they have learnt responsibility as they get older.

⁂

CHAPTER 64

The election of an abbot or abbess

IN THE PROCESS THROUGH WHICH AN ABBOT OR abbess is elected the principle to be borne in mind is that the one finally elected should be the choice of the whole community acting together in the fear of God or else of a small group in the community, however small they may be in numbers, provided they have sounder judgement. The grounds on which a candidate is elected abbot or abbess must

---

* For the same reasons an abbess is called 'lady abbess' and nuns in a monastic community address each other as 'sister' or 'mother'.

be the quality of their monastic life and the wisdom of their
teaching, even if they are the last in order in the community.

If it should happen – and may God forbid it – that the whole
community should conspire to elect one who will consent
to their evil way of life, and if their corrupt ways become
known to the bishop of the local diocese or to the abbots
or abbesses or ordinary Christians living nearby, they
should intervene to prevent so depraved a conspiracy and
provide for the appointment of a worthy guardian for the
house of God. They may be sure that they will receive a
rich reward for this good act, if it is done out of pure
intentions and zeal for the Lord, while if they neglect to
intervene in such a situation it will be accounted sinful.

The abbot or abbess, once established in office, must often
think about the demands made on them by the burden they
have undertaken and consider also to whom they will have
to give an account of their stewardship.[1] They must
understand that the call of their office is not to exercise
power over those who are their subjects but to serve and
help them in their needs. They must be well-grounded in
the law of God so that they may have the resources to
bring forth what is new and what is old in their teaching.[2]
They must be chaste, sober and compassionate and should
always let mercy triumph over judgement[3] in the hope of
themselves receiving like treatment from the Lord. While
they must hate all vice, they must love their brothers or
sisters. In correcting faults they must act with prudence
being conscious of the danger of breaking the vessel itself
by attacking the rust too vigorously. They should always
bear their own frailty in mind and remember not to crush
the bruised reed.[4] Of course I do not mean that they should
allow vices to grow wild but rather use prudence and
charity in cutting them out, so as to help each one in their
individual needs, as I have already said. They should seek
to be loved more than they are feared.

They should not be trouble-makers nor given to excessive
anxiety nor should they be too demanding and obstinate,
nor yet interfering and inclined to suspicion so as never to
be at rest. In making decisions they should use foresight
and care in analysing the situation, so that whether they are
giving orders about sacred or about secular affairs they
should be far-seeing and moderate in their decisions. They
might well reflect on the discretion of the holy patriarch
Jacob when he said: if I force my flock to struggle further
on their feet, they will all die in a single day.[5] They should
take to heart these and other examples of discretion, the
mother of virtues, and manage everything in the monastery
so that the strong may have ideals to inspire them and the
weak may not be frightened away by excessive demands.
Above all they must remain faithful to this Rule in every
detail, so that after fulfilling their ministry well they may
hear the words uttered to that good servant who provided
bread for fellow servants at the proper time: I tell you
solemnly the Lord sets his faithful servant over all that he
possesses.[6]

CHAPTER 65

The prior or prioress of the monastery

IT HAS OFTEN HAPPENED THAT UNFORTUNATE
conflicts have arisen in monasteries as a result of the
appointment of a prior or prioress as second in authority
to the superior. There have been instances when some of
these officials have conceived out of an evil spirit of self-
importance that they also are superiors and for that
reason have assumed the powers of a tyrant, so that they

encourage scandalous divisions in the community. This sort of thing is most likely to happen in those regions where the prior or prioress is appointed by the same bishop or priest who appointed the abbot or abbess. It is clear how very foolish this arrangement is, because it provides the grounds for these subordinate officials to think proudly from the very beginning that they are exempt from the superior's authority on the specious grounds that their own authority derives from the same source as their superior's. That simply encourages the development of envy, quarrels, slander, rivalry, divisions and disorderly behaviour. The result is that, because of the conflict between the superior and the second in command, their own souls are at risk and their subjects take sides in the dispute, which brings ruin on them too. The responsibility for this and all the danger and evil it brings rests on the heads of those who devised such a confusing method of appointment.

We have no doubt, therefore, that it is best in the interests of preserving peace and charity that the authority for the whole administration of the monastery should rest with the abbot or abbess. If possible, as noted above, it is best that everything should be organized through deans according to the wishes of the superior. Then, since power is delegated to many, there is no room for pride to take hold of any individual. However, if local needs suggest it and if the community makes the request with good reason and deference and the superior thinks it the right course to follow, the superior should take counsel with God-fearing seniors and appoint a second in command. Then the prior or prioress so appointed must carry out the duties delegated to them with due respect for the superior, against whose expressed wishes nothing must be attempted by them. The higher the position thus conferred on anyone the greater must be his or her devotion to the observance of the Rule.

If the prior or prioress is subsequently found to be led astray
by pride into serious faults and shows scant respect for the
holy Rule, then up to four times they must be rebuked in
words. If there is no improvement the discipline of the
Rule must be applied. If that brings no improvement, then
there is nothing for it but dismissal from this position so
that another more worthy candidate may be promoted.
If a dismissed prior or prioress cannot live in peace and
obedience in the community, then they must be expelled
from the monastery. But the superior must take care not to
be seared in soul by the flames of jealousy or envy and to
remember always the account we shall have to give to God
of all the judgements we make.

CHAPTER 66

The porter or portress of the monastery

AT THE ENTRANCE TO THE MONASTERY THERE
should be a wise senior who is too mature in stability to
think of wandering about and who can deal with enquiries
and give whatever help is required. This official's room
should be near the main door so that visitors will always
find someone there to greet them. As soon as anyone
knocks on the door or one of the poor calls out, the
response, uttered at once with gentle piety and warm
charity, should be 'thanks be to God' or 'your blessing,
please'. If the porter or portress needs help, then a junior
should be assigned to this task.

The monastery itself should be constructed so as to include
within its bounds all the facilities which will be needed,

that is water, a mill, a garden and workshops for various crafts. Then there will be no need for monks and nuns to wander outside which is far from good for their monastic development. We intend that this Rule should be read at regular intervals in the community so that no one may have the excuse of ignorance.

�֍

CHAPTER 67

Those who are sent on a journey

THOSE WHO ARE SENT ON A JOURNEY SHOULD commend themselves to the prayers of all the community as well as of the superior and, at the last prayer of the work of God in the oratory, there should always be a memento of all who may be absent. Any who come back from a journey should lie prostrate in the oratory at the end of each of the Hours to ask the prayer of the whole community in case they have chanced to suffer any harm from what they have seen or heard or from idle gossip on their journey. None of them should be foolish enough to give an account to anyone in the community of what they may have seen or heard while away from the monastery, because this can do much harm. If any dare to do so they must receive the punishment of the Rule. The same must apply to anyone who presumes to go outside the enclosure of the monastery or to go anywhere or do anything, however small, without the superior's permission.

�֍

CHAPTER 68

The response to orders that seem impossible

IF INSTRUCTIONS ARE GIVEN TO ANYONE IN THE
community which seem too burdensome or even impossible,
then the right thing is to accept the order in a spirit of
uncomplaining obedience. However, if the burden of this
task appears to be completely beyond the strength of the
monk or nun to whom it has been assigned, then there
should be no question of a rebellious or proud rejection,
but it would be quite right to choose a good opportunity
and point out gently to the superior the reasons for
thinking that the task is really impossible. If the superior
after listening to this submission still insists on the original
command, then the junior must accept that it is the right
thing and with loving confidence in the help of God obey.

CHAPTER 69

No one should act as advocate for another

GREAT CARE MUST BE TAKEN TO AVOID ANY
tendency for one of the community to take the side of and
try to protect another, even though they may be closely
related through ties of blood. Such a thing must not happen
in the monastery because it would provide a very serious
occasion of scandal. Anyone who acts against this principle
must be sharply deterred by punishment.

CHAPTER 70

The offence of striking another

EVERY OCCASION FOR PRESUMPTUOUS BEHAVIOUR IN a monastery must be avoided, so we insist that no one in the community may excommunicate or strike another unless given the power to do so by the superior. Those guilty of such wrongdoing should be rebuked before everyone so that all others may fear.[1] Everyone, however, should have some responsibility for the control and supervision of children up to the age of fifteen, but they must be moderate and sensible in the way they exercise it. Just as among the adults any who assume power over others must be punished so anyone who flares up immoderately against children must be subjected to the discipline of the Rule, for it is written in scripture; do not do to another what you would be unwilling to suffer yourself.[2]

CHAPTER 71

Mutual obedience in the monastery

OBEDIENCE IS OF SUCH VALUE THAT IT SHOULD BE shown not only to the superior but all members of the community should be obedient to each other in the sure knowledge that this way of obedience is the one that will take them straight to God. Of course any commands from the abbot or abbess or those they have delegated must take precedence and cannot be over-ridden by unofficial orders, but when that has been said, all juniors should obey their seniors showing them love and concern. Anyone objecting to this should be corrected.

Any monk or nun who is corrected for anything by abbot or abbess or one of the seniors and perceives that the senior is upset by feelings of anger, even though they may be well in control, then that junior should at once prostrate on the ground in contrition and not move until the senior gives a blessing which will heal the upset. Anyone who disdains to do so should receive corporal punishment or in a case of real rebellion be expelled from the monastery.

✲

CHAPTER 72

The good spirit which should inspire monastic life

IT IS EASY TO RECOGNIZE THE BITTER SPIRIT OF wickedness which creates a barrier to God's grace and opens the way to the evil of hell. But equally there is a good spirit which frees us from evil ways and brings us closer to God and eternal life. It is this latter spirit that all who follow the monastic way of life should strive to cultivate, spurred on by fervent love. By following this path they try to be first to show respect to one another with the greatest patience in tolerating weaknesses of body or character. They should even be ready to outdo each other in mutual obedience so that no one in the monastery aims at personal advantage but is rather concerned for the good of others.[1] Thus the pure love of one another as of one family should be their ideal. As for God they should have a profound and loving reverence for him. They should love their abbot or abbess with sincere and unassuming affection. They should value nothing whatever above Christ himself and may he bring us all together to eternal life.

☙

CHAPTER 73

This Rule is only a beginning

THE PURPOSE FOR WHICH WE HAVE WRITTEN THIS rule is to make it clear that by observing it in our monasteries we can at least achieve the first steps in virtue and good monastic practice. Anyone, however, who wishes to press on towards the highest standards of monastic life may turn to the teachings of the holy Fathers, which can lead those who follow them to the very heights of perfection. Indeed, what page, what saying from the sacred scriptures of the Old and New Testaments is not given us by the authority of God as reliable guidance for our lives on earth? Then there are the Conferences and the Institutes and the Lives of the Fathers and the rule of our holy father Basil. What else are these works but the means of true progress in virtue for those aiming at high standards of observance and obedience in monastic life? We, however, can only blush with shame when we reflect on the negligence and inadequacy of the monastic lives we lead.

Whoever you may be, then, in your eagerness to reach your Father's home in heaven, be faithful with Christ's help to this small Rule which is only a beginning. Starting from there you may in the end aim at the greater heights of monastic teaching and virtue in the works which we have mentioned above and with God's help you will then be able to reach those heights yourself. Amen.

Notes

Prologue

1 Rom. 13:11
2 Ps. 94(95):8
3 Rev. 2:7
4 Ps. 33(34):11
5 John 12:35
6 Ps. 33(34):12
7 Ps. 33(34):13–14
8 Isa. 58:9
9 Ps. 14(15):1
10 Ps. 14(15):2–3
11 Ps. 14(15):4 &
   cf Ps. 136(137):9
12 Ps. 113:9 (Ps. 115:1)
13 1 Cor. 15:10
14 2 Cor. 10:17
15 Matt. 7:24–25
16 Rom. 2:4
17 Ezek. 33:11

Chapter 2

1 Rom. 8:15
2 Ps. 39(40):10; Isa. 1:2
3 Ps. 49(50):16–17
4 Matt. 7:3
5 cf Rom. 2:11
6 cf 2 Tim. 4:2
7 1 Kings 2:27; 1 Sam. 2:27–36
8 Prov. 18:2
9 Prov. 23:14
10 Luke 12:48
11 Matt. 6:33
12 Ps. 33(34):10

Chapter 3

1 Ecclus. 32:24

Chapter 4

1 Gal. 5:16
2 Matt. 23:3
3 Matt. 5:44–45; Eph. 4:26
4 1 Cor. 2:9

Chapter 5

1 Ps. 17(18):44
2 Luke 10:16
3 Matt. 7:14
4 John 6:38
5 Luke 10:16
6 2 Cor. 9:7

Chapter 6

1 Ps. 38(39):1–2
2 Prov. 10:19
3 Prov. 18:21

Chapter 7

1 Luke 14:11
2 Ps. 130(131):1
3 Ps. 130(131):2. In this case, as in many others, the Latin translation available to St Benedict differed from the original Hebrew and therefore from modern translations of the same. To accept the Latin translator's interpretation is necessary if we are to make some sense of St Benedict's comment.
4 Gen. 28:12
5 Ps. 7:9
6 Ps. 93(94):11
7 Ps. 138(139):2

8 Ps. 75(76):10
9 Ps. 17(18):23
10 Ecclus. 18:30
11 Prov. 16:25
12 Ps. 13(14):1
13 Ps. 37(38):9
14 Ecclus. 18:30
15 Ps. 13(14):2
16 Ps. 49(50):21
17 John 6:38
18 *cf* 2 Tim. 4:8; Rev. 2:10
19 Phil. 2:8
20 Matt. 10:22
21 Ps. 26(27):14
22 Ps. 43(44):22; Rom. 8:36
23 Rom. 8:37
24 Ps. 65(66):10–11
25 *Ibid.* 12
26 Matt. 5:39–41
27 *cf* 1 Cor. 4:12
28 Ps. 36(37):5
29 Ps. 105(106):1
30 Ps. 31(32):5
31 Ps. 72(73):22–23
32 Ps. 21(22):6
33 Ps. 87(88):16
34 Ps. 118(119):71
35 Prov. 10:19
36 Ps. 139(140):11
37 Ecclus. 21:20
38 Luke 18:13
39 Ps. 37(38):6

Chapter 9

1 Ps. 50(51):15

Chapter 13

1 Matt. 6:13

Chapter 16

1 Ps. 118(119):164
2 Ps. 118(119):62
3 Ps. 118(119):164

Chapter 19

1 Ps. 2:11
2 Ps. 46(47):7
3 Ps. 137(138):1

Chapter 25

1 1 Cor. 5:5

Chapter 27

1 Matt. 9:12
2 2 Cor. 2:7–8
3 Ezek. 34:3–4

Chapter 28

1 1 Cor. 5:13
2 1 Cor. 7:15

Chapter 31

1 1 Tim. 3:13
2 Ecclus. 18:16
3 Matt. 18:6

Chapter 33

1 Acts 4:32

Chapter 34

1 Acts 4:35

Chapter 35

1 Ps. 85(86):17
2 Ps. 69(70):1

Chapter 36

1 Matt. 25:36, 40

Chapter 38

1 Ps. 50(51):15

Chapter 39

1 Luke 21:34

Chapter 40

1 1 Cor. 7:7
2 Ecclus. 19:2

Chapter 49

1 *cf* 1 Thess. 1:6

Chapter 53

1 Matt. 25:35
2 Gal. 6:10

Chapter 54

1 Eph. 4:27

Chapter 55

1 Acts 4:35

Chapter 57

1 Acts 5:1–11
2 1 Pet. 4:11

Chapter 58

1 1 John 4:1
2 Ps. 118(119):116

Chapter 60

1 Matt. 26:50

Chapter 61

1 Tobit 4:15

Chapter 63

1 1 Sam. 3:10–18; Dan. 13:44–64
2 Rom. 12:10

Chapter 64

1 Luke 16:2
2 Matt. 13:52
3 Jas. 2:13
4 Isa. 42:3
5 Gen. 33:13
6 Matt. 24:47

Chapter 70

1 1 Tim. 5:20
2 Tobit 4:15

Chapter 72

1 Rom. 12:10

Part Two

Tools of Benedictine Spirituality

The Work of God

One of the most readily recognizable passages in the Rule of St Benedict concerns the public prayer of the monastic community: 'Indeed, nothing is to be preferred to the work of God' (Chapter 43, first paragraph). When Benedict uses such an unusual expression as 'work of God' for the public prayer of the monastery, he is drawing on monastic tradition, where the term probably refers to God's prior claim on human activity as opposed to merely human projects or ambitions.

In any case, Benedict emphasizes the importance of this public prayer by devoting no less than twelve chapters of the Rule to his description of how the 'work of God' is to be structured. He is also very concerned about the timetable for public prayer as he sets aside seven distinct periods during the day when the monks are to drop whatever work may be engaging their attention in order to gather for prayerful recognition of God's claim on their lives.

Time is one of the most precious gifts that we humans receive from God. It is clear that Benedict wants his monks to acknowledge this gift by returning choice portions of their time each day to God. In this way, they will practise the most basic form of hospitality, which is to make room in their schedules for the entertainment of God's real but mysterious presence. All other forms of hospitality, whether it is welcoming guests or respecting nature, derive from this profound respect for the mystery of God. Thus, the apparent folly of 'wasting' time on God becomes the wisest possible use of this precious gift.

This public prayer of the monastic community is made up

primarily of biblical psalms, but there are also readings from other parts of Scripture, as well as special prayers, such as the Lord's Prayer. The constant chanting of the psalms is intended to immerse the monk in a world where God's presence is felt and where God's goodness is praised. This world is made access-ible to the monk through personal faith, which finds the gift of God at the centre of all reality, in spite of much evil and violence on the surface of human life.

For the purpose of achieving this prayerful immersion, Benedict prescribed that his monks should memorize the entire Psalter. This must have been a daunting task for the younger members of the monastery. But they would have been greatly assisted and encouraged by the older members, for we can well imagine that they were carried along, as it were, on the waves of biblical words provided by their elders. Over the years, the effect would be that the minds and memories of all the monks would be filled more and more with expressions of praise and gratitude.

Living with the psalms in this way would become like a second nature and would colour the consciousness of the monks in every circumstance of life. This would in turn gradually realize the ideal of monastic holiness, namely, a constant, loving aware-ness of the reality and presence of God in all of human life. With this awareness would also come a deep inner sense of peace and harmony, regardless of external chaos or even the final disruption we call death.

These unvarying and regular periods of praise and thanks-giving were thus intended to bring about that spiritual conver-sion which Benedict valued so highly. Such a transformation finds expression ultimately in liberation from self-centred pre-occupation and anxiety as the monk commits himself to unselfish love and service. The inner peace and calm realized through prayer will then permit greater awareness of the needs of others and the freedom to respond to those needs.

Such generosity is made possible through an ever-deeper trust in God's goodness as reflected in the reality of divine promises. The future will accordingly be changed from a time of threat and darkness to an illuminated horizon producing invincible hope and joyful expectation. The monastic tradition has recognized this dimension of Benedictine spirituality by making Benedict the patron of a happy death.

It is well worth noting that Benedict, in spite of his meticulous concern for the structure of this public prayer of the community, makes explicit provision for the right of future abbots to modify the timetable and structure of this prayer. This makes it quite clear that Benedict did not believe that an exact, much less a scrupulous, observance of the 'work of God' would produce the salvation of monks in some magical or mechanical way. Such prayerful attention to God will greatly assist them, however, in the painful conversion demanded by unselfish and sensitive behaviour in all areas of their lives.

This public monastic prayer is not to be understood, therefore, as scheduled moments of explicit prayers totally divorced from the rest of the monks' lives. They are to be understood rather as times when God's loving presence is at centre stage, as it were, while at other times of the day God is not totally forgotten but is allowed to recede to the wings. From there his presence can be recalled at any moment, especially when there is that atmosphere of silence and recollection that Benedict wishes his monks to foster in the cloister.

We know that Benedict's spiritual wisdom is valid for all Christians. Many lay people would like to share in that wisdom and they can do so even when they are prevented from regular participation in the public prayer of the monastery. There are breviaries available, which contain prayers very similar to those used in monasteries. By saying these prayers, lay people will also be able to consecrate each day to God and to enter into that same loving awareness of the divine presence in their lives.

Demetrius R. Dumm OSB

The Art of *Lectio Divina*

As it is now used, *lectio divina* is understood as the prayerful meditation on the text of the Bible and of other writings that embody the faith of the Church. The term lectio divina originally referred to the reading of the scriptures during the liturgy. As literacy and the availability of books increased, the context of this reading became less communal and more personal, as can be seen from St Benedict's provision of individual books for reading during Lent. This personal reading served as a complement to the liturgy, and became a characteristic feature of Benedictine spirituality. It ceased to be principally an oral-aural and communal experience and became more and more an internal dialogue of the heart with the text, and through the text with God.

Dynamic

Lectio differs substantially from the ordinary act of reading, even 'spiritual reading'. Lectio is at the service of prayer and goes beyond the act of merely absorbing the contents of a page. The classical formulation of this dynamic was given by Guigo the Carthusian (d. 1188): *lectio, meditatio, oratio, contemplatio*: reading, meditation, prayer, contemplation. What is read must first be digested and assimilated through a process of quiet repetition, in which we aim to become progressively attuned to its subtle echoes in the heart. The text thus serves as a mirror that brings inner realities to consciousness. This heightened awareness exposes our need for divine help and readily leads to prayer.

Sometimes, in this dialogue with God, we become more aware of God than of our own needs and pass into the simpler and more profound state of contemplation. Lectio can thus be viewed as a pathway towards contemplation. This is not, however, to say that the four steps constitute a sequential method to be followed, or that each is present in every lectio. Often the various phases are spread throughout the day as mindfulness of the Word is prolonged, and we keep responding to what we have read in the way that we live.

Practice

Initially we need to acquire the discipline of close reading, paying attention to every word and sentence, and not allowing ourselves to pass over anything. This deliberateness is helped by reading out loud, learning to articulate or vocalize the words as a means of slowing down and avoiding distraction. Lectio is like reading poetry; the sound of the words creates interior assonances, which in turn trigger intuitive connections which lodge more effectively in the memory. In lectio the intention is affective not cognitive, it is a work of a heart that desires to make contact with God and, thereby, to reform our lives.

Some wider reading can help us to sidestep speculative questions which would otherwise disperse our energies. This preparation is not lectio, but it serves it well.

Attention to the ambience of our lectio will often help to lead us more smoothly into prayer. Anything that we can do in terms of choice of place or posture, or to secure silence will keep potential disturbances at bay. Using an icon or a candle, or offering reverence to the book of the scriptures will often help us to move into a more prayerful space.

The Benedictine Spirit

There are three terms found in monastic tradition that describe an appropriate attitude to lectio. Our reading must be assiduous or generous, that is to say it must involve a sustained expenditure of forethought and energy and will often demand a sacrifice of time which could have been devoted to other things. Lectio must be done in a spirit of reverence, expressed in the manner in which we treat the sacred book itself, in our posture and in the way in which we make practical provision to exclude from this space whatever is not sacred. It is reverence which makes us keep silent and receptive so that we can listen to the word that speaks to our souls and brings salvation. When we open the sacred book we also open ourselves; we let ourselves become vulnerable – willing to be pierced by God's two-edged sword. This is what St Benedict refers to as compunction, allowing ourselves to experience the double dynamic of every genuine encounter with God: the growing awareness of our urgent need for forgiveness and healing on the one hand and, on the other, a more profound confidence in God's superabundant mercy.

Challenges

Two areas call for constant vigilance. First we must be not only hearers but doers of the word. Unless we come to our lectio with an antecedent will for conversion, the exercise is vain. Our lectio will thrive most fully when we aim to incarnate what we read in the way we act. When God seems silent, it is usually because either there is a latent resistance, or there is too much inner noise coming from a multiplicity of other concerns. Sometimes the difficulties we experience in lectio serve as a summons to re-examine our lives and to seek to establish there a greater harmony with what we read. Second, we have to renounce the search for novelty. Lectio needs to be regular and not erratic. We need, as St Benedict insisted, to read whole books of Scripture from beginning to end, quietly working our way through a Gospel or an Old Testament prophet, willing to be surprised, resisting the temptation to exercise total control over what we read.

Joy

Lectio demands much of us, but it is an enriching experience that constantly renews our spiritual life. God's word adds perspective to our experience, gives meaning to our struggles and keeps alive the flame of hope. Above all, contact with the scriptures is a source of joy and delight to the heart, bringing us into an ever-deeper relationship to the God whom we seek and to Jesus who calls us.

Michael Casey OCSO

Bibliography

Benedict of Nursia, *Rule for Monasteries*, Ch. 48.

Casey, Michael, *The Art of Sacred Reading*, Dove, Melbourne, 1995.

Casey, Michael, *Sacred Reading*, Triumph Books, Liguori, 1996.

Guigo II, *The Ladder of Monks and Twelve Meditations*, Cistercian Publications, Kalamazoo, 1981, pp. 67–86.

Prayer

Prayer for Benedictines is a relationship with God which opens one to the awareness of God's presence permeating all of one's life. Prayer for ancient monastics was spoken of in terms of *memor Dei* ('remembrance of God'), who is always remembering everything which has been created. Benedict does not present any detailed treatise on personal prayer in his Rule; rather he assumes that prayer derives from the two main monastic practices of formal prayer, that of the *Opus Dei*, or liturgy of hours, and *lectio divina*, the activity of reading, pondering, ruminating and reflecting on the scriptures.

Prayer is an invitation to 'listen with the ear of your heart', the first words of the Prologue that opens the whole Rule of St Benedict. Listening is both a grace given by God and an act of love, for listening requires setting aside one's own preoccupations so as to give oneself time and space to be present to the 'Other'. This 'Other' longs to reveal to us how much we are beloved and to make possible in us our coming to know that we are made in the Divine image and likeness. As one is led more deeply into a relationship with the God whose love is beyond imagining, one is taught by the Spirit how to see every event and person, all creation and happenings from the divine perspective. Gregory the Great describes Benedict's contemplation of 'the whole world . . . brought before his eyes, gathered up, as it were, under a single ray of sun',[1] such that 'the mind of the seer was enlarged: caught up in God, it could see without difficulty all that is under God'.[2] Thus the aim of prayer is that of widening one's vision such that one begins to see as God sees, to love all that God has created as God has, to view life's situations as God does.

How does one come to be such a contemplative? Divine grace makes possible what is not possible by human effort, as the pray-er uncovers the mysteries of the biblical words chanted in the Divine Office and pondered during lectio divina hidden in one's own life. One discovers that the psalms, parables, wisdom sayings, stories and events of Scripture are living words. As they are prayed over under the Spirit's guidance, the particular phrases and scenes become 'real' in one's life. The practice of prayer spills over into the practice of remembering how God is forming the dynamism of those words in one's life. In turn, the living of the words of prayer is manifest in encountering Christ in one's monastic leader, in the community members, in the exchange of hospitality with strangers and guests, and in the service of others in various ministries.

The realization of God's activity in the soul has been expressed in a variety of ways over the centuries, so that prayer forms have changed in response to the larger movements of prayer within differing cultures. In the early centuries of Benedictine life, prayer grew out of the practice of lectio divina, the reading, memorization and contemplation of the Word of God. The phrases which touched the heart during engagement in lectio were carried in the memory and repeatedly considered as the monastic engaged in manual labour. With the Carolingian reform of Charlemagne, monasteries became centres for learning as well as prayer. Those monastics involved in copying manuscripts of the Bible and biblical commentaries in the scriptorium began to portray the fruit of their lectio in illuminations and decorated letters, which, in turn, would serve as material for reflection for others. Commentaries on Scripture multiplied out of a need to explain the scriptures to the people.

As devotion to Mary and the saints began developing in the eleventh and twelfth centuries, along with meditation on Christ's suffering, meditation handbooks became important for those who could read. Prayer books were a means of introducing the educated to reflections drawn from Scripture. Those laity who were unable to read were taught to pray the Lord's Prayer 150 times, a practice which coincided with the praying of 150 psalms of the *Opus Dei* in the monasteries. As devotion to Mary increased in the twelfth century, then *Aves* ('Hail Mary') replaced the 150 *Paters* ('Our Father') and beads were designed to help people visually remember the number of prayers. Along with devotional prayers a flourishing of mystical prayer arose in the high middle ages, often the fruit of pondering the Song of Songs. Commentaries on this biblical book of love poetry abounded in Cistercian and Benedictine monasteries in the twelfth and thirteenth centuries. For example, the influence of the commentaries by Bernard of Clairvaux and William of St Thierry are clearly apparent in the Revelations of Gertrude of Helfta.

As the *devotio moderna* movement spread among the laity in the fourteenth century under the influence of Carthusian monks,[3] the stress on meditation of interior contemplative themes, which were more affective in tone than speculative, also permeated monasteries. Books like Thomas a Kempis' *Imitation of Christ* popularized the practice of twice daily meditations on the life and passion of Christ. Such books of meditations, designed to lead people to interior mental recollection on the mysteries in Christ's life, became over time 'spiritual reading' and often replaced the practice of lectio divina, particularly in women's monasteries of the nineteenth and twentieth centuries prior to the monastic renewal following Vatican Council II.

In the years following Vatican II, study, workshops and publications on lectio divina have brought a return to this practice of Benedictine prayer. In addition, various forms of centring prayer, as taught by John Main OSB, Basil Pennington OCSO and Thomas Keating OCSO, have been a means of attending to the presence of God in contemplative prayer.

Mary Forman OSB

Notes

1 Gregory the Great, *The Life of Saint Benedict*, Commentary by Adalbert de Vogüé, translated by Hilary Costello and Eoin de Bhaldraithe, St Bede's Publications, Petersham, MA, 1993, p. 164.
2 Ibid., p. 165.
3 Peter King, *Western Monasticism: A History of the Monastic Movement in the Latin Church*, Cistercian Studies 185, Cistercian Publications, Kalamazoo, MI/Spencer, MA, 1999, p. 246.

Work*

Working to Rule

What is monastic?

What sort of things do we think are holy? The question seems silly and easy to answer at first. God is holy, so whatever is to do with God is holy too. This leads us very naturally to think about prayer, going to church, acting justly and other spiritual things. All of these are holy and worthwhile, but if we concentrate on them alone, we miss out some very large parts of our lives. Most people spend much of their time working for their living, and working for and within their families. Our daily lives often seem to have nothing holy about them at all. This is a thoroughly un-Christian way of looking at things and the Rule of St Benedict provides something of an antidote.

In Chapter 48 of the Rule, Benedict makes arrangement for the work of the monks. He begins with a remark that has become a proverb, 'Idleness is the enemy of the soul.' He goes on to describe the timetable and anticipates that some communities will be so small or poor that they will have to do quite a lot of work, including bringing in the harvest, by themselves. At this daunting prospect he says, 'Let them not be distressed . . . For when they live by the labour of their hands, as our fathers the apostles did, then they are really monks.' It is worth reflection that the only practice St Benedict explicitly commends as mon-

* This piece is a shortened version of an original article which appeared in *The Journal*, vol. 102, Autumn 1997.

astic in the whole of the Rule is that the monks should earn their living.

Yet work is not often seen as a part of the spiritual life. St Benedict meets this head on. For Benedict, idleness is the enemy because monks who do not work well will not pray well. Therefore he says, monks 'should have specified periods for manual labour as well as for prayerful reading'. Work is given a protected place in the monastic timetable, just as much as prayer and the *Opus Dei*. This is quite a radical position. The force of St Benedict's commendation of work is not simply that it is another good monastic practice, but there is something about work which sums up the goals of monastic, and hence of Christian life.

Toil and trouble

Today there is a large degree of confusion about the purpose and value of work. For many, the word 'work' is synonymous with 'toil'. There are two opposing tendencies, which to some degree are present in everyone. One is to minimize work as much as possible, 'clocking' on and off, with little regard for what is done in between or the sense of purpose in it. The other is the workaholic, who cannot stop, who stays late at work, or even brings it home at weekends. Work becomes a person's life. It would be unwise to rhapsodize about the supreme Christian value of work unless we understand that work for many is a kind of trap into either futility or hectic pursuit of rewards that there is little time to enjoy.

The issue can be put very simply. Many people feel alienated from their work. While some individuals have work which is fulfilling, many more feel no connection with the actual work they do and drudge away at something whose only direct bearing on their lives is that it provides them, if they are lucky, with the means to survive and perhaps raise children. Others feel alien-ated because the process of working for gain can itself be dehumanizing. People who do rotten jobs, or none at all, are easily seen as inferior, and easily see themselves as inferior. There is also a third level of alienation, which gives some clue to a way forward. It is a curious phenomenon of social history that at some point work became something one went out to do. We talk of domestic work, but it is not seen in the same way as, say, ploughing a field or brokering a deal. The trouble with this division is that we end up with a very artificial conception of what work is. It is seen as something which earns money from 'outside' and is judged by what it brings in, whether to the family or society as a whole. The worker is also judged in the same way. The focus is on *what* is done and for whom. We have to look instead at *who* is doing it.

The Work of God

If we wish to arrive at a Christian understanding of work, we have to begin with the basic facts of the faith. Work can easily become bound up with judgements about status. By contrast, St Paul's letter to the Philippians gives us a hymn about Christ, who though in the form of God, accepted the human state and became obedient even to the shameful death of a criminal. The Word became flesh and dwelt among us. Everything is changed by this, including our work.

To get the right view of work, we have to get the right view of humanity. Instead of valuing certain types of work above others, we should think that each is being done by a human being, created and loved by God. If we really want to know what is valuable, we should look at what Christ did. Having found him performing simple and humble tasks at the carpenter's bench, we have to ask more searching questions about our value judgements.

What is work, seen in the context of God's revelation in Christ? There are ambiguities in the way that Christians talk about work. On the one hand, Genesis 1 depicts God as working for six days to create the world and implies that human work is a reflection of that divine toil. On the other hand, work is seen as a consequence of the Fall, a part of Adam's curse in Genesis 2. One approach gives us the much-derided 'work ethic', while the other leaves little room for seeing value in anything we do. There are two important points to note here. The first is that the problem is not with work itself, but the way we regard it. It is not our power to work which has resulted in today's sorry mess, but our tendency to use that power to do things other than love and serve the God who gave it. The correct understanding of work therefore is not to be found in socio-economic analyses, but in an examination of the human condition itself. The second point is found in these words from the Prologue to St Benedict's Rule:

> The labour of obedience will bring you back to him from whom you had drifted through the sloth of disobedience ... Seeking his workman in a multitude of people, the Lord calls out to him and lifts his voice ... (Prologue, first and fourth paragraphs)

What we might be tempted to see as a necessary evil or as a punishment is in fact the means used by God for our salvation. There is an ascetical quality to work in that it involves (often reluctant) effort. But the deeper point is that the incarnation of the Word has given us a gospel of work, the first tenet of which is that work has value precisely because it is done by human beings. Jesus slaving away at the carpenter's bench can encourage us to plod on with our column of figures or heap of bricks. However, the fact that it was God who was doing it changes everything; that apparently pointless drudge is given eternal value because God bothered to do it. Whatever we do in our God-given capacity for action can be grace-bearing since we may do it as human beings fully restored to the full image of God who took on our nature. Perhaps this seems too grand a vision of the daily round of the office or factory, but we must bear in mind *who* is doing that daily grind: a human person made in the image of God.

To know what an authentically human life looks like, we have to look at Christ. The incarnation of the Son of God ended in agony at Calvary. The central mystery of our redemption is that it comes through suffering and death. Just as significant as the life of God in Christ is the death of God in Christ. We have to set the glossy picture of work as participation in God's creative power against the starker vision of work as part of the sufferings of the body of Christ. Here we find reflected the barren nature of so much social life and exchange. The difference for Christian workers is that they accept their burden in the same spirit as Christ did. That spirit was one of saving love and such faith in God that the issue of that death was resurrection. Christians are meant to transform society and that is done by participation in its woes in faith and hope. Work we are reluctant to do, or the unwelcome idleness of unemployment or destitution, are part of what God has taken to himself on the cross. Idleness is the enemy of the soul because it springs from the conviction that God is not found in those things that bore or hurt us. It prevents us from accepting those burdens in the redeeming spirit of Christ. As such, work, whether it be designing planes or washing dishes, is part of the 'labour of obedience' which brings us back to God, just as much as the daily round of prayer and *lectio*.

Laurence McTaggart

Perseverance

Choices cause consequences. As one leaves the centre of Sydney the road forks. Going to the left up King's Street can lead eventually to Melbourne; continuing straight ahead one may find oneself in Perth: two very different cities separated by over 3,000 km. People beginning a journey need to be clear about their goal or they may find themselves in a very different place from what they had hoped. In the Rule of St Benedict, Chapter 72, Benedict contrasts the bitter zeal that makes a barrier to God's grace and the good zeal that opens us to divine and human love. Zeal, or perseverance, can be a two-edged sword. Constantly on our journey we need to ask ourselves how our spiritual disciplines and practices are furthering our journey to the Kingdom of God.

Consider the contrast between two monastics I have known. Sister A and Brother B have both been exemplary in their monastic observance, both contributed greatly to the physical wellbeing of their communities – yet the contrast in spirit is stark. Sr A suffered greatly towards the end of her life – changes in religious practice undermined her belief in God, her rigid personality kept her emotionally distant from her community. Did anyone grieve at her passing? – who knows, nothing showed but relief. In contrast, Br B is not only at the heart of his community, but also the bearer of God's life far beyond. His funeral will be a celebration of life in the midst of many tears.

What made the difference? The disciplines they chose to feed the life of faith. The only personal practice of Sr A that I know of is significant: each day she made her bed the same way as an expression of her Vow of Stability. No, don't laugh. There is a good lesson here. An ordered woman, she wanted to offer all to God, even the small things. So far so good. But she focused on what came easily, baptized her own preferences, and did not leave herself open to God's love and the demands of others.

Br B's actions seem to point to a decision made early in his monastic life to never let pass an act of charity he could possibly do. Thus open to God's providence and to serving others, he radiates equanimity and joy. Significantly he is also a most astute, if most kind, judge of character.

We all need practices to feed the life of faith and Benedictine spirituality provides a rich variety of resources: the work of God, *lectio divina*, prayer, work, hospitality, etc. At differing stages of life these resources will sustain our faith in differing ways. Discerning what is appropriate at any point in time is a challenge, but necessary if we are to run the way of God's commandments with joyful hearts.

In the midst of our first enthusiasm, we need to take stern stock of ourselves and embrace a disciplined spirituality. Chesterton has said that we inveigh against the sins we are least likely to commit. Unless we can recognize our genuine weakness we become sadly lost like Sr A. In this the comments of others on our personalities can be so helpful. If talkative, we could develop our listening skills, if naturally withdrawn, become sociable, if moody, emotional self-discipline works wonders, if reserved, play may be the challenge we need. Rarely will we overturn who God has made us to be but rather with balance we can flourish to God's glory.

Such early challenges are relatively easy to discern. The real difficulty comes further on the journey when we are called to negotiate the times and seasons that are the natural part of growth. Dramatic conversion is rarely the stuff of the journey and often it takes time before we realize we are on the wrong road. How can we recognize such? First, a sense of drudgery pervades our life. Notice this is not difficulty or suffering – both means by which God can foster growth – but rather a sense that we are not getting anywhere. Our prayers seems routine and we feel disengaged from others. This malaise can be good. It is as though God is letting us run out of petrol in the hope that we must stop and ask direction. Again, at this time, the comments of others can be enlightening. Once I had a call to change from a passing remark of a shopkeeper – nothing said unkindly but an observation that brought me up and made me reconsider the balance of my life.

At such times we need to reassess our lives in the light of the two great Commandments of Jesus, using the resources of our Benedictine spirituality. We who have prayed much may be called to shift the balance to service, we who have been hospitable may be called to withdraw in silent prayer, we who have been still may be called to study. The purpose of this testing is to make us sensitive to the Spirit at work in our hearts and so be schooled to love God and others more creatively.

Over time, the decisions we make and the practices we embrace form us, hopefully into Christ. Shaped by his Gospel and supported by others we may persevere to the fullness of everlasting life in the Kingdom of God.

Kym Harris OSB

The Vows

The Second Vatican Council's teaching about religious life in the Constitution on the Church starts with a discussion of the three evangelical counsels: chastity, poverty and obedience. The same is true of Pope John Paul II's Apostolic Exhortation 'Vita consecrata'.

The Rule of St Benedict never speaks of the evangelical counsels as such. However, St Benedict certainly believed that monks were called to chastity, poverty and obedience. In Chapter 33 he gives a fine description of the three evangelical counsels when he writes that 'no one may presume to give, receive or retain anything . . . especially since monks may not have the free disposal even of their own bodies and wills'.

The monk does not own property, does not have the free disposition of his body, and is not allowed to follow his own will: these are the three renunciations involved in the evangelical counsels of poverty, chastity and obedience.

When modern writers say that all religious profess the evangelical counsels, they are using a formula which did not emerge until several hundred years after St Benedict wrote. However, what St Benedict says in Chapter 33 reminds us that the three evangelical counsels are closely related to each other. When religious say that they have given up the right to possess property, as well as control of the body and of the will, this is another way of saying that they have given up everything: if you have given up your body, will and possessions, there is nothing left for you to own. That is why we can say that religious are dedicated totally and unreservedly to the service of God, out of love for him. That is what the evangelical counsels involve, and that is also what St Benedict calls for from his monks.

St Benedict says that newcomers spend a year as novices. Modern Church law requires that they then spend at least three years in temporary vows – that is, commitment for a period of time, to allow for a longer period of training and discernment. At the end of this period, they may make profession for life. This is what St Benedict describes in Chapter 58 of his Rule.

St Benedict writes that the candidate 'comes before the whole community in the oratory and promises stability, fidelity to monastic life and obedience'.

This promise is central to the commitment made by the monk, and it is helpful to explore the meaning of this promise, though it would be a mistake to try and define each of the three expressions in precise legal terms.

'Fidelity to monastic life' is an attempt to translate the Latin words *conversatio morum*. The meaning of this term has foxed scholars and commentators for years. One way of approaching it is to see it as the core element in the monastic commitment, and to examine what that commitment is. Cassian tells us that the monk's ultimate aim is to come to the Kingdom of God, and that his immediate goal is purity of heart, without which we shall never attain our ultimate aim.[1] A good way of describing *conversatio morum* is that it is the monk's commitment to pursuing this goal, through adopting the monastic programme of asceticism and prayer, as well as the monastic structure of life which is designed to support that programme.

If *conversatio morum* is the core of the monk's commitment, 'stability' and 'obedience' give more precision to the Benedictine way of leading the monastic life. 'Stability' implies perseverance, sticking to the programme once undertaken, 'faithfully observing his (God's) teaching in the monastery until death' (Prologue). Obedience recognizes the need for guidance. The Benedictine is a cenobite, serving 'under a rule and an abbot' (Chapter 1).

A mediaeval commentator, Bernard of Monte Cassino, thought that the threefold promise Benedict asks of his monks distinguishes them from the three other types of monk we find in Chapter 1.[2] Bernard wrote that Benedictine monks are stable, unlike gyrovagues, who wander from one place to another; they are under a superior, unlike hermits, who have been tried and tested and no longer need the guidance of a superior; they seek a true monastic way of life, unlike sarabaites, who have no rule and whose characters are as soft as lead.

While St Benedict may not have thought in these terms, it is quite a useful way of looking at the promise he asks of his monks. If someone wants to be a member of a Benedictine community, he needs to know that stability, conversatio morum and obedience are the ground rules for community membership.

However, it would be a mistake to see profession simply in terms of accepting the rules of a club. It is, above all, an act of self-dedication to God, made out of love since, as St Benedict tells us (Chapter 5), it is love that impels the monk to pursue everlasting life. And this act of self-dedication is vividly expressed in the ritual St Benedict prescribes when a monk is professed.

The monk, after making his promise, draws up a written document and places this on the altar. When we celebrate the Mass, gifts of bread and wine are placed on the altar. These gifts are received by the Church and will be used exclusively for the honour and glory of God, as they are destined to become the Body and Blood of Christ. Like the bread and the wine, the monk's document is placed on the altar. It becomes a symbol of the monk's self-giving to the Lord. Monks, through making their profession, are totally dedicated to the honour and glory of God, and to his service.

Richard Yeo OSB

Notes

1 Cassian, *Conferences*, I, IV.
2 Bernard of Monte Cassino, *Expositio in Regulam*, c. 58.

Hospitality

An acquaintance once said to me, 'You are wrong when you say that hospitality is at the centre of the Christian Church. It isn't hospitality,' she insisted, 'it's fear.' The woman, a Catholic convert, was responding to a chapter in my book, *The Cloister Walk*, in which I talk about how monastic hospitality opened the doors of Christian faith to me, overcoming what had seemed insurmountable obstacles of doubt and dread, including the fear of a God who wants to punish me for being who I am.

The world could use more of the fear of the Lord, which is the first stage of wisdom, the healthy fear of wonder and reverence before a God who knows us better than we know ourselves and loves us anyway. But we would do well to let go of the narcissistic fear that makes us anxious under circumstances and with people we can't control. When misfortune strikes, and we fall victim to accident, illness, or the bad intentions of others, we can choose how to respond, either falling back on our own resources and withdrawing from a dangerous world, or remaining open to what God has placed before us. The latter, Benedict insists, is always our best response. Hospitality is a tool that keeps us focused, not on ourselves, but on 'the divine presence [that] is everywhere' (the Rule of St Benedict, Chapter 19). The stranger at our door may bring new dangers and temptations, or be an angel in disguise. But Benedict trusts that in the play of hospitality, in learning how to give and to receive that which we cannot truly give or earn, we will be brought closer to the mystery of the Incarnation.

It is remarkable that in the Rule, which is otherwise so humane and flexible, there is no leeway regarding hospitality: 'All guests who present themselves are to be welcomed as Christ' (Chapter 53, first paragraph). No wriggle room, no way out, no chance to respond to a visitor's demands by saying, in an exasperated tone, 'Can't you see we're trying to run a monastery here?' The monk I know who did say that to a guest asking one too many questions about monastic life spent the next day apologizing to her, and the next ten years telling the story on himself.

Benedict places his chapter on the reception of guests late in the Rule, after he has established the sort of place a monastery is to be. This is proper, for only those who are truly at home in themselves can offer genuine hospitality, which is not controlling or manipulative, but welcomes us as we are. For the guest the most refreshing thing about monastic hospitality is that it does not seek to turn you into a 'monklet', a celibate, or a Roman Catholic, but guides you in honouring your own vows, in my case as a married Presbyterian lay preacher and deacon.

Unlike commercial hospitality, which provides a comforting sameness, monastic hospitality is always surprising, as it liberates guests to discern their true needs. People who go to a monastery to rest begin working hard instead, writing a poem for the first time in years, or composing a conciliatory letter to an estranged friend. But a pilgrim who comes prepared to work may find it impossible. On my first retreat, when I complained to an elderly monk that I had been too sleepy to even begin the spiritual books I had intended to read, he said, 'Maybe sleep is the most spiritual thing you can do right now.'

Benedict demands a radical hospitality from monks, but he also knows that they need to keep some time and space reserved for themselves alone: 'The kitchen for the abbot and guests ought to be separate, so that guests – and monasteries are never without them – need not disturb the brothers when they present themselves at unpredictable hours' (Chapter 53, fifth paragraph). This is not fussiness or exclusivity but a wise acknowledgement of a deep psychological truth. People who give so much of themselves that they lose their own identity are not truly hospitable, and neither the monastery nor the pilgrim is well served if monks use guests as a means of escaping dull routine, or an unhappy community life. In *Seeking God* Esther de Waal reminds us that monastic hospitality has two simple ends: Did they see Christ in us? Did we see Christ in them?

To Benedict, the mundane hospitality we offer others has a divine purpose, and he uses a judgement text in Matthew to underscore this point: 'All guests who present themselves are to be welcomed as Christ, for he himself will say, "I was a stranger and you welcomed me"' (Chapter 53, first paragraph). Christ will recognize is in the new creation, as he has already encountered us in this one. The Incarnation is God's hospitality to us, a means of welcoming us not only as friends, but as family. We, in turn, are called to be fully present to one another now, and to live our lives keeping in mind St Paul's admonition to 'Welcome one another . . . just as Christ has welcomed you, for the glory of God' (Rom. 15:7).

Kathleen Norris

Bibliography

de Waal, Esther, *Seeking God: The Way of St Benedict*, Collins Fount, London, 1984. New Edition, Canterbury Press, Norwich, 1999.
Norris, Kathleen, *The Cloister Walk*, Lion, Oxford, 1999.

Part Three

The Benedictine Experience of God

A Simple Daily Office –
Morning and Evening Prayer

Introduction

There is nothing particularly Benedictine about the monastic
Office, or, as Benedict calls it, the *Opus Dei*, the 'Work of God'.
Like the sacraments, daily prayer belongs to the whole Church,
and the whole people of God are called to sanctify their own
history by the practice of constant prayer. When Benedict gave
his instructions on the Opus Dei in the Rule, it is likely that he
himself was following 'best practice' as it was in Rome in the
sixth century, combined with what he had seen of some monastic
uses, and some 'novelty items', such as the Ambrosian hymns
which he adds.

Indeed, one might go so far as to say that the most character-
istically 'Benedictine' approach to the Opus Dei is in its regular
practice, its becoming a natural part of the interplay between
work and rest in the fabric of any day, a natural part of the life
of those who pray it. It becomes a habit, much more than any
monastic dress could ever be, and a habit in which there is a
constant interchange between familiarity and novelty, since
what we pray in the Opus Dei is, above all, the Word of God
in Scripture, whether it be in the psalmody, the short readings,
or the prayers and antiphons which those readings have inspired
over the past 1,500 years.

To this end, the following scheme is offered. In no way does
it aim at completeness, as Benedict did when he insisted on the
entire cursus of 150 psalms being recited, with the customary
canticles, over the course of a week. Rather, it is offered as a

selection, an aid and beginning to prayer, not as an end in itself. It is deliberately much shorter than either the Rule's version of the Office, or the version available since Vatican II for the use of the Church as a whole, in the hope that its very brevity will aid both use and memorization. This last point is important. For the early monks, and for Benedict's disciples, the psalms were not only an external discipline, but also a help to the internal life. Little by little, when combined with silence and *lectio*, external words, the words of the world, are gradually abandoned, until all that is heard is the Word of God. When that Word is all that there is to shape the mind, the thought, the conversation of the disciple, then it has begun to be internalized, and it can begin the work of transforming the heart, what Paul calls 'having the mind in you which was in Christ Jesus' (Phil. 2:5). The words of God become our words, so that we become the Word's.

The selection has therefore aimed at offering some of the more memorable psalms, along with some well-known passages of Scripture, in the hope that they may more easily be learned, and then more freely prayed (there is nothing more distracting in prayer – at least in my experience – than constantly having to find the right page!). Antiphons selected from the tradition have been used to illustrate and illuminate the psalms when they are prayed during the great seasons of Advent, Lent and Eastertide. They are, however, only an option.

In line with the theology of the Work of God proposed in the General Instruction on the Liturgy of the Hours of Vatican II, the selection of texts for morning prayer is largely from the Old Testament, highlighting the prophetic promise of salvation as a way of greeting each new day, with all the opportunities it offers. Texts for evening prayer make fuller use of the New Testament, and culminate in Mary's song of thanksgiving, the 'Magnificat', as we contemplate what God has done for us in Christ at the close of each day's labours. The prayer texts have been selected from those offered in the Roman Office, both for daily and for Sunday use, since they often illustrate a particular aspect of the theology of the psalms and readings.

For many, use of this version of the Office will be in private prayer, but originally it was conceived for use in one of the school houses at Ampleforth Abbey. It can therefore be used in communal recitation, with one or more people acting as leader for the versicles, antiphons and prayers, and all responding.

SUNDAY – MORNING PRAYER – WEEK I

V.* Lord, open my lips.
R.† And my mouth shall proclaim your praise.
Glory be to the Father, and to the Son, and to the Holy
    Spirit,
as it was in the beginning, is now and ever shall be,
world without end. Amen. Alleluia.

One psalm is used at each hour. During the great seasons of the year (Advent, Lent and Eastertide) the psalm is preceded and concluded with a proper antiphon. In Ordinary Time, the antiphons are omitted.

ANTIPHONS

Advent: We shall see the glory of the Lord, the splendour of
        our God (cf. Isa. 35:2).
Lent: They seek me day after day, and long to know my
        ways (Isa. 58:2).
Easter: This day was made by the Lord; we rejoice and are
        glad. Alleluia (Ps. 117:24).

Psalm 62

This psalm has been used at morning prayer since the earliest days of the Church. The psalmist speaks of his longing for God, and of his joy at God's abiding presence, which is a presence for salvation.

* Versicle
† Response

O God, you are my God, for you I long;
for you my soul is thirsting.
My body pines for you
like a dry, weary land without water.

So I gaze on you in the sanctuary
to see your strength and your glory.
For your love is better than life,
my lips will speak your praise.

So I will bless you all my life,
in your name I will lift up my hands.
My soul shall be filled as with a banquet,
my mouth shall praise you with joy.

On my bed I remember you.
On you I muse through the night
for you have been my help;
in the shadow of your wings I rejoice.

My soul clings to you;
your right hand holds me fast.
Those who seek to destroy my life
shall go down to the depths of the earth.

They shall be put into the power of the sword
and left as the prey of the jackals.
But the king shall rejoice in God;
all that swear by him shall be blessed
for the mouth of liars shall be silenced.

Glory be to the Father ... *(and at the end of all psalms)*

SCRIPTURE READING   *(Rom. 13:11–14)*

Besides this, you know what hour it is, how it is full time now for
you to wake from sleep. For salvation is nearer to us now than
when we first believed; the night is far gone, the day is at hand.
Let us then cast off the works of darkness and put on the armour
of light; let us conduct ourselves becomingly as in the day, not

in revelling and drunkenness, not in debauchery and licentious-
ness, not in quarrelling and jealousy. But put on the Lord Jesus
Christ, and make no provision for the flesh, to gratify its desires.

Pause for silent reflection

> **V.** Rejoice in the Lord, O you just.
> **R.** For praise is fitting for loyal hearts.

BENEDICTUS ANTIPHON

> Blessed be Jesus Christ, whose saving light shines upon
> us like the rising sun at dawn. Alleluia.

BENEDICTUS *(See p. 207)*

OUR FATHER . . .

CONCLUDING PRAYER *(may be replaced by the prayer for
the occurring Sunday)*

> Lord God,
> On this day you opened for us the way to eternal life
> through your Son's victory over death.
> Grant that as we celebrate his resurrection
> we may be renewed by your Holy Spirit
> and rise again in the light of life.
> We make our prayer through Christ our Lord.

> May the peace of God, which passes all understanding,
> be with us throughout this day.
> And with all those we love. Amen.

SUNDAY – EVENING PRAYER – WEEK I

> **V.** O God, come to my assistance.
> **R.** O Lord, make haste to help me.

Glory be to the Father, and to the Son, and to the Holy
  Spirit,
as it was in the beginning, is now and ever shall be,
world without end. Amen. Alleluia.

Antiphons

Advent: Behold, the Lord is coming with all his power on the
  clouds of heaven.
Lent: O Lord, I will bless you all my life; in your name I
  will lift up my hands.
Easter: This day was made by the Lord; we rejoice and are
  glad. Alleluia (Ps. 117:24).

Psalm 150

*This, the last psalm in the psalter, is a great song of rejoicing.
All creation joins together to sing the praise of the God who
created us, and who, through Christ, has re-created us.*

Praise God in his holy place,
praise him in his mighty heavens.
Praise him for his powerful deeds,
praise his surpassing greatness.

O praise him with sound of trumpet,
praise him with lute and harp.
Praise him with timbrel and dance,
praise him with strings and pipes.

O praise him with resounding cymbals,
praise him with clashing of cymbals.
Let everything that lives and that breathes
give praise to the Lord.

Scripture Reading   (2 Cor. 1:3–5)

Blessed be the God and Father of our Lord Jesus Christ, the
Father of mercies and God of all consolation, who comforts us

in all our affliction, so that we may be able to comfort those who are in any affliction, with the comfort which we ourselves have received from God. For as we share abundantly in Christ's sufferings, so too, through Christ, we share abundantly in consolation.

Pause for silent reflection

V. Let my prayer rise before you like incense.
R. The raising of my hands like an evening sacrifice.

MAGNIFICAT ANTIPHON

ORDINARY: Let us praise God through Jesus Christ, whose light conquers the darkness of our earthly night. Alleluia.

MAGNIFICAT *(See p. 208)*

OUR FATHER . . .

CONCLUDING PRAYER *(may be replaced by the prayer for the occurring Sunday)*

God our Father,
we have celebrated today the mystery of the Lord's
    resurrection;
grant our humble prayer:
free us from all harm that we may sleep in peace
and rise in joy to sing your praise.
We make our prayer through Christ our Lord.

May the almighty and merciful God,
Father, Son ✠ and Holy Spirit,
bless and preserve us.
And all those we love. Amen.

MONDAY – MORNING PRAYER – WEEK I

V. Lord, open my lips.
R. And my mouth shall proclaim your praise.
Glory be to the Father, and to the Son, and to the Holy
    Spirit,
as it was in the beginning, is now and ever shall be,
world without end. Amen. Alleluia.

ANTIPHONS

Advent: Jerusalem, lift up your head and see the power of your
            king. Behold, your Saviour is coming to free you
            from your chains.
Lent: Behold, now is the acceptable time; behold, this is the
            day of salvation.
Easter: Your sadness will be turned to joy. Alleluia.

Psalm 97

*This is a psalm of rejoicing. All creation sings a new song to
greet the dawning day, and to praise the God of glory – the
God who brings light and life to all people.*

> Sing a new song to the Lord
> for he has worked wonders.
> His right hand and his holy arm,
> have brought salvation.
>
> The Lord has made known his salvation;
> has shown his justice to the nations.
> He has remembered his truth and love
> for the house of Israel.
>
> All the ends of the world have seen
> the salvation of our God.
> Shout to the Lord all the earth,
> ring out your joy.

Sing psalms to the Lord with the harp
with the sound of music.
With trumpets and the sound of the horn
acclaim the King, the Lord.

Let the sea and all within it, thunder;
the world, and all its peoples.
Let the rivers clap their hands
and the hills ring out their joy –

at the presence of the Lord: for he comes,
he comes to rule the earth.
He will rule the world with justice
and the peoples with fairness.

SCRIPTURE READING   *(Tobit 4:14–16, 19)*

Watch yourself in everything you do, and be disciplined in all
your conduct. What you hate, do not do to any one. Give of
your bread to the hungry, and of your clothing to the naked.
Give all your surplus to charity, and do not let your eye begrudge
the gift when you make it.

Bless the Lord God in everything; beg him to guide your ways,
and bring your paths and purposes to their end. For wisdom is
not given to every nation; the Lord himself gives all good things.

Pause for silent reflection

V. O Lord, rescue my soul from death
R. And keep my feet from stumbling.

BENEDICTUS ANTIPHON

Blessed be the Lord, the God of Israel; he has come to
his people and set them free. (Alleluia).

BENEDICTUS *(See p. 207)*

Our Father...

Concluding Prayer

> Father of might and power,
> every good and perfect gift comes down to us from you.
> Plant in our hearts the love of your name,
> increase our zeal for your service,
> nourish what is good in us
> and tend it with watchful care.
> We make our prayer through Christ our Lord.
>
> May the peace of God, which passes all understanding,
> be with us throughout this day.
> And with all those we love. Amen.

Monday – Evening Prayer – Week I

V. O God, come to my assistance.
R. O Lord, make haste to help me.
Glory be to the Father, and to the Son, and to the Holy
  Spirit,
as it was in the beginning, is now and ever shall be,
world without end. Amen. Alleluia.

Antiphons

Advent: Behold, I am sending my angel to prepare my way
            before you.
Lent: He will give his angels charge over you, to keep you
            in all your ways.
Easter: In the presence of the angels I will bless you. Alleluia.

Psalm 137

*St Benedict tells us that we are in the presence of God and his
angels whenever we pray together. Confident that our loving*

The Benedictine Experience of God

Father will hear us, let us bless his name for all that he has given us during this day.

> I thank you, O Lord, with all my heart,
> you have heard the words of my mouth.
> In the presence of the angels I will bless you.
> I will adore before your holy temple.
>
> I thank you for your faithfulness and love
> which excel all we ever knew of you.
> On the day I called, you answered;
> you increased the strength of my soul.
>
> All the kings of the earth shall thank you
> when they hear the words of your mouth.
> They shall sing of the ways of the Lord:
> How great is the glory of the Lord!
>
> The Lord is high yet he looks on the lowly
> and the haughty he knows from afar.
> Though I walk in the midst of affliction
> you give me life and frustrate my foes.
>
> You stretch out your hand and save me,
> your hand will do all things for me.
> Your love, O Lord, is eternal,
> discard not the work of your hands.

SCRIPTURE READING   (*1 John 3:1–2*)

Think of the love that the Father has lavished on us, by letting us be called God's children; and that is what we are. Because the world refused to acknowledge him, therefore it does not acknowledge us. My dear people, we are already the children of God, but what we are to be in the future has not yet been revealed; all we know is, that when it is revealed, we shall be like him, because we shall see him as he really is.

Pause for silent reflection

V. Let my prayer rise before you like incense.
R. The raising of my hands like an evening sacrifice.

MAGNIFICAT ANTIPHON

My soul magnifies the Lord, for he has looked on the
lowliness of his servant. (Alleluia).

MAGNIFICAT *(See p. 208)*

OUR FATHER . . .

CONCLUDING PRAYER

We give you thanks, Lord God Almighty,
for bringing us safely to the evening of this day;
we humbly ask that the prayer we make with uplifted hearts
may be an offering pleasing in your sight.
We make our prayer through Christ our Lord.

May the almighty and merciful God,
Father, Son ✠ and Holy Spirit,
bless and preserve us.
And all those we love. Amen.

TUESDAY – MORNING PRAYER – WEEK I

V. Lord, open my lips.
R. And my mouth shall proclaim your praise.
Glory be to the Father, and to the Son, and to the Holy
    Spirit,
as it was in the beginning, is now and ever shall be,
world without end. Amen. Alleluia.

ANTIPHONS

Advent: The mountains and hills are brought low, and the rough
            places are made a plain for the coming of our God.

Lent: Too heavy for us our offences; but you, O Lord, rejoice
             in steadfast love.
Easter: We are filled with blessings of your house. Alleluia.

Psalm 64

*This psalm combines both prayer to God in humility and praise
of God in joy for his many gifts. Beginning a new day, both
attitudes should be in our hearts, as we ask God to help us
grow in our knowledge and love of him and of our neighbour.*

To you our praise is due in Zion, O God.
To you we pay our vows – you who hear our prayer.
To you all flesh will come with its burden of sin.
Too heavy for us, our offences – but you wipe them
    away.

Blessed are those whom you choose and call to dwell in
    your courts.
We are filled with the blessings of your house – of your
    holy temple.
You keep your pledge with wonders – O God our
    saviour,
the hope of all the earth and of far distant isles.

You uphold the mountains with your strength,
you are girded with power.
You still the roaring of the seas – the roaring of their
    waves
and the tumult of the peoples.

The ends of the earth stand in awe at the sight of your
    wonders.
The lands of sunrise and sunset you fill with your joy.
You care for the earth, give it water – you fill it with
    riches.
Your river in heaven brims over to provide its grain.

And thus you provide for the earth – you drench its
   furrows,
you level it, soften it with showers – you bless its growth.
You crown the year with your goodness.
Abundance flows in your steps,
in the pastures of the wilderness it flows.

The hills are girded with joy,
the meadows covered with flocks,
the valleys are decked with wheat.
They shout and sing together for joy.

SCRIPTURE READING   *(1 Kgs. 8:27–30)*

Will God really live with us on the earth? The heavens and the
earth cannot contain you. How much less this house that I have
built! Listen to the prayer and entreaty of your servant, O Lord
my God; listen to the cry and to the prayer which your servant
makes to you today. Day and night let your eyes watch over
this house, over this place of which you have said, 'My name
shall be there'. Listen to the prayer that your servant will offer
in this place.

   Hear the entreaty of your servant and of Israel your people
as they pray in this place. From heaven where your dwelling is,
hear; and, as you hear, forgive.

Pause for silent reflection

   V. How many are your works, O Lord!
   R. In wisdom, you have made them all.

BENEDICTUS ANTIPHON

   The Lord has raised up for us a mighty Saviour, born of
   the house of his servant David. (Alleluia).

BENEDICTUS *(See p. 207)*

OUR FATHER . . .

CONCLUDING PRAYER

> Almighty Lord and God,
> protect us by your power throughout the course of this
>   day,
> even as you have enabled us to begin it:
> do not let us turn aside to any sin,
> but let our every thought, word and deed
> aim at doing what is pleasing in your sight.
> We make our prayer through Christ our Lord.
>
> May the peace of God, which passes all understanding,
> be with us throughout this day.
> And with all those we love. Amen.

TUESDAY – EVENING PRAYER – WEEK I

V. O God, come to my assistance.
R. O Lord, make haste to help me.
Glory be to the Father, and to the Son, and to the Holy
  Spirit,
as it was in the beginning, is now and ever shall be,
world without end. Amen. Alleluia.

ANTIPHONS

Advent: The Lord himself will arise over you, O Jerusalem, and
           you will see his glory.
Lent: The Lord is compassion and love.
Easter: Great are the works of the Lord. Alleluia.

Psalm 110

*This is a song of thanksgiving. The psalmist recalls God's faith-
fulness to his promise of mercy, and his remembrance calls forth
a shout of praise. At the evening hour, let us too recall God's*

*mercy towards us, and, with the psalmist and Mary in her Mag-
nificat, ponder the works of the Lord.*

> I will thank the Lord with all my heart
> in the meeting of the just and their assembly.
> Great are the works of the Lord;
> to be pondered by all who love them.
>
> Majestic and glorious his work,
> his justice stands firm for ever.
> He makes us remember his wonders.
> The Lord is compassion and love.
>
> He gives food to those who fear him;
> keeps his covenant ever in mind.
> He has shown his might to his people
> by giving them the lands of the nations.
>
> His works are justice and truth:
> his precepts are all of them sure,
> standing firm for ever and ever:
> they are made in uprightness and truth.
>
> He has sent deliverance to his people
> and established his covenant for ever.
> Holy his name, to be feared.
>
> The fear of the Lord is the beginning of wisdom
> all who do so prove themselves wise.
> His praise shall last for ever!

SCRIPTURE READING   *(1 Pet. 5:5b–7)*

Wrap yourselves in humility to be servants of each other,
because God refuses the proud and will always favour the
humble. Bow down, then, before the power of God now, and
he will raise you up on the appointed day. Unload all your
worries on to him, since he is looking after you.

Pause for silent reflection

V. Let my prayer rise before you like incense.
R. The raising of my hands like an evening sacrifice.

MAGNIFICAT ANTIPHON

My spirit exults in God my Saviour. (Alleluia).

MAGNIFICAT *(See p. 208)*

OUR FATHER ...

CONCLUDING PRAYER

Lord,
help us always
both to love and fear your holy name,
for you never withdraw your guiding hand
from those whom you establish on the firm foundation of
    your love.
We make our prayer through Christ our Lord.

May the almighty and merciful God,
Father, Son ✠ and Holy Spirit,
bless and preserve us.
And all those we love. Amen.

WEDNESDAY – MORNING PRAYER – WEEK I

V. Lord, open my lips.
R. And my mouth shall proclaim your praise.
Glory be to the Father, and to the Son, and to the Holy
    Spirit,
as it was in the beginning, is now and ever shall be,
world without end. Amen. Alleluia.

ANTIPHONS

Advent: Sion, have no fear. Behold, your God is coming.

Lent: I will watch for you before dawn, that I may see your
          strength, O Lord.
Easter: The Lord I will sing, he is covered in glory. Alleluia.

Canticle of Judith   *(Judith 16:2–3a, 13–15)*

*Judith was one of the great women of the Old Testament, a
woman who not only took care of her people, but also fought
valiantly and with cunning against their enemies. In this song,
she praises God – whose example of care and protection she
sought to copy in her own life. Even though the very world is
shaken, she understands that nothing can shake the love of God
for those who fear him.*

> Begin a song to my God with tambourines,
> sing to my Lord with cymbals.
> Raise to him a new psalm;
> exalt him, and call upon his name.
> For God is the Lord who crushes wars.
> I will sing a new song to my God;
> Lord you are great, you are glorious,
> wonderfully strong, full of power.
>
> May your whole creation serve you,
> for you spoke and they came into being.
> You sent your breath and they were put together,
> and no one can resist your voice.
>
> Should mountains topple to mingle with the waves,
> should rocks melt like wax before your face
> to those who fear you
> you would still be merciful.

SCRIPTURE READING   *(Isa. 43:1–3a)*

> But now, thus says the Lord,
> he who created you, Jacob,
> he who formed you, O Israel:

'Fear not, for I have redeemed you;
I have called you by your name, you are mine.

When you pass through the waters, I will be with you;
and through the rivers, they shall not overwhelm you;
when you walk through fire you shall not be burned,
and the flames will not harm you.
For I am the Lord your God, the Holy One of Israel,
  your Saviour.'

Pause for silent reflection

> **V.** I will bless the Lord at all times.
> **R.** His praise always on my lips.

BENEDICTUS ANTIPHON

Save us, O Lord, from our enemies, from the hands of all
  who hate us. (Alleluia).

BENEDICTUS (*See p. 207*)

OUR FATHER . . .

CONCLUDING PRAYER

Lord God, protector of all who trust in you,
without you nothing is strong, nothing is holy;
support us always by your love.
Guide us so to use the good things of this world,
that even now, we may hold fast to what endures for
  ever.
We make our prayer through Christ our Lord.

May the peace of God, which passes all understanding,
be with us throughout this day.
And with all those we love. Amen.

WEDNESDAY – EVENING PRAYER – WEEK I

V. O God, come to my assistance.
R. O Lord, make haste to help me.
Glory be to the Father, and to the Son, and to the Holy
  Spirit,
as it was in the beginning, is now and ever shall be,
world without end. Amen. Alleluia.

ANTIPHONS

Advent: Let the darkness around me be light.
Lent: Search me, O God, and know my heart.
Easter: O Lord my God, lead me in the paths of life eternal.
  Alleluia.

Psalm 138 'The Hound of Heaven'

*This is a complex psalm, which echoes some of the ideas of
Judith's canticle. God's care and protection is universal – there
is nowhere he cannot reach us to save and comfort us. In the
same way, he knows us better than we know ourselves, even
before we are born. We can thus take confidence in God at the
end of the day, knowing that there is nothing we can do which
he will not forgive, nothing we have done which will alter his
love for us.*

> O Lord, you search me and you know me
> you know my resting and my rising,
> you discern my purpose from afar.
> You mark when I walk or lie down,
> all my ways lie open to you.
>
> Before ever a word is on my tongue
> you know it, O Lord, through and through.
> Behind and before you besiege me,
> your hand ever laid upon me.

Too wonderful for me, this knowledge,
too high, beyond my reach.

O where can I go from your spirit,
or where can I flee from your face?
If I climb the heavens, you are there.
If I lie in the grave, you are there.

If I take the wings of the dawn
and dwell at the sea's furthest end,
even there your hand would lead me,
your right hand would hold me fast.

If I say: Let the darkness hide me
and the light around me be night;
even darkness is not dark for you
and the night is as clear as the day.

For it was you who created my being,
knit me together in my mother's womb.
I thank you for the wonder of my being,
for the wonders of all your creation.

Already you know my soul,
my body held no secret from you,
when I was being fashioned in secret
and moulded in the depths of the earth.

Your eyes saw all my actions,
they were all of them written in your book;
every one of my days was decreed
before one of them came into being.

To me, how mysterious your thoughts, O God!
The sum of them not to be numbered!
If I count them, they are more than the sand;
to finish, I must be eternal, like you.

Search me, O God, and know my heart.
O test me and know my thoughts.

See that I follow not the wrong path
and lead me in the path of life eternal.

SCRIPTURE READING *(Rom. 11:33–36)*

O the depths of the riches and wisdom and knowledge of
God!
How unsearchable are his judgements, and how
inscrutable his ways!
'For who has known the mind of the Lord,
or who has been his counsellor?
Or who has given a gift to him that he might be repaid?'
For from him and through him and to him are all things.
To him be glory for ever. Amen.

Pause for silent reflection

V. How many are your works, O Lord.
R. In wisdom you have made them all.

MAGNIFICAT ANTIPHON

The Lord has looked on his lowly servant, and he who is
powerful has saved me. (Alleluia).

MAGNIFICAT *(See p. 208)*

OUR FATHER . . .

CONCLUDING PRAYER

Lord,
be present with your servants,
and pour out your everlasting love on those who call
you,
that you may both freely redeem
and lovingly guard

all those who rejoice to have you as their creator and
   their guide.
We ask this through Christ our Lord.

May the almighty and merciful God,
Father, Son ✠ and Holy Spirit,
bless and preserve us.
And all those we love. Amen.

THURSDAY – MORNING PRAYER – WEEK I

V. Lord, open my lips.
R. And my mouth shall proclaim your praise.
Glory be to the Father, and to the Son, and to the Holy
   Spirit,
as it was in the beginning, is now and ever shall be,
world without end. Amen. Alleluia.

ANTIPHONS

Advent: In the morning I offer you my prayer – watching and
         waiting.
Lent: O Lord my God, let me lead my life in your presence.
Easter: Those you protect shall be glad and ring out their joy.
         Alleluia.

Psalm 5

*This is a morning psalm of hope and trust. The psalmist ponders
God's love for those who at least try to do his will, his hatred
for those who simply do their own will, practising deceit, slander
and all types of evil. More importantly, perhaps, the psalmist –
like us – is at prayer, waiting on God, hoping that God will
come to his aid. If we too trust, we will know the sheltering
protection of God's hand during the day.*

To my words give ear, O Lord, give need to my
   groaning.
Attend to the sound of my cries, my King and my God.
It is you whom I invoke, O Lord, in the morning you
   hear me;
In the morning I offer you my prayer – watching and
   waiting.

You are no God who loves evil; no sinner is your guest.
The boastful shall not stand their ground before your
   face.
You hate all who do evil: – you destroy all who lie.
The deceitful and bloodthirsty man the Lord detests.

But I through the greatness of your love – have access to
   your house.
I bow down before your holy temple, filled with awe.
Lead me, Lord, in your justice, because of those who lie
   in wait;
make clear your way before me.

No truth can be found in their mouths, their heart is all
   mischief
their throat a wide-open grave – all honey their speech.
Declare them guilty, O God.
Let them fail in their designs.
Drive them out for their many offences – for they have
   defied you.

Those you protect shall be glad and ring out their joy.
You shelter them; in you they rejoice, those who love
   your name.
It is you who bless the just, O Lord:
you surround them with favour as with a shield.

SCRIPTURE READING   *(Micah 6:6–8)*

With what gift shall I come into the Lord's presence
   and bow down before God on high?

154

Shall I come with burnt offerings, with calves one year
  old?
Will he be pleased with rams by the thousand, with
  libations of oil in torrents?
Must I give my first-born for what I have done wrong,
  the fruit of my body for my own sin?
What is good has been explained to you;
this is what the Lord asks of you:
only this, to act justly, to love tenderly, and to walk
  humbly with your God.

Pause for silent reflection

> **V.** Pay your sacrifice of thanksgiving to God.
> **R.** And render him your votive offerings.

BENEDICTUS ANTIPHON

> In holiness let us serve the Lord, he will free us from our
>   enemies. (Alleluia).

BENEDICTUS *(See p. 207)*

OUR FATHER . . .

CONCLUDING PRAYER

> Let us praise you, O Lord,
> with voice and mind and deed throughout this day:
> and since life itself is your gift,
> may all we have and are be yours.
> We ask this through Christ our Lord.
>
> May the peace of God, which passes all understanding,
> be with us throughout this day.
> And with all those we love. Amen.

Thursday – Evening Prayer – Week I

V. O God, come to my assistance.
R. O Lord, make haste to help me.
Glory be to the Father, and to the Son, and to the Holy Spirit,
as it was in the beginning, is now and ever shall be,
world without end. Amen. Alleluia.

Antiphons

Advent: Let us live just and holy lives as we await our blessed
hope, the coming of our Saviour Jesus Christ.
Lent: Let us be holy and blameless before him.
Easter: In Christ, we have redemption through his blood.
Alleluia.

Canticle from Ephesians   *(Eph. 1:3–10)*

*Some sections of the New Testament are very like early hymns
– and this may indeed be the reason for their writing. In this
canticle from the letter of St Paul to the Ephesians, Paul gives
glory to God for the wonders of our salvation, and especially
for the great mystery of 'election' or choice by which God makes
us his children. We do not know why God has chosen us – since
we are all sinners – but with Paul we are certain that God's
choice is real. Having made us his daughters and sons, he will
never go back on his choice.*

Blessed be the God and Father
of our Lord Jesus Christ,
who has blessed us in Christ
with every spiritual blessing in the heavenly places.

He chose us in him
before the foundation of the world,
that we should be holy
and blameless before him.

He destined us in love
to be his children through Jesus Christ,
according to the purpose of his will,
to the praise of his glorious grace
which he freely bestowed on us in the Beloved.

In him, we have redemption through his blood,
the forgiveness of our trespasses,
according to the riches of his grace
which he lavished upon us.

He has made known to us
in all wisdom and insight
the mystery of his will,
according to his purpose
which he set forth in Christ.

His purpose he set forth in Christ,
as a plan for the fullness of time,
to unite all things in him,
things in heaven and things on earth.

SCRIPTURE READING   *(1 John 4:7–12)*

My dear people, let us love one another, since love comes from
God, and everyone who loves is begotten by God and knows
God. Anyone who fails to love can never have known God,
because God is love. God's love for us was revealed when he
sent into the world his only Son so that we could have life
through him; this is the love I mean: not our love for God, but
God's love for us when he sent his Son to be the sacrifice which
takes our sins away.

My dear people, since God has loved us so much, we too
should love one another. No one has ever seen God; but as long
as we love one another God will live in us, and his love will be
complete in us.

Pause for silent reflection

V. Let your love be upon us, O Lord.
R. Since we place all our trust in you.

MAGNIFICAT ANTIPHON

O God, show forth the power of your arm. Scatter the proud and exalt the humble. (Alleluia).

MAGNIFICAT *(See p. 208)*

OUR FATHER . . .

CONCLUDING PRAYER

Lord God,
you have prepared for those who love you
what no eye has seen, no ear has heard.
Fill our hearts with your love,
so that loving you above all, and in all,
we may come to the inheritance you promise us
which exceeds all our hearts can desire.
We make our prayer through Christ our Lord.

May the almighty and merciful God,
Father, Son ✠ and Holy Spirit,
bless and preserve us.
And all those we love. Amen.

FRIDAY – MORNING PRAYER – WEEK I

V. Lord, open my lips.
R. And my mouth shall proclaim your praise.
Glory be to the Father, and to the Son, and to the Holy Spirit,
as it was in the beginning, is now and ever shall be,
world without end. Amen. Alleluia.

ANTIPHONS

Advent: Repent and believe the good news; the kingdom of
God is at hand.
Lent: Do not leave me alone in my distress; come close, there
is none else to help.
Easter: You are holy, O Lord our God, and enthroned on the
praises of Israel. Alleluia.

Psalm 21a   *(Ps. 21:1–22)*

*On Fridays, the Church commemorates the sacrifice of Christ
on the Cross, the death which brings us new life. Jesus himself
sang this psalm on the Cross as he lay dying – offering in his
death all the futility, tragedy and shattered hope of humanity
in his cry of abandonment. When we pray this psalm, we are
uniting our hearts to Jesus' heart. We also take on something
of his priestly role, for when we pray for ourselves and for
others in the midst of our own troubles and sorrows, we are
offering ourselves to the Father just as Christ did for the sake
of all who suffer.*

My God, my God, why have you forsaken me?
You are far from my plea and the cry of my distress.
O my God, I call by day and you give no reply;
I call by night and I find no peace.

Yet you, O God, are holy,
enthroned on the praises of Israel.
In you our fathers put their trust; –
they trusted and you set them free.
When they cried to you, they escaped.
In you they trusted and never in vain.

But I am a worm and no man,
the butt of men, laughing-stock of the people.
All who see me deride me.
They curl their lips, they toss their heads.

'He trusted in the Lord – let him save him;
let him release him for this is his friend.'

For it was you who took me from the womb,
entrusted me to my mother's breast.
To you I was committed from my birth,
from my mother's womb you have been my God.
Do not leave me alone in my distress;
come close, there is none else to help.

I am poured out like water
and all my bones are disjointed.
My heart has become like wax,
it is melted within my breast.
Parched as burnt clay is my throat,
my tongue cleaves to my jaws.

Many dogs have surrounded me,
a band of the wicked beset me.
They tear holes in my hands and my feet
and lay me in the dust of death.

I can count every one of my bones.
These people stare at me and gloat;
they divide my clothing among them.
They cast lots for my robe.

O Lord, do not leave me alone,
my strength, make haste to help me!
Rescue my soul from the sword,
my life from the grip of these dogs.
Save my life from the jaws of these lions,
my poor soul from the horns of these oxen.

SCRIPTURE READING   *(Isa. 53:1–6)*

Who would believe what we have heard, and to whom has the
power of the Lord been revealed? Like a sapling, he grew up in
front of us, like a root in arid ground. Without beauty, without
majesty we saw him, no looks to attract our eyes; a thing

despised and rejected by men, a man of sorrows and familiar with suffering, a man to make people screen their faces; he was despised, and we took no account of him.

And yet ours were the sufferings he bore, ours the sorrows he carried. But we, we thought of him as someone punished, struck by God and brought low. Yet he was pierced through for our faults, crushed for our sins. On him lies a punishment that brings us peace, and through his wounds we are healed.

Pause for silent reflection

V. O Lord, rescue my soul from death.
R. And keep my feet from stumbling.

BENEDICTUS ANTIPHON

In the tender compassion of our God, the dawn from on high shall break upon us. (Alleluia).

BENEDICTUS *(See p. 207)*

OUR FATHER . . .

CONCLUDING PRAYER

Lord God,
the Cross reveals the mystery of your love:
a stumbling block indeed for unbelief,
but the sign of your power and wisdom to us who
    believe.
Teach us so to contemplate your Son's glorious Passion
that we may always trust and glory in his Cross.
We ask this in the name of Jesus the Lord.

May the peace of God, which passes all understanding,
be with us throughout this day.
And with all those we love. Amen.

FRIDAY – EVENING PRAYER – WEEK I

V. O God, come to my assistance.
R. O Lord, make haste to help me.
Glory be to the Father, and to the Son, and to the Holy Spirit,
as it was in the beginning, is now and ever shall be,
world without end. Amen. Alleluia.

ANTIPHONS

Advent: The Lord is our king; he himself will come to save us.
Lent: Spare us, O Lord, for you do not scorn the poverty of
the poor.
Easter: You who fear the Lord, give him praise. Alleluia.

Psalm 21b   *(Ps. 21:23–32)*

*This is the continuation of the psalm which was said at morning
prayer, but it is almost totally different in character. It is a psalm
of trust, not a psalm of abandonment; a psalm of praise, not of
dejection. The Cross too has this double character. Although
the agony of Christ's death is very real, without it, we could
never have been saved. Although the reality of our own suffering
and death is unquestionable, we too look forward in hope and
praise to the resurrection. Both these aspects, the sorrowful and
the joyful, meet in the Cross, the sign of our salvation.*

I will tell of your name to my brethren
and praise you amid the assembly.
You who fear the Lord give him praise,
all sons of Jacob, give him glory.
Worship him, O children of Israel.

For he has never despised
nor scorned the poverty of the poor.
From them he has not hidden his face,
but he heard the poor when they cried.

You are my praise in the great assembly.
My vows I will pay before those who fear him.
The poor shall eat and shall have their fill.
They shall praise the Lord, those who seek him.
May your hearts live for ever and ever!

All the earth shall remember and return to the Lord,
all families of the nations worship before him
for the kingdom is the Lord's; he is ruler of the nations.
They shall worship him, all the mighty of the earth;
before him shall bow all who go down to the dust.

And my soul shall live for him, my children serve him.
They shall tell of the Lord to generations yet to come,
proclaim his salvation to peoples yet unborn:
'These things the Lord has done.'

SCRIPTURE READING   *(Gal. 2:20; 5:13–14)*

I have been crucified with Christ; it is no longer I who live, but
Christ who lives in me; and the life I now live in the flesh, I live
by faith in the Son of God, who loved me and gave himself for
me.

   For you were called to freedom; only do not use your freedom
as an opportunity for the flesh, but through love be servants of
one another. For the whole law is fulfilled in one saying, 'You
shall love your neighbour as yourself.'

Pause for silent reflection

   V. Uphold me by your promise, Lord, and I shall live.
   R. Let my hopes not be in vain.

MAGNIFICAT ANTIPHON

   He has cast down the mighty who persecuted his people,
      and has exalted those who humbly follow Christ.
      (Alleluia).

163

MAGNIFICAT *(See p. 208)*

OUR FATHER . . .

CONCLUDING PRAYER

> Holy Father and Lord,
> you willed that Christ, your Son,
> should be the price of our salvation.
> Give us the grace so to live,
> that through sharing his sufferings
> we may be strengthened by the power of his resurrection,
> who lives and reigns with you and the Holy Spirit,
> one God, for ever and ever.

> May the almighty and merciful God,
> Father, Son ✠ and Holy Spirit,
> bless and preserve us.
> And all those we love. Amen.

SATURDAY – MORNING PRAYER – WEEK I

V. Lord, open my lips.
R. And my mouth shall proclaim your praise.
Glory be to the Father, and to the Son, and to the Holy
 Spirit,
as it was in the beginning, is now and ever shall be,
world without end. Amen. Alleluia.

ANTIPHONS

Advent: Our mighty Lord comes forth from Sion, that he might
 save his flock.
Lent: Let our hearts not be hardened in your presence, O
 God.
Easter: With songs let us hail the Lord. Alleluia.

Psalm 94

St Benedict recommends that his monks use this psalm every day at the beginning of their prayer. It is a prayer of praise as we come into the presence of the God who made us and the God who has saved us through his Son. But it is also a psalm with a warning; unless we walk in the ways of truth, and avoid the temptation to ignore God's voice in favour of our own plans, we too – like those in the psalm – will find it hard to enter the peaceful rest of God's kingdom.

Come, let us sing to the Lord;
hail the rock who saves us.
Let us come before him, giving thanks,
with songs let us hail the Lord.

A mighty God is the Lord,
a great king above all gods.
In his hand are the depths of the earth;
the heights of the mountains are his.
To him belongs the sea, for he made it
and the dry land shaped by his hands.

Come in; let us bow and bend low;
let us kneel before the God who made us
for he is our God
and we the people who belong to his pasture,
the flock that is led by his hand.

O that today you would listen to his voice!
'Harden not your hearts as at Meribah,
as on that day at Massah in the desert
when your fathers put me to the test;
when they tried me, though they saw my work.

For forty years I was wearied of these people
and I said: "Their hearts are astray,
these people do not know my ways."

Then I took an oath in my anger: "Never shall they enter
my rest."'

SCRIPTURE READING   *(Sirach 2:7–11)*

You who fear the Lord, wait for his mercy;
    and do not turn aside, lest you fall.
You who fear the Lord, trust in him,
    and your reward will not fail;
You who fear the Lord, hope for good things,
    for everlasting joy and mercy.
Consider the ancient generations and see:
    who ever trusted in the Lord and was put to shame?
Or who ever persevered in the fear of the Lord and was
        forsaken?
    Or who ever called upon him and was overlooked?
For the Lord is compassionate and merciful;
    he forgives sins and saves in time of affliction.

Pause for silent reflection

> **V.** Turn aside from evil and do good.
> **R.** Seek and strive after peace.

BENEDICTUS ANTIPHON

Shine on those who dwell in darkness O Lord; guide our
feet on the road of peace. (Alleluia).

BENEDICTUS *(See p. 207)*

OUR FATHER . . .

CONCLUDING PRAYER

Lord,
creator and ruler of the whole world,
look mercifully upon us:

give us grace to serve you with all our heart
so that we may come to know the power of your
   forgiveness and love.
We ask this through Christ our Lord.

May the peace of God, which passes all understanding,
be with us throughout this day.
And with all those we love. Amen.

SATURDAY – EVENING PRAYER – WEEK I

V. O God, come to my assistance.
R. O Lord, make haste to help me.
Glory be to the Father, and to the Son, and to the Holy Spirit,
as it was in the beginning, is now and ever shall be,
world without end. Amen. Alleluia.

ANTIPHONS

Advent: O sing to the Lord a new song; his praise to the ends
           of the earth.
Lent: The Lord crowns the poor with salvation.
Easter: Let us rejoice in our maker, let us exult in our King.
           Alleluia.

Psalm 149

*This is a song of thanksgiving, a fitting way to end the week.
The end of the psalm speaks of God's vengeance over his enemies
– which has sometimes been interpreted as his triumph over our
sins. As St Paul says, let us put to death the deeds of the body,
and walk in the Spirit and in thanksgiving.*

Sing a new song to the Lord,
his praise in the assembly of the faithful.
Let Israel rejoice in its Maker,
let Zion's sons exult in their king.

Let them praise his name with dancing
and make music with timbrel and harp.
For the Lord takes delight in his people.
He crowns the poor with salvation.

Let the faithful rejoice in their glory,
shout for joy and take their rest.
Let the praise of God be on their lips
and a two-edged sword in their hand,

to deal out vengeance to the nations
and punishment on all the peoples;
to bind their kinds in chains
and their nobles in fetters of iron;

to carry out the sentence pre-ordained:
this honour is for all his faithful.

SCRIPTURE READING   *(Wisd. 7:25–30)*

Wisdom is a breath of the power of God,
    and a pure emanation of the glory of the Almighty;
        therefore nothing defiled gains entrance into her.
For she is a reflection of the eternal light,
    a spotless mirror of the working of God,
    and an image of his goodness.
Though she is one, she can do all things,
    and while remaining in herself, she renews all things;
in every generation she passes into holy souls
    and makes them friends of God and prophets;
    for God loves nothing so much as those who love
        wisdom.
For she is more beautiful than the sun
    and excels every constellation of the stars.
Compared with the light she is found to be superior,
    for it is succeeded by the night,
        but against wisdom, evil does not prevail.

Pause for silent reflection

V. How great are your works, O Lord.
R. In wisdom you have made them all.

MAGNIFICAT ANTIPHON

The Lord has come to the help of his servant,
remembering his mercy. (Alleluia).

MAGNIFICAT *(See p. 208)*

OUR FATHER . . .

CONCLUDING PRAYER

Lord our God,
you guide and govern our lives with unfailing wisdom
and love,
drive away from us all that is harmful this night
and grant us all that will be for our good.
We ask this through Christ our Lord.

May the almighty and merciful God,
Father, Son ✠ and Holy Spirit,
bless and preserve us.
And all those we love. Amen.

SUNDAY – MORNING PRAYER – WEEK II

V. Lord, open my lips.
R. And my mouth shall proclaim your praise.
Glory be to the Father, and to the Son, and to the Holy
Spirit,
as it was in the beginning, is now and ever shall be,
world without end. Amen. Alleluia.

ANTIPHONS

Advent: Let the wilderness and the dry land exult; let it flower
for the Lord who saves us.
Lent: Let your face shed its light upon us, O Lord.
Easter: Let the peoples praise you, O God. Alleluia.

Psalm 66

*This psalm was originally a harvest thanksgiving. It has been
sung by the Church on Sundays since the fifth century, since in
this psalm we give thanks for the resurrection of Christ, the first
fruits of those who sleep, the beginning of the new harvest of
Mankind to salvation.*

O God, be gracious and bless us
and let your face shed its light upon us.
So will your ways be known upon earth
and all nations learn your saving help.

Let the peoples praise you, O God;
let all the peoples praise you.

Let the nations be glad and exult
for you rule the world with justice.
With fairness you rule the peoples,
you guide the nations on earth.

Let the peoples praise you, O God;
let all the peoples praise you.

The earth has yielded its fruit
for God, our God, has blessed us.
May God still give us his blessing
till the ends of the earth revere him.

Let the peoples praise you, O God;
let all the peoples praise you.

Glory be to the Father ... *(and at the end of all psalms)*

The Benedictine Experience of God

SCRIPTURE READING   *(Ezek. 36:24–28)*

I will take you from among the nations, and gather you from
all the countries, and bring you into your own land. I will
sprinkle clean water upon you, and you shall be clean from all
your uncleannesses, and from all your idols I will cleanse you.
A new heart I will give you, and a new spirit I will put within
you; and I will take out of your flesh the heart of stone and give
you a heart of flesh. And I will put my Spirit within you, and
cause you to walk in my statutes and be careful to observe my
ordinances. You shall dwell in the land which I gave to your
fathers; and you shall be my people, and I will be your God.

Pause for silent reflection

> **V.** Rejoice in the Lord, O you just.
> **R.** For praise is fitting for loyal hearts.

BENEDICTUS ANTIPHON

> Blessed be Jesus Christ, whose saving light shines upon
> us like the rising sun at dawn. Alleluia.

BENEDICTUS *(See p. 207)*

OUR FATHER . . .

CONCLUDING PRAYER *(may be replaced by the prayer for
the occurring Sunday)*

> O God,
> let your people always rejoice,
> for you have renewed the life of our souls.
> May we, who rejoice in the glory of your adopted
>   children,
> look forward in hope and joy to the day of our own
>   resurrection.
> We ask this through Christ our Lord.

May the peace of God, which passes all understanding,
be with us throughout this day.
And with all those we love. Amen.

SUNDAY – EVENING PRAYER – WEEK II

V. O God, come to my assistance.
R. O Lord, make haste to help me.
Glory be to the Father, and to the Son, and to the Holy
   Spirit,
as it was in the beginning, is now and ever shall be,
world without end. Amen. Alleluia.

ANTIPHONS

Advent: Behold, our King is coming, the Lord of all the earth.
           He himself will break the yoke of our captivity.
Lent: If the Lord comes to my help, why should I fear what
           man will do to me.
Easter: This day was made by the Lord; we rejoice and are
           glad. Alleluia.

Psalm 117   *(Ps. 117:1–9, 13–29)*

*This has been the classic Easter psalm of the Church since at least
the fourth century – and used in Sunday prayer as a memorial of
our baptism. It is a song of worship in praise of the God who
saves us, and who has made this day the day of salvation through
the Resurrection of Christ his Son.*

> Give thanks to the Lord for he is good,
> for his love has no end.
> Let the sons of Israel say:
> 'His love has no end.'
> Let the sons of Aaron say:
> 'His love has no end.'

Let those who fear the Lord say:
'His love has no end.'

I called to the Lord in my distress;
he answered and freed me.
The Lord is at my side; I do not fear.
What can man do against me?
The Lord is at my side as my helper:
I shall look down on my foes.

It is better to take refuge in the Lord
than to trust in men:
it is better to take refuge in the Lord
than to trust in princes.

I was thrust, thrust down and falling
but the Lord was my helper.
The Lord is my strength and my song;
he was my saviour.
There are shouts of joy and victory
in the tents of the just.

The Lord's right hand has triumphed;
his right hand raised me up.
The Lord's right hand has triumphed;
I shall not die, I shall live
and recount his deeds.
I was punished, I was punished by the Lord,
but not doomed to die.

Open to me the gates of holiness:
I will enter and give thanks.
This is the Lord's own gate
where the just may enter.
I will thank you for you have answered
and you are my saviour.

The stone which the builders rejected
has become the corner stone.

This is the work of the Lord,
a marvel in our eyes.
This day was made by the Lord;
we rejoice and are glad.

O Lord, grant us salvation;
O Lord, grant success.
Blessed is he who comes
in the name of the Lord.
We bless you from the house of the Lord;
the Lord God is our light.

Go forward in procession with branches
even to the altar.
You are my God, I thank you.
My God, I praise you.
Give thanks to the Lord for he is good;
for his love has no end.

SCRIPTURE READING   *(Rom. 6:3–5, 9–11)*

Do you not know that all of us who have been baptized into
Christ Jesus were baptized into his death? We were buried therefore with him by baptism into death, so that as Christ was raised
from the dead by the glory of the Father, we too might walk in
newness of life. For if we have been united with him in a death
like his, we shall certainly be united with him in a resurrection
like his.

For we know that Christ being raised from the dead will never
die again; death no longer has power over him. The death he
died he died to sin, once for all, but the life he lives he lives to
God. So you also must consider yourselves dead to sin, and alive
to God in Christ Jesus.

Pause for silent reflection

> V. Let my prayer rise before you like incense.
> R. The raising of my hands like an evening sacrifice.

Magnificat Antiphon

Let us praise God through Jesus Christ, whose light
conquers the darkness of our earthly night. Alleluia.

Magnificat *(See p. 208)*

Our Father . . .

Concluding Prayer *(may be replaced by the prayer for the occurring Sunday)*

God our Father,
from you comes our salvation
and our adoption as your children,
grant that all who believe in Christ
may receive true freedom
and the eternal life you have promised.
We ask this through Christ our Lord.

May the almighty and merciful God,
Father, Son ✠ and Holy Spirit,
bless and preserve us.
And all those we love. Amen.

Monday – Morning Prayer – Week II

V. Lord, open my lips.
R. And my mouth shall proclaim your praise.
Glory be to the Father, and to the Son, and to the Holy
  Spirit,
as it was in the beginning, is now and ever shall be,
world without end. Amen. Alleluia.

Antiphons

Advent: Come to us, O Lord, and visit us with your peace, that
we may serve you with all our heart.

Lent: Do not remember the sins of my youth.

Easter: The Lord's friendship is for those who revere him. Alleluia.

Psalm 24

This is a morning prayer of trust and self-abandonment. All of us are sinners; all need the constant help and teaching and support of our Father as we struggle with the temptations and pitfalls of each day. Only through prayer and trust can we hope to remain faithful to our calling.

To you, O Lord, I lift up my soul.
I trust you let me not be disappointed;
do not let my enemies triumph.
Those who hope in you shall not be disappointed,
but only those who wantonly break faith.

Lord, make me know your ways.
Lord, teach me your paths.
Make me walk in your truth, and teach me
for you are God my saviour.

In you I hope all the day long
because of your goodness, O Lord.
Remember your mercy, Lord,
and the love you have shown from of old.
Do not remember the sins of my youth.
Remember me in your love.

The Lord is good and upright.
He shows the path to those who stray,
he guides the humble along the right path;
he teaches his way to the poor.

His ways are faithfulness and love
for those who keep his covenant and will.
Lord, for the sake of your name
forgive my guilt; for it is great.

If anyone fears the Lord
he will show him the path he should choose.
His soul shall live in happiness
and his children shall possess the land.

The Lord's friendship is for those who revere him;
to them he reveals his covenant.
My eyes are always on the Lord;
for he rescues my feet from the snare.

Turn to me and have mercy
for I am lonely and poor.
Relieve the anguish of my heart
and set me free from my distress.

See my affliction and my toil
and take all my sins away.
See how many are my foes;
how violent their hatred for me.

Preserve my life and save me.
Do not disappoint me, you are my refuge.
May innocence and uprightness protect me:
for my hope is in you, O Lord.
Redeem Israel, O God, from all his distress.

SCRIPTURE READING   *(Eph. 4:1–7)*

I beg you to lead a life worthy of your calling, with humility
and patience, forbearing one another in love, eager to maintain
the unity of the Spirit in the bond of peace. There is one body
and one Spirit, just as you were called into the one hope by which
you were called. There is one Lord, one faith, one baptism, and
one God and Father of us all, who is above all and through all
and in all. But grace was given to each of us according to the
measure of Christ's gift.

Pause for silent reflection

177

V. O Lord, rescue my soul from death
R. And keep my feet from stumbling.

Benedictus Antiphon

Blessed be the Lord, the God of Israel; he has come to his people and set them free. (Alleluia).

Benedictus *(See p. 207)*

Our Father . . .

Concluding Prayer

O God,
you have promised to remain
in the hearts of those who seek to do your will.
Grant us, through your grace,
that our life and work
may make us a fitting dwelling place for you.
We ask this through Christ our Lord.

May the peace of God, which passes all understanding,
be with us throughout this day.
And with all those we love. Amen.

Monday – Evening Prayer – Week II

V. O God, come to my assistance.
R. O Lord, make haste to help me.
Glory be to the Father, and to the Son, and to the Holy Spirit,
as it was in the beginning, is now and ever shall be,
world without end. Amen. Alleluia.

Antiphons

Advent: Your almighty Word descends from his heavenly throne to save us.

Lent: The Lord is kind and full of compassion.
Easter: We shall sing of your splendour and glory. Alleluia.

Psalm 144a

A song of praise to the God whose mercy has supported us throughout the course of the day. In this psalm we join the whole Church, on earth and in heaven, and in the daily prayer which is poured out from age to age – an eternal offering of thanksgiving to the God who made us, and who saves us through his Son.

I will give you glory, O God my King,
I will bless your name for ever.
I will bless you day after day
and praise your name for ever.
The Lord is great, highly to be praised,
his greatness cannot be measured.

Age to age shall proclaim your works,
shall declare your mighty deeds,
shall speak of your splendour and glory,
tell the tale of your wonderful works.

They will speak of your terrible deeds,
recount your greatness and might.
They will recall your abundant goodness;
age to age shall ring out your justice.

The Lord is kind and full of compassion,
slow to anger, abounding in love.
How good is the Lord to all,
compassionate to all his creatures.

SCRIPTURE READING   *(Rev. 7:9–12)*

I looked, and behold, a great multitude which no one could number, from every nation, from all tribes and peoples and languages, standing before the throne and before the Lamb, clothed in white robes with palm branches in their hands, and crying out with a loud voice, 'Salvation belongs to our God who sits on the throne, and to the Lamb!' And all the angels stood round the throne and round the elders and the four living creatures, and they fell on their faces before the throne, and worshipped God, saying, 'Amen! Blessing and glory and wisdom and thanksgiving and honour and power and might be to our God for ever and ever! Amen!'

Pause for silent reflection

> **V.** Let my prayer rise before you like incense.
> **R.** The raising of my hands like an evening sacrifice.

Magnificat Antiphon

> My soul magnifies the Lord, for he has looked on the lowliness of his servant. (Alleluia).

Magnificat *(See p. 208)*

Our Father . . .

Concluding Prayer

> Lord,
> may our evening prayer ascend to the throne of your
>   mercy,
> and may your blessing come down upon us,
> that we may be made worthy to receive your salvation,
> both now and for ever,
> through the help of your grace.
> We ask this through Christ our Lord.
>
> May the almighty and merciful God,
> Father, Son ✠ and Holy Spirit,
> bless and preserve us.
> And all those we love. Amen.

TUESDAY – MORNING PRAYER – WEEK II

V. Lord, open my lips.
R. And my mouth shall proclaim your praise.
Glory be to the Father, and to the Son, and to the Holy
   Spirit,
as it was in the beginning, is now and ever shall be,
world without end. Amen. Alleluia.

ANTIPHONS

Advent: Look towards him and be radiant, for behold, our light
          is coming.
Lent: From all my terrors set me free, O Lord.
Easter: Taste and see that the Lord is good. Alleluia.

Psalm 33

Benedict quotes from this psalm in the Prologue to his Rule.
He makes it the 'Covenant Charter' for God's workers, a guide
to the Christian life, and a never-ending call to all those who
long for life. Let us commit our lives to the Lord again, and
tasting, find that he alone can satisfy us.

> I will bless the Lord at all times,
> his praise always on my lips;
> in the Lord my soul shall make its boast.
> The humble shall hear and be glad.
>
> Glorify the Lord with me.
> Together let us praise his name.
> I sought the Lord and he answered me;
> from all my terrors he set me free.
>
> Look towards him and be radiant;
> let your faces not be abashed.
> This poor man called; the Lord heard him
> and rescued him from all his distress.

The angel of the Lord is encamped
around those who revere him, to rescue them.
Taste and see that the Lord is good.
He is happy who seeks refuge in him.

Revere the Lord, you his saints.
They lack nothing, those who revere him.
Strong lions suffer want and go hungry
but those who seek the Lord lack no blessing.

O children, come and hear me
that I may teach you the fear of the Lord.
Who is he who longs for life
and many days, to enjoy his prosperity?

Then keep your tongue from evil
and your lips from speaking deceit.
Turn aside from evil and do good;
seek and strive after peace.

The Lord turns his face against the wicked
to destroy their remembrance from the earth.
The Lord turns his eyes to the just
and his ears to their appeal.

The Lord hears their cry
and rescues them in all their distress.
The Lord is close to the broken-hearted;
those whose spirit is crushed he will save.

The trials of the just man are many
but from them all the Lord will rescue him.
He will keep guard over all his bones,
not one of his bones shall be broken.

Evil brings death to the wicked;
those who hate the good are doomed.
The Lord ransoms the souls of his servants.
Those who hide in him shall not be condemned.

Scripture Reading   *(Jer. 31:31, 33–34)*

See, the days are coming – it is the Lord who speaks – when I will make a new covenant with the house of Israel and the house of Judah, but not a covenant like the one I made with their ancestors on the day I took them by the hand to bring them out of the land of Egypt.

This is the covenant I will make with the house of Israel when those days come – it is the Lord who speaks. Deep within them I will plant my Law, writing it on their hearts. Then I will be their God and they shall be my people. There will be no further need for neighbour to try to teach neighbour, or brother to say to brother, 'Learn to know the Lord!' No, they will all know me, the least no less than the greatest – it is the Lord who speaks – since I will forgive their iniquity and never call their sin to mind.

Pause for silent reflection

> **V.** How many are your works, O Lord!
> **R.** In wisdom, you have made them all.

Benedictus Antiphon

> The Lord has raised up for us a mighty Saviour, born of the house of his servant David. (Alleluia).

Benedictus *(See p. 207)*

Our Father . . .

Concluding Prayer

> O God,
> the strength of all who trust in you,
> be present with us as we pray;
> and as we are weak, and can do nothing without you,
> grant us always the help of your grace,
> so that running in the path of your commands

our every deed and desire may please you.
We make our prayer through Christ our Lord.

May the peace of God, which passes all understanding,
be with us throughout this day.
And with all those we love. Amen.

TUESDAY – EVENING PRAYER – WEEK II

V. O God, come to my assistance.
R. O Lord, make haste to help me.
Glory be to the Father, and to the Son, and to the Holy
    Spirit,
as it was in the beginning, is now and ever shall be,
world without end. Amen. Alleluia.

ANTIPHONS

Advent: With joy you will draw water from the wells of sal-
         vation.
Lent: My soul is thirsting for God, the God of my life.
Easter: I will praise my saviour and my God. Alleluia.

Psalm 41

*Originally, this psalm may have been a pilgrim song, sung by
those making their way to the House of God. We too are pilgrims, yearning for our true home, yearning to be set free from
all that holds us back, yearning for the presence of the Lord,
and content with nothing less.*

    Like the deer that yearns for running streams,
    so my soul is yearning for you, my God.
    My soul is thirsting for God, the God of my life;
    when can I enter and see the face of God?

    My tears have become my bread,
    by night, by day,

as I hear it said all the day long:
'Where is your God?'

These things will I remember as I pour out my soul:
how I would lead the rejoicing crowd into the house of
    God,
amid cries of gladness and thanksgiving,
the throng wild with joy.

Why are you cast down, my soul,
why groan within me?
Hope in God, I will praise him still,
my saviour and my God.

My soul is cast down within me as I think of you,
from the country of Jordan and Mount Hermon, from
    the Hill of Mizar.
Deep is calling on deep in the roar of waters:
your torrents and all your waves swept over me.

By day the Lord will send his loving kindness;
by night I will sing to him, praise the God of my life.
I will say to God, my rock: 'Why have you forgotten me?
Why do I go mourning oppressed by the foe?'

With cries that pierce me to the heart, my enemies revile
    me,
saying to me all the day long: 'Where is your God?'
Why are you cast down, my soul, why groan within me?
Hope in God; I will praise him still, my saviour and my
    God.

SCRIPTURE READING   (Rom. 8:18-23)

I think that what we suffer in this life can never be compared
to the glory, as yet unrevealed, which is waiting for us. The
whole creation is eagerly waiting for God to reveal his children.
It was not for any fault on the part of creation that it was made
unable to attain its purpose, it was made so by God; but creation
still retains the hope of being freed, like us, from its slavery to

decadence, to enjoy the same freedom and glory as the children of God. From the beginning until now the entire creation, as we know, has been groaning in one great act of giving birth; and not only creation, but all of us who possess the first-fruits of the Spirit, we too groan inwardly as we wait for our bodies to be set free.

Pause for silent reflection

V. Let my prayer rise before you like incense.
R. The raising of my hands like an evening sacrifice.

MAGNIFICAT ANTIPHON

My spirit exults in God my Saviour. (Alleluia).

MAGNIFICAT *(See p. 208)*

OUR FATHER . . .

CONCLUDING PRAYER

O God,
to whom all hearts are open, all desires known,
and from whom no secret lies hidden,
cleanse the thoughts of our hearts
by the indwelling of your Holy Spirit,
that we may perfectly love you
and worthily praise your name.
We make our prayer through Christ our Lord.

May the almighty and merciful God,
Father, Son ✠ and Holy Spirit,
bless and preserve us.
And all those we love. Amen.

WEDNESDAY – MORNING PRAYER – WEEK II

V. Lord, open my lips.
R. And my mouth shall proclaim your praise.
Glory be to the Father, and to the Son, and to the Holy
　Spirit,
as it was in the beginning, is now and ever shall be,
world without end. Amen. Alleluia.

ANTIPHONS

Advent:　Look! Our God is coming to save us.
Lent:　　Be still, and know that I am God.
Easter:　Proclaim to the nations 'God is King!' Alleluia.

Psalm 45

*There is none like the Lord, who is our stronghold. If we cling
to him, dashing all our fears and temptations against the rock
who is Christ, then we need fear nothing. If we drink deeply of
the water which he brings forth from the side of the crucified
Christ, that same water in which we were baptized, then we
need never thirst for anything but him.*

　　God is for us a refuge and strength,
　　a helper close at hand, in time of distress:
　　so we shall not fear though the earth should rock,
　　though the mountains fall into the depths of the sea,
　　even though its waters rage and foam,
　　even though the mountains be shaken by its waves.

　　The waters of a river give joy to God's city,
　　the holy place where the Most High dwells.
　　God is within, it cannot be shaken;
　　God will help it at the dawning of the day.
　　Nations are in tumult and kingdoms are shaken:
　　he lifts his voice, the earth shrinks away.

The Lord of hosts is with us:
the God of Jacob is our stronghold.

Come, consider the works of the Lord
the redoubtable deeds he has done on the earth.
He puts an end to wars over all the earth;
the bow he breaks, the spear he snaps.
He burns the shields with fire.
'Be still and know that I am God,
supreme among the nations, supreme on the earth!'

The Lord of hosts is with us:
the God of Jacob is our stronghold.

SCRIPTURE READING   *(Micah 4:1–3)*

It shall come to pass in days to come
   that the mountain of the house of the Lord
   shall be established as the highest of the mountains,
   and shall be raised above the hills;
and peoples shall flow to it, and many nations shall come
      and say:
   'Come, let us go up to the mountain of the Lord,
   to the house of the God of Jacob;
   that he may teach us his ways, and we may walk in his
      paths.'
For out of Zion shall go forth the law,
   and the word of the Lord from Jerusalem.
He shall judge between many peoples,
   and shall decide for strong nations afar off;
and they shall beat their swords into ploughshares,
   and their spears into pruning-hooks;
nation shall not lift up sword against nation,
   neither shall they learn war any more.

Pause for silent reflection

V. I will bless the Lord at all times.
R. His praise always on my lips.

BENEDICTUS ANTIPHON

Save us, O Lord, from our enemies, from the hands of all
who hate us. (Alleluia).

BENEDICTUS *(See p. 207)*

OUR FATHER . . .

CONCLUDING PRAYER

Almighty God,
grant, we beseech you,
that we who now offer you our morning praise
may one day sing with even greater joy
with all your saints in your kingdom.
We make our prayer through Christ our Lord.

May the peace of God, which passes all understanding,
be with us throughout this day.
And with all those we love. Amen.

WEDNESDAY – EVENING PRAYER – WEEK II

V. O God, come to my assistance.
R. O Lord, make haste to help me.
Glory be to the Father, and to the Son, and to the Holy
Spirit,
as it was in the beginning, is now and ever shall be,
world without end. Amen. Alleluia.

ANTIPHONS

Advent: Who is like the Lord our God, who has stooped from
the throne of his glory?

Lent: Raise us to yourself, O Lord, and free us from our
            sins.
Easter: From the rising of the sun to its setting, let us praise
            the Lord's name. Alleluia.

Psalm 112

An evening prayer of praise for salvation. This great cry of thanksgiving celebrates God's ability to turn our lives upside-down, to bring order out of chaos and joy out of misery. Whatever this day has brought us, let us thank God with full hearts, and ask him for his gift of perseverance in both our prayer and our service.

> Praise, O servants of the Lord,
> praise the name of the Lord!
> May the name of the Lord be blessed
> both now and for evermore!
> From the rising of the sun to its setting
> praised be the name of the Lord!
>
> High above all nations is the Lord,
> above the heavens his glory.
> Who is like the Lord, our God,
> who has risen on high to his throne
> yet stoops from the heights to look down,
> to look down upon heaven and earth?
>
> From the dust he lifts up the lowly,
> from the dungheap he raises the poor
> to set him in the company of princes,
> with the princes of his people.
> To the childless wife he gives a home
> and gladdens her heart with children.

SCRIPTURE READING   *(Col. 3:12–17)*

Bear with one another; forgive each other as soon as a quarrel begins. The Lord has forgiven you: now you must do the same.

The Benedictine Experience of God

Over all these clothes, to keep them together and complete them, put on love. And may the peace of Christ reign in your hearts, because it was for this that you were called together as parts of one body. Always be thankful.

Let the message of Christ, in all its richness, find a home with you. Teach each other, and advise each other in all wisdom. With gratitude in your hearts sing psalms and hymns and inspired songs to God; and never say or do anything except in the name of the Lord Jesus, giving thanks to God the Father through him.

Pause for silent reflection

> **V.** How many are your works, O Lord.
> **R.** In wisdom you have made them all.

MAGNIFICAT ANTIPHON

> The Lord has looked on his lowly servant, and he who is powerful has saved me. (Alleluia).

MAGNIFICAT *(See p. 208)*

OUR FATHER . . .

CONCLUDING PRAYER

> O God,
> whose name is holy
> and whose mercy is sung from generation to generation;
> receive the prayer of your people,
> and let them magnify your name with everlasting praise.
> We ask this through Christ our Lord.
>
> May the almighty and merciful God,
> Father, Son ✠ and Holy Spirit,
> bless and preserve us.
> And all those we love. Amen.

191

THURSDAY – MORNING PRAYER – WEEK II

V. Lord, open my lips.
R. And my mouth shall proclaim your praise.
Glory be to the Father, and to the Son, and to the Holy
  Spirit,
as it was in the beginning, is now and ever shall be,
world without end. Amen. Alleluia.

ANTIPHONS

Advent: May the Lord send from heaven and save us. May God
        send his truth and his love.
Lent: In the shadow of your wings I take refuge. Lord, have
        mercy on me.
Easter: Your love reaches to the heavens. Alleluia.

Psalm 56

*A morning psalm for help. As in many of the psalms, the first
anguished cry for mercy gradually gives way to a cry of praise
to the God who brings us into light with each new day, and
who gives us again a chance to work out our salvation through
our obedience to his loving will.*

Have mercy on me, O God, have mercy
for in you my soul has taken refuge.
In the shadow of your wings I take refuge
till the storms of destruction pass by.

I call to God the Most High,
to God who has always been my help.
May he send from heaven and save me
and shame those who assail me.
May God send his truth and his love.

My soul lies down among lions,
who would devour the sons of men.

Their teeth are spears and arrows,
their tongue a sharpened sword.

O God, arise above the heavens;
may your glory shine on earth!

They laid a snare for my steps,
my soul was bowed down.
They dug a pit in my path
but fell in it themselves.

My heart is ready, O God, my heart is ready.
I will sing, I will sing your praise.
Awake my soul, awake lyre and harp,
I will awake the dawn.

I will thank you Lord among the peoples,
I will praise you among the nations;
for your love reaches to the heavens
and your truth to the skies.

O God, arise above the heavens;
may your glory shine on earth!

SCRIPTURE READING   *(Hosea 14:1–3, 5–9)*

Return, O Israel, to the Lord your God; your iniquity was the
cause of your downfall. Provide yourself with words and come
back to the Lord. Say to him, 'Take all iniquity away, so that
we may have happiness again and offer you our words of praise.'
   I will heal their disloyalty, I will love them with all my heart,
for my anger has turned from them. I will fall like a dew on
Israel. He shall bloom like a lily, and thrust out roots like a
poplar, his shoots will spread far; he will have the beauty of the
olive, and the fragrance of Lebanon. They will come back to
live in my shade; they will grow corn that flourishes, they will
cultivate vines as renowned as the wine of Helbon. What has
Ephraim to do with idols any more, when it is I who hear his
prayer and care for him? I am like a cypress, ever green, all your
fruitfulness comes from me.

Pause for silent reflection

> **V.** Pay your sacrifice of thanksgiving to God.
> **R.** And render him your votive offerings.

BENEDICTUS ANTIPHON

> In holiness let us serve the Lord, he will free us from our enemies. (Alleluia).

BENEDICTUS (*See p. 207*)

OUR FATHER . . .

CONCLUDING PRAYER

> Lord God,
> yours is the day and yours is the night;
> grant that the Sun of Justice may shine so constantly in
>   our hearts
> that we may come at last to that light in which you
>   dwell.
> We ask this through Christ our Lord.

> May the peace of God, which passes all understanding,
> be with us throughout this day.
> And with all those we love. Amen.

THURSDAY – EVENING PRAYER – WEEK II

> **V.** O God, come to my assistance.
> **R.** O Lord, make haste to help me.
> Glory be to the Father, and to the Son, and to the Holy
>   Spirit,
> as it was in the beginning, is now and ever shall be,
> world without end. Amen. Alleluia.

ANTIPHONS

Advent: To you will I offer the sacrifice of praise, and call on
         your name, O Lord.
Lent: Your servant, Lord, your servant am I; Lord, help my
         unbelief.
Easter: The cup of salvation I will raise. Alleluia.

Psalm 115

*The psalmist asks a question: How can I repay the Lord for his
goodness? It is in offering ourselves, together with Christ, that
we repay God for all that he has done for us, offering ourselves
in obedience, in love and in trust to the God who has already
accepted us as his children.*

I trusted, even when I said:
I am sorely afflicted;
and when I said in my alarm:
No man can be trusted.

How can I repay the Lord
for his goodness to me?
The cup of salvation I will raise;
I will call on the name of the Lord.

I will pay my vows to the Lord
before all his people.
O precious in the eyes of the Lord
is the death of his faithful.

Your servant, Lord, your servant am I;
you have loosened my bonds.
A thanksgiving sacrifice I make:
I will call on the name of the Lord.

I will pay my vows to the Lord
before all his people,
in the courts of the house of the Lord,
in your midst, O Jerusalem.

SCRIPTURE READING (*1 Cor. 11:23–27*)

For this is what I received from the Lord, and in turn passed on to you: that on the same night that he was betrayed, the Lord Jesus took some bread, and thanked God for it and broke it, and he said, 'This is my body, which is for you; do this as a memorial of me.' In the same way he took the cup after supper, and said, 'This cup is the new covenant in my blood. Whenever you drink it, do this as a memorial of me.' Until the Lord comes, therefore, every time you eat this bread and drink this cup, you are proclaiming his death.

Pause for silent reflection

> **V.** Let your love be upon us, O Lord.
> **R.** Since we place all our trust in you.

MAGNIFICAT ANTIPHON

> He has filled the hungry with good things, and the rich sent empty away. (Alleluia).

MAGNIFICAT *(See p. 208)*

OUR FATHER . . .

CONCLUDING PRAYER

> God our Father,
> you redeemed all peoples
> through the Paschal Mystery of Christ your Son;
> protect the grace which your work of mercy has planted
> in us
> that, continually mindful of the mystery of our salvation,
> we may be worthy to enjoy its fruits.
> We make our prayer through Christ our Lord.

May the almighty and merciful God,
Father, Son ✠ and Holy Spirit,
bless and preserve us.
And all those we love. Amen.

FRIDAY – MORNING PRAYER – WEEK II

V. Lord, open my lips.
R. And my mouth shall proclaim your praise.
Glory be to the Father, and to the Son, and to the Holy
  Spirit,
as it was in the beginning, is now and ever shall be,
world without end. Amen. Alleluia.

ANTIPHONS

Advent: Give us again the joy of your help; in your goodness
       show favour to Sion.
Lent: O wash me more and more from my guilt, and cleanse
       me from my sin.
Easter: Our mouths shall proclaim your praise. Alleluia.

Psalm 50

*The Church's classic psalm of repentance. Whenever we confess
our guilt, we acknowledge our need for God, the most basic
need that we have as his creatures. Equally, however, we confess
our faith in God as the one who has power to save us from
ourselves, and who has made us new through the blood of his
Son. With confidence, then, let us ask the Father's mercy, for
he is full of gentleness and compassion.*

Have mercy on me, O God, in your kindness.
In your compassion blot out my offence.
O wash me more and more from my guilt
and cleanse me from my sin.

My offences truly I know them;
my sin is always before me.
Against you, you alone, have I sinned;
what is evil in your sight I have done.

That you may be justified when you give sentence
and be without reproach when you judge
O see, in guilt I was born,
a sinner was I conceived.

Indeed you love truth in the heart;
then in the secret of my heart teach me wisdom;
O purify me, then I shall be clean;
O wash me, I shall be whiter than snow.

Make me hear rejoicing and gladness,
that the bones you have crushed you may thrill.
From my sins turn away your face
and blot out all my guilt.

A pure heart create for me, O God,
put a steadfast spirit within me.
Do not cast me away from your presence,
nor deprive me of your holy spirit.

Give me again the joy of your help;
with a spirit of fervour sustain me,
that I may teach transgressors your ways
and sinners may return to you.

O rescue me, God my helper,
and my tongue shall sing of your goodness.
O Lord, open my lips
and my mouth shall declare your praise.

For in sacrifice you take no delight,
burnt offering from me you would refuse,
my sacrifice, a contrite spirit.
A humbled, contrite heart you will not spurn.

In your goodness show favour to Zion:
rebuild the walls of Jerusalem.
Then you will be pleased with lawful sacrifice,
burnt offerings wholly consumed,
then you will be offered young bulls on your altar.

SCRIPTURE READING   *(Lam. 3:19–24)*

Remember my affliction and my bitterness,
    the wormwood and the gall!
My soul continually thinks of it
    and is bowed down within me.
But this I call to mind,
    and therefore I have hope.

The steadfast love of the Lord never ceases,
    his mercies never come to an end;
they are new every morning;
    great is thy faithfulness.
'The Lord is my portion,' says my soul,
    'therefore I will hope in him.'

Pause for silent reflection

V. O Lord, rescue my soul from death.
R. And keep my feet from stumbling.

BENEDICTUS ANTIPHON

In the tender compassion of our God, the dawn from on
high shall break upon us. (Alleluia).

BENEDICTUS *(See p. 207)*

OUR FATHER . . .

CONCLUDING PRAYER

> Lord God,
> the Cross reveals the mystery of your love:
> a stumbling block indeed for unbelief,
> but the sign of your power and wisdom to us who
>   believe.
> Teach us so to contemplate your Son's glorious Passion
> that we may always trust and glory in his Cross.
> We ask this in the name of Jesus the Lord.
>
> May the peace of God, which passes all understanding,
> be with us throughout this day.
> And with all those we love. Amen.

FRIDAY – EVENING PRAYER – WEEK II

V. O God, come to my assistance.
R. O Lord, make haste to help me.
Glory be to the Father, and to the Son, and to the Holy Spirit,
as it was in the beginning, is now and ever shall be,
world without end. Amen. Alleluia.

ANTIPHONS

Advent: My soul is longing for the Lord's coming, more than
          watchman for daybreak.
Lent: With you is found forgiveness; for this we revere you.
Easter: With the Lord there is mercy, and fullness of redemp-
          tion. Alleluia.

Psalm 129

*A prayer for help in the midst of distress, but also a prayer of
hope and trust in the God in whom all find redemption and
healing. As we come to the close of the day, let us pray for
forgiveness for ourselves and for all those whom we have
wronged, trusting that the Guardian of Israel is close to us.*

Out of the depths I cry to you, O Lord,
Lord, hear my voice!
O let your ears be attentive
to the voice of my pleading.

If you, O Lord, should mark our guilt,
Lord, who would survive?
But with you is found forgiveness:
for this we revere you.

My soul is waiting for the Lord,
I count on his word.
My soul is longing for the Lord
more than the watchman for daybreak.
Let the watchman count on daybreak
and Israel on the Lord.

Because with the Lord there is mercy
and fullness of redemption,
Israel indeed he will redeem
from all its iniquity.

SCRIPTURE READING   *(Eph. 2:13–18)*

But now in Christ Jesus you who once were far off have been
brought near in the blood of Christ. For he is our peace, who
has made us both one, and has broken down the dividing wall
of hostility, by abolishing in his flesh the law of commandments
and ordinances, that he might create in himself one new man
in place of the two, so making peace, and might reconcile us
both to God in one body through the cross, thereby bringing
hostility to an end. And he came and preached peace to you
who were far off and peace to those who were near; for through
him, we both have access in one Spirit to the Father.

Pause for silent reflection

V. Uphold me by your promise, Lord, and I shall live.
R. Let my hopes not be in vain.

MAGNIFICAT ANTIPHON

> He has cast down the mighty who persecuted his people,
> and has exalted those who humbly follow Christ.
> (Alleluia).

MAGNIFICAT *(See p. 208)*

OUR FATHER . . .

CONCLUDING PRAYER

> Holy Father and Lord,
> you willed that Jesus Christ your Son
> should be the price of our redemption,
> grant us so to live
> that by sharing in his sufferings
> we may be found worthy of a share in his
>   resurrection.
> We ask this through the same Christ our Lord.

> May the almighty and merciful God,
> Father, Son ✠ and Holy Spirit,
> bless and preserve us.
> And all those we love. Amen.

SATURDAY – MORNING PRAYER – WEEK II

V. Lord, open my lips.
R. And my mouth shall proclaim your praise.
Glory be to the Father, and to the Son, and to the Holy Spirit,
as it was in the beginning, is now and ever shall be,
world without end. Amen. Alleluia.

ANTIPHONS

Advent: Come and save us, O Lord; we are your people, the
        sheep of your flock.

Lent: How good is the Lord to all; eternal his merciful love.
Easter: Serve the Lord with gladness. Alleluia.

Psalm 99

A song of thanksgiving and praise to God, the true shepherd of his people. In early Christian art, Jesus is often represented as the Good Shepherd, surrounded by the Apostles, his flock. Benedict, too, often returns to this same image, in his description of the abbot and his care for the community. Each of us is called to be both sheep following the Master and to be shepherds to those in need of our love and care.

    Cry out with joy to the Lord, all the earth.
    Serve the Lord with gladness.
    Come before him singing for joy.

    Know that he, the Lord, is God.
    He made us, we belong to him,
    we are his people, the sheep of his flock.

    Go within his gates, giving thanks.
    Enter his courts with songs of praise.
    Give thanks to him and bless his name.

    Indeed, how good is the Lord,
    eternal his merciful love.
    He is faithful from age to age.

SCRIPTURE READING   *(Ezek. 34:11–12, 15–16)*

For thus says the Lord God: Behold, I, I myself will search for my sheep, and will seek them out. As a shepherd seeks out his flock when some of his sheep have been scattered abroad, so I will seek out my sheep; and I will rescue them from all the places where they have been scattered on a day of clouds and thick darkness.

    I myself will be shepherd of my sheep, and I will make them lie down, says the Lord God. I will seek the lost, and I will bring back the strayed, and I will bind up the crippled, and I will strengthen the weak, and the fat and the strong I will watch over; I will feed them in justice.

Pause for silent reflection

> **V.** Turn aside from evil and do good.
> **R.** Seek and strive after peace.

BENEDICTUS ANTIPHON

> Shine on those who dwell in darkness O Lord; guide our feet on the road of peace. (Alleluia).

BENEDICTUS *(See p. 207)*

OUR FATHER . . .

CONCLUDING PRAYER

> O God,
> you show the light of your truth to all those who stray,
> that they might return to the right way:
> grant that all who bear the name of Christian
> may reject whatever is contrary to their calling,
> and strive for what is worthy of it.
> We ask this through Christ our Lord.
>
> May the peace of God, which passes all understanding,
> be with us throughout this day.
> And with all those we love. Amen.

SATURDAY – EVENING PRAYER – WEEK II

V. O God, come to my assistance.
R. O Lord, make haste to help me.
Glory be to the Father, and to the Son, and to the Holy Spirit,
as it was in the beginning, is now and ever shall be,
world without end. Amen. Alleluia.

ANTIPHONS

Advent: Behold, the light is coming; he will reveal to us his glory.

Lent: Lord, we look for your salvation; grant us your peace.

Easter: Our own eyes have seen the salvation which the Lord has won for us. Alleluia.

Canticle of Simeon   *(Luke 2:29–32)*

This canticle from the Gospel of St Luke is sung by Simeon, an old man who waited in the Temple for the coming of God, and was finally rewarded by his meeting with the infant Jesus when he was brought to be circumcised. It is normally sung at Compline – the last of the monastic Offices – every day. In it we give thanks to God, because we too have seen salvation with our own eyes in the face of Christ, we too have shared in the light of Christ which enlightens both this world and the next.

Now, Lord, you have kept your word:
let your servant go in peace.
With my own eyes I have seen the salvation
which you have prepared in the sight of every people:

a light to reveal you to the nations
and the glory of your people Israel.

Glory be to the Father, and to the Son,
and to the Holy Spirit,
as it was in the beginning, is now and ever shall be,
world without end. Amen.

SCRIPTURE READING   *(1 John 1:1–4)*

That which was from the beginning, which we have heard, which we have seen with our own eyes, which we have looked upon and touched with our hands, concerning the word of life – that life was made visible, and we saw it and testify to it, and proclaim to you the eternal life which was with the Father and was made manifest to us – that which we have seen and heard we proclaim also to you, so that you may have fellowship with us; and our fellowship is with the Father and with his Son Jesus Christ. And we are writing this to you that our joy may be complete.

Pause for silent reflection

> V. How great are your works, O Lord.
> R. In wisdom you have made them all.

MAGNIFICAT ANTIPHON

> The Lord has come to the help of his servant,
> remembering his mercy. (Alleluia).

MAGNIFICAT *(See p. 208)*

OUR FATHER . . .

CONCLUDING PRAYER

> Visit, we beseech you, O Lord,
> this house and family,
> and drive far from it all the snares of the enemy.
> Let your holy angels dwell herein, who may keep us in peace,
> and let your blessing be always upon us.
> We ask this through Christ our Lord.

> May the almighty and merciful God,
> Father, Son ✠ and Holy Spirit,
> bless and preserve us.
> And all those we love. Amen.

COMMON TEXTS

CANTICLE OF ZECHARIAH   *(Luke 1:68–79)*

This text has been used at morning prayer since the first centuries of the Church's life. In this prophecy over John the Baptist, we hear Zechariah's praise of God for the dawning of the light of salvation, a light which shone in John, who came as a witness to the true Light, and a light which, in Jesus, our mighty saviour, the darkness cannot overpower. As each day dawns, and the light returns, we too give thanks for another chance to live out the mystery of our salvation.

Blessed be the Lord, the God of Israel;
he has come to his people and set them free.
He has raised up for us a mighty saviour,
born of the house of his servant David.

Through his holy prophets he promised of old
that he would save us from our enemies,
from the hands of all who hate us.
He promised to show mercy to our fathers
and to remember his holy covenant.

This was the oath he swore to our father Abraham:
to set us free from the hand of our enemies
free to worship him without fear,
holy and righteous in his sight all the days of our life.

You, my child, shall be called the prophet of the Most
   High
for you will go before the Lord to prepare his way,
to give his people knowledge of salvation
by forgiving them their sins.

In the tender compassion of our God
the dawn from on high shall break upon us,
to shine on those who dwell in darkness and the shadow
   of death,
and to guide our feet on the road of peace.

Glory be to the Father . . .

CANTICLE OF THE BLESSED
VIRGIN MARY   *(Luke 1:46–55)*

This canticle, the 'Magnificat' is Mary's song of joy at the Incarnation of Jesus. It has been sung by the Church at evening prayer for many centuries. God has a habit of turning the world, and our expectations, completely upside-down; this can be very disturbing, but in this song of praise we can see that God's purpose is our salvation, not our destruction. Let us, then, be prepared to be surprised by the action of the God who looks on the lowly.

My soul proclaims the greatness of the Lord,
my spirit rejoices in God my Saviour;
for he has looked with favour on his lowly servant,
and from this day all generations will call me blessed.

The Almighty has done great things for me:
holy is his Name.
He has mercy on those who fear him
in every generation.

He has shown the strength of his arm,
he has scattered the proud in their conceit.
He has cast down the mighty from their thrones,
and has lifted up the lowly.

He has filled the hungry with good things
and has sent the rich away empty.

He has come to the help of his servant Israel
for he has remembered his promise of mercy,
the promise he made to our fathers,
to Abraham and his children for ever.

Glory be to the Father . . .

Little Hours

These short psalms and prayers are intended for those who wish to mark other key points in the day apart from morning and evening prayer. They have been deliberately chosen to be short, simple and unvarying (as was Benedict's version of Compline), so that they can be easily committed to memory – thus obviating the need to find the book!

PRAYER ON RISING

V. In the name of the Father, and of the Son ✠ and of the Holy Spirit. Amen.

Psalm 3

Benedict uses this psalm as a sort of 'pre-invitatory' psalm in the Rule. It is a suitable prayer for committing oneself to God's care at the beginning of each day. Traditionally, the use of the rather powerful language in such psalms has been interpreted by the Christian Fathers as a prayer against our common foe, the Devil, and against our true enemies, the temptations and sins which so often beset us.

How many are my foes, O Lord!
How many are rising up against me!
How many are saying about me:
'There is no help for him in God.'

But you, O Lord, are a shield about me,
my glory, who lifts up my head.
I cry aloud to the Lord.
He answers from his holy mountain.

I lie down to rest and I sleep.
I wake, for the Lord upholds me.
I will not fear even thousands of people
who are ranged on every side against me.

Arise, O Lord; save me, my God,
you who strike all my foes on the mouth,
you who break the teeth of the wicked!
O Lord of salvation, bless your people!

PRAYER

Grant us, Almighty God,
throughout this day which is now beginning
the continual help of your grace;
may we at all times avoid sin,
and in thought, word and deed do your holy will.
Through Christ our Lord. Amen.

PRAYER DURING THE DAY

V. In the name of the Father, and of the Son ✠ and of
the Holy Spirit. Amen.

Psalm 120

*This is one of the so-called 'Gradual' psalms, originally pilgrim
songs for those ascending to the Temple. As we make our own
pilgrimage through the day, it is good to be reminded of the
help that God offers us in all the circumstances of our daily life,
and to turn to him in prayer for strength and protection.*

I lift up my eyes to the mountains:
from where shall come my help?
My help shall come from the Lord
who made heaven and earth.

May he never allow you to stumble!
Let him sleep not, your guard.

No, he sleeps not nor slumbers,
the watchman of Israel.

The Lord is your guard and your shade;
at your right side he stands.
By day the sun shall not smite you
nor the moon in the night.

The Lord will guard you from evil,
he will guard your soul.
The Lord will guard your going and coming
both now and for ever.

PRAYER

Almighty and merciful God,
you grant us rest amidst our labours;
look kindly on the works we have begun,
make good our defects,
and bring all things to that fulfilment
which best accords with your will.
We ask this through Christ our Lord. Amen.

PRAYER BEFORE RETIRING

V. In the name of the Father, and of the Son ✠ and of
the Holy Spirit. Amen.

Psalm 4

This is one of the psalms which Benedict chooses for use at Compline each day. Clearly, it has been used as a 'bedtime' prayer since Old Testament times, but it is also a prayer for insight into God's truth, and a prayer of rejoicing in God's merciful care. What better way to end the day.

When I call, answer me, O God of justice;
from anguish you released me, have mercy and hear me!

O men, how long will your hearts be closed,
will you love what is futile and seek what is false?

It is the Lord who grants favours to those whom he
    loves;
the Lord hears me whenever I call him.
Fear him; do not sin:
ponder on your bed and be still.

Make justice your sacrifice
and trust in the Lord.
'What can bring us happiness?' many say.
Lift up the light of your face on us, O Lord.

You have put into my heart a greater joy
than they have from abundance of corn and new wine.
I will lie down in peace and sleep comes at once
for you alone, Lord, make me dwell in safety.

PRAYER

    Lord, in your kindness,
    we ask you to lighten the darkness of this night,
    and grant that your servants may sleep in peace;
    that rejoicing in the light of a new day
    we may rise to praise your name.
    We ask this through Christ our Lord. Amen.

Benedictine Prayers

PRAYERS FROM THE RULE

At the beginning of every work (Chapter 35, fourth paragraph)

> O God, come to my assistance;
> O Lord, make haste to help me.

An Act of Commitment (Chapter 58, fourth paragraph)

> Receive me, Lord, according to your promise
> and I shall live;
> and do not disappoint me of my hope.

At the conclusion of every work (Chapter 35, fourth paragraph)

> Blessed are you, O Lord my God,
> for you have helped me and strengthened me.

A meditation on Chapter 72 of the Rule

> Almighty God and ever-loving Father,
> grant us that good zeal
> which separates from Hell and leads to life.
> Grant us always to be first to love and serve,
> always last to think first of ourselves.
> Grant us grace to love all those we meet
> with your chaste and humble love.
> Grant that we may come to love your will
> in all the ways you make it known to us,
> so that, putting nothing whatever before the love of
>   Christ,
> we may come at last to everlasting life. Amen.

PRAYERS IN HONOUR OF ST BENEDICT

A Prayer for those who follow St Benedict (Roman Missal)

> Lord,
> arouse in your Church
> the spirit which guided our Holy Father Benedict.
> Fill us with that spirit,
> and grant that we may love what he loved,
> and put into practice what he taught.
> We ask this through Christ our Lord. Amen.

Collect for the feast of the Translation of St Benedict
(11 July)

> God our Father,
> you willed that your blessed confessor Benedict
> should be filled with the spirit of all the just.
> Grant that we, your servants,
> who celebrate his feast,
> may be filled with that same spirit,
> so that we may faithfully fulfil
> all that by your grace we have promised.
> We ask this through Christ our Lord. Amen.

Preface of St Benedict (21 March)

> Father, all-powerful and ever-living God,
> we do well always and everywhere to give you thanks,
> for you willed that the blessed Abbot Benedict
> should reflect the great light of Christ's grace.
> Preferring nothing to the love of Christ,
> he consecrated himself and his disciples
> in the service of the one true King.
> You chose him as a Master in the way of perfection
> so that, inspired by his work and his example,
> your people might seek you in truth,

and strive for the rewards you have promised.
And so we sing your praise
with all the company of saints,
through Jesus Christ our Lord. Amen.

Preface of St Benedict (11 July)

Father, all-powerful and ever-living God,
we do well always and everywhere to give you thanks.
You gave the most blessed Benedict,
learned in the ways of heaven,
to be leader and teacher of countless hosts of sons and
　　daughters.
In him lived fully the spirit of all the just,
and, when he was rapt in ecstasy,
you poured into his heart the radiance of your light.
It was in the brilliance of this inward vision
that his mind grew in larger understanding,
so that he perceived how narrow are all the values of the
　　world.
And so today, with great happiness,
the whole monastic company throughout the world
　　rejoices
through Jesus Christ our Lord. Amen.

*Magnificat Antiphon 'O caelestis norma vitae' – for the feast
of the Translation of St Benedict (11 July)*

O guide of heavenly life, Saint Benedict,
our teacher and leader,
whose spirit now exults with Christ in heaven.
Guard your flock, O loving shepherd,
strengthen it by your holy prayers;
grant that we may safely walk the path to heaven
following the light of your example.

A prayer for St Scholastica's Day (10 February)

> O God,
> you made the soul of Saint Scholastica
> to fly with all the beauty of a dove
> up to your heavenly courts,
> to show us all the path of innocence.
> Grant us, through her merits and prayers,
> that we too may lead such innocent lives
> that we may follow her to everlasting joy.
> We ask this through Christ our Lord. Amen.

PRAYERS BY BENEDICTINES

Two prayers of St Bede (c. AD 673–735)

> I pray you, O good Jesus,
> that as you have given me the grace
> to drink in with joy
> the Word that gives knowledge of you,
> so, in your goodness,
> you will grant me to come at last to yourself,
> the source of all wisdom,
> and to stand before your face forever. Amen.

A meditation on Christ

> Christ is the Morning Star,
> who, when the night of this dark world is past,
> brings to his Saints the promise of the light of life,
> and opens everlasting day.

Prayers of Herimann of Reichenau (AD 1013–54)

The 'Salve Regina'

> Hail, holy Queen, mother of mercy,

hail, our life, our sweetness and our hope.
To thee do we cry, poor banished children of Eve.
To thee do we send up our sighs,
mourning and weeping in this vale of tears.
Turn then, most gracious Advocate,
thine eyes of mercy towards us,
and after this our exile
show unto us the blessed fruit of thy womb, Jesus.
O clement, O loving, O sweet Virgin Mary.

The 'Alma Redemptoris Mater'

O sweet Mother of our Redeemer,
you are the Gate,
which opens for us the way to heaven;
O star of the sea arise,
you who care for us all
grant your aid to those who sink beneath the waves.
O Mother who, whilst nature marvelled,
bore as your Son the Holy One of God,
who himself had first created you;
O Virgin both before and ever after
you received God's 'Hail' from Gabriel,
have mercy on us, sinners.

Prayers of St Anselm of Canterbury (c. AD 1033–1109)

A prayer for his friends

O Lord, O sweet and kind Jesus Christ,
you have shown forth a love which none can excel,
and whose equal none can have;
for you – doing nothing deserving death –
yet laid down your life for your sinful servants,
and prayed even for those who killed you,
that they might be your brothers,
that you might make them just,

and might reconcile them to yourself and to your
merciful Father.

You, O Lord, you who showed such love to your
enemies,
you yourself have commanded your friends to love.
O good Lord, with what love can I think on your
immeasurable love?
How can I repay such an immense kindness?
For your kindness in its sweetness exceeds all love,
and your goodness in its greatness conquers all
punishment for sin.

How can I repay my creator and my re-creator?
How can I repay him who had mercy on me and
redeemed me?
For Lord, *you are my God, and my goods you do not
seek,*
for yours is the earth and its fullness.
So then, how can I repay my God,
I who am a poor beggar, a poor worm, dust and ashes,
except that with all my heart I might obey his command?
For it is your command that we should love one another.

O good man and good God, good Lord, good friend,
you who are the greatest good of whatever is,
your humble and contemptible servant longs to fulfil
your command.
You know, O Lord that I love that love which you
command,
that I long for that love, that I yearn for that love.
This I seek, for this I search,
for this your poor beggar knocks and calls at the door of
your mercy.
And though I have already received sweet alms
from your boundless generosity,
so that I can love all in you and for your sake,

yet I do not love as much as I ought or as much as I
   would:
and for all this I pray for your mercy.
For there are many whom your love imprints on my
   heart
as being special and close because of their love,
so that more fervently I long for their good,
and more devotedly wish to pray for them.

O sweet Lord, your servant longs and longs again
to pray to you for his friends,
but recalls your judgement on his sins.
I am not worthy to ask mercy for myself,
how then should I presume to ask your grace for others?
I myself anxiously seek those to pray for me,
with what faith should I intercede for others?
You order me to pray for them, and the desire is strong,
but my conscience cries out that I should look to my
   own sins
so that I tremble to plead for others.
Should I, therefore, forget what you command,
since I have done what you forbid?
No – rather, having dared to do what is forbidden
I should fulfil what is commanded,
so that perhaps obedience might heal the fault,
and love, perhaps, cover the multitude of my sins.

So I pray you, O sweet and good God,
for those who love me for your sake
and whom I love in you;
and more devotedly I pray for those
whose love for me, like mine for them,
you know to be the deeper.
I do not do this, my God,
as if I were just, free from my sins,
but as one in some way moved by love for others.
Love them, you fount and source of love,

you who command and give me strength to love them.
And even if my prayer is not worthy to help them,
since it is offered to you by a sinner,
let it help them, since it is done at your command.

For your own sake then, O Lord,
you who are author and giver of love,
for your sake and not for mine
love them,
and grant that they may love you
with all their heart, with all their mind and with all their
    strength,
that they may will and speak and do
only those things which are pleasing to you and for their
    own good.
My prayer is so lukewarm, my God, so lukewarm,
just as the fervour of my love is but little;
O you who are rich in mercy,
do not measure out your good gifts to them
according to the weakness of my love;
but just as your goodness exceeds all human loving
so may your response surpass the love in my prayer.
O Lord, do with them and for them
all that will help them according to your will,
so that ruled and protected by you at all times and in all
    places,
they may come at last to your glorious and eternal
    kingdom,
you who live and reign, God for ever and ever. Amen.

A prayer before an image of the Holy Cross

O Holy Cross,
by which that Cross is brought to mind
on which our Lord Jesus Christ,
through his own death
raised us up from that eternal death

220

(towards which, in our misery, we all journeyed)
to the eternal life, that life which by our sin we threw
    away.
O Cross, I adore, I venerate and I glorify in you
that Cross which you now represent to us,
and in that Cross I honour our merciful Lord,
and all that he has mercifully done for us through that
    Cross.
O lovely Cross, in which is our salvation, our life and
    our resurrection!
O precious wood, by which we are saved and made free!
O holy sign, by which we are sealed for God!
O glorious Cross, in you alone should we glory!

O Cross, you were chosen and prepared to bring such
    good,
that neither tongue nor mind of angels or of men
can sing your praise or raise you up so high
as does the work which was achieved through you.
You, O Cross, in whom and through whom is my
    salvation and my life:
You, O Cross, in whom and through whom is all my
    good:
forbid it that I should glory save in you.

For what good to me could my conception be,
my birth, my life,
and even the enjoyment of all the good things of this
    world,
if then I must descend into the pit?
And if it should be thus with me,
then better that I should not have been, than be.
And most surely would this have been my lot,
if I had not once been redeemed through you.

And so let all my glory be through you and in you,
let my true hope be through you and in you.
Through you all my sins are wiped clean;

through you my soul dies to its old life
and is raised up again in the new life of righteousness.
O Cross, I beseech you,
grant that, just as you cleansed me from all my sins in
    baptism,
in which I was conceived and reborn,
so too may you cleanse me from all those sins
which after my rebirth I have committed,
that through you
I may come to that glory for which we were created
through the power of our Lord Jesus Christ
who is blessed to endless ages. Amen.

Prayers of St Hildegard of Bingen (AD 1098–1179)

A prayer to the Blessed Virgin Mary

Hail, noble and glorious maiden.
You are the perfection of chastity,
the very source of holiness,
because God took such delight in you
that, through the grace he poured into you from heaven,
he caused the Word to take flesh in your womb.
You are like a white lily
on which rested the loving gaze of God,
before any other creature saw it.
O maiden, you are so beautiful and gentle
that when God's love embraced you with its creative warmth
you became the Mother of his Son,
and nursed him in your arms.
All the choirs of angels sang with joy
when, in your virginal womb,
you bore the Son of God,
while, at the selfsame time,
your chastity was praised before God's throne.
As dew that falls on grass gives us delight
by making all that growth spring fresh and green again,

so too your womb, through this his birth,
was for us a source of great joy,
O you who are mother of all our joys.
Now that joy takes fire through all the Church
and breaks forth in one united song
in honour of so gentle a virgin,
and in praise of Mary, the Mother of God.

The Song of the Blessed of the Virgin Mary (Vision XIII)

O most splendid jewel,
most worthy to be suffused by the serene light of the
    Sun,
that Sun who is like a fountain from the heart of God
    the Father,
that Sun who is his unique Word,
through whom he created the world,
the first Light which Eve darkened.

That Word our God made man in you,
and you are that shining gem,
from which the Word himself brought forth all virtue,
just as he had formed all creatures from the dust of
    earth.

You are that most sweet branch, springing from the
    stock of Jesse!
O how great is this wonder:
that the divinity should look on his most fair daughter,
as the eagle fixes his eyes on the sun,
when the Father Most High awaits the brightness of the
    Virgin,
and wills that his Word should take flesh in her very
    body.

For the Virgin's heart was mystically illumined by the
    mystery of God,
and the bright flower sprang forth wondrously from her
    virginity.

Prayers of St Gertrude the Great (AD 1256–c.1302)

A prayer to the Blessed Virgin Mary (The Herald of Divine Love, Bk. III. 19)

Hail, O white lily
of the bright and ever-peaceful Trinity!
Hail, O fairest rose of heaven's bliss!
Of you, the King willed to be born,
On your milk, he willed to feed!
O feed our souls too
by the inpouring of divine graces.

A prayer for conversion (Spiritual Exercises II)
(A meditation on the Song of Songs for the anniversary of her clothing)

O Jesus,
best-beloved of my heart,
no spiritual gift can bear fruit,
unless it is strengthened by your Spirit,
unless that strength is warmed by your love.
Be merciful, then, to me;
receive me into the arms of your love,
set me wholly on fire with your Spirit!
Behold, here are my soul and my body:
these I give you, that you might possess them.
O my beloved, my beloved!
Pour out upon me your blessing.
Open the door to me,
and lead me into the fullness of your sweetness.
With both my heart and my soul I desire you,
I beg you that you alone might possess me.
Behold, I am yours, and you are mine:
grant that I may grow again,
ever in the fire of your Spirit,
ever in the liveliness of your love;

grant that by your grace I may flower
like the lily of the valley
that grows by the water's edge.

Come, O Holy Spirit!
Come, O God, O Love
fill my heart
which is all too empty of good.
Set me ablaze, that I may love you.
Enlighten me, that I may recognize you.
Draw me to yourself, that I may delight in you.
Change me, that I may come to perfection in you.

A morning prayer of commitment (twentieth century)

Lord Jesus, you have made me for yourself,
and my heart is restless until it rests in you;
have mercy on me, and let your will be done.

Lord Jesus, you have brought me to this day,
to this place, and to the service of those around me;
have mercy on me, and let your will be done.

Lord Jesus, you have spared yourself nothing for my
   good,
even the very life which you poured out for me;
have mercy on me, and let your will be done.

A Benedictine Who's Who

Benedict

Those who have visited the great Benedictine Abbey of Monte Oliveto Maggiore outside Siena will have walked around its great cloister, and gazed at the frescoes of the life of St Benedict by Sodoma and Signorelli. They are supremely beautiful, with the saint and his contemporaries depicted in a graceful Umbrian landscape. The inspiration for the frescoes, and indeed the main source of information about Benedict, aside from the Rule of St Benedict itself, was the life of the saint recorded in the second book of the *Dialogues* of Pope Gregory the Great. Composed between 593 and 594, some forty years after the saint's death, Pope Gregory was concerned to propagate his belief that the Church in Italy was as capable of nurturing holy people, worthy of emulation, as other parts of the Church. His work proved to be enormously popular, and in the centuries that followed contributed to the growing influence of the Benedictine Rule across mediaeval Europe.

Reading the *Life and Miracles of Saint Benedict* today is a somewhat bizarre experience. Unlike Augustine who, like most late Antique men, could be credulous without being necessarily superstitious, this was not true of Pope Gregory and his contemporaries. They lived and breathed a different air from that of earlier generations of Christians, a supernatural air in a world where visions and miracles were commonplace, and where demonic intervention was a fact of life to be contended with. We are presented not so much with history as hagiography, a selection of vignettes and miraculous episodes chosen to illustrate Benedict's sanctity, and from which we have to assemble the story of his life.

Benedict was born in Nursia, central Italy, around 480. The date is significant because only four years before, in 476, the line of the Western emperors ended with the deposition of the boy emperor, Romulus Augustulus. Control of the Western Empire passed to Odoacer, a barbarian king, and seventeen years later following his defeat in battle, to another barbarian, Theodoric the Ostrogoth. Under Theodoric, Italy enjoyed seventeen years of strong government and peace. His death in 526, however, ushered in a period of turmoil and war – far worse than anything that had preceded it. The emperor of the East, Justinian, seeing his chance, resolved to recover Italy. For the next twenty years the so-called Gothic War raged across the Italian peninsula, causing untold havoc and destruction. Benedict was thus born at a turning point in history, and lived through one of the great periods of transition in which the face of the world changed. He witnessed political instability, widespread famine and war, and it is against this dark backcloth that his Rule is set.

Benedict's early years – The old structures of the Roman Empire were already disintegrating when as a young man Benedict was sent by his parents to study in Rome. Pope Gregory does not give us the names of his parents, but tells us only of a sister, Scholastica – later to become a nun – and of a devoted nurse who accompanied Benedict to Rome. We do not know how long he remained there, but we do know that at some point he abruptly broke off his studies, appalled by the decadence of the city, and that he went with his nurse to Affile, some forty miles north-east of the city. It was in Affile that Gregory tells us that Benedict first attracted attention. His nurse had borrowed an earthenware sieve and accidentally broke it. She appealed to Benedict for help, and he mended it, apparently miraculously. But finding himself at the centre of local interest, he left the town (and his nurse) as abruptly as he had left Rome, and sought complete solitude some five miles further north at Subiaco.

Subiaco – For the next three years, Benedict settled in a cave in the valley of the river Anio, and lived the life of a hermit. At some juncture he made the acquaintance of a local monk called Romanus who cared for him, providing him with bread and clothing. Benedict was probably about twenty at this time. There can be no doubt that this period of intense solitude was supremely formative of Benedict's monastic vocation. In due course, monks at Vicovaro, some eighteen miles downstream, asked him to become their abbot. Benedict consented, but it was not long before conflict emerged when he attempted to reform their monastic observance. According to Gregory, the monks tried (unsuccessfully) to poison his wine at dinner, which is why in some statues of Benedict he is shown holding not only his Rule, but also a chalice with a serpent emerging out of it.

Not surprisingly, Benedict returned to his hermitage where he attracted more worthy disciples. A small monastery was built by the side of the lake, and very quickly Benedict found himself at the head of a monastic colony. Gregory tells us that it was at Subiaco that two patricians of Rome entrusted their sons Maurus and Placid to Benedict's care. The custom of giving children to monasteries in this way was already established by the sixth century: that they were children of the nobility indicates the level of the acceptance and influence of monasticism in the Christian West.

Benedict organized the colony into small monasteries, each with twelve monks over which he set a prior, while remaining himself in overall charge. The model would seem to have been Jesus and the twelve disciples. For some twenty-five years Benedict presided over the Subiaco colony, and doubtless it was during this period that he began to distil the substance of his Rule. Perhaps his antipathy to the role of the prior in a monastery can also be dated from this period. Around 525, a disaffected faction, led by a jealous priest from the neighbourhood called Florentius, tried to sow dissension among the monks and even poison Benedict's bread. The plot failed, but the experience profoundly disturbed Benedict and it led him to the painful decision to leave Subiaco for Monte Cassino.

Monte Cassino – Monte Cassino overlooked, as it still does, a small town, some eighty miles south of Rome. When Benedict and his band of loyal monks arrived, they took over the old hill fortress complete with temple dedicated to Apollo. Within its walls they constructed their new monastery, turning the pagan sanctuary of Apollo into an oratory dedicated to St Martin, and later also building a church dedicated to St John the Baptist.

According to Gregory, it was at Monte Cassino towards the end of his life, that Benedict wrote his Rule. Scholars think it highly likely that he utilized the text of an existing monastic document, The Rule of the Master, adapting, modifying and adding to the text in the light of his own experience. He was certainly well qualified to do so, bringing forth from the inner treasury, 'things new and old'. Unlike many other monastic documents, Benedict's Rule has the virtue of being moderate, humane and *short*. It is only seventy-three chapters long. It is also said that unlike others, Benedict did not expect his monks to be heroes. The pattern of his life reveals why he was so realistic and compassionate about his fellow human beings. As Pope Gregory noted, Benedict 'wrote a Rule for Monks that is remarkable for its discretion and its clarity of language. Anyone who wishes to know more about his life and character can discover exactly what he was like as an abbot from his Rule, for his life cannot have differed from his teaching.'

Benedict died during the course of the Gothic War. Gregory tells us that the war brought famine and devastation to the region, but the monks ministered among the local population, feeding them from their own reserves, and intervening to prevent cruelty. Even Totila, King of the Goths, came seeking Benedict's counsel. According to Gregory, Benedict's sister, Scholastica, who lived not far from Monte Cassino and who visited him once a year, predeceased him and was buried in the monastery in the very grave that Benedict had prepared for himself. Benedict himself did not long survive her, but died on 21 March, probably in 550.

Swami Abhishiktananda (1910–73)

Henri le Saux was born in Brittany in France. His early years in monastic life, some nineteen in total, were spent as a Benedictine monk in the monastery of Kergonan near Briac. In 1948, however, he left Europe for India, desiring to bring the Benedictine life to India. Initially he lived at Shantivanam, an ashram in Tamil Nadu, which he founded with another French Catholic priest, Fr Jules Monchanin. Their aim was to live a Christian monastic life of the utmost poverty and simplicity, in harmony with the spirit of traditional Hindu ashrams. Following a meeting with the great Indian sage Sri Ramana Maharshi, however, he became so attached to silence and solitude that thereafter he spent long periods as a hermit in the Himalayas. Known as Abhishiktananda and wearing the saffron robes of a Hindu *sadhu*, he remained Christian and faithful to his Benedictine roots, and became one of the great Christian explorers of Indian spirituality and of interfaith dialogue.

Aelfric of Eynsham (*c*.955–*c*.1020)

Aelfric, known as 'The Grammarian', entered monastic life at Winchester and became in due course the greatest scholar of the English Benedictine revival, promoting the ideals of St Dunstan. In 1005 he was appointed Abbot of Eynsham in Oxfordshire. Among his many writings is a series of writings on the *Lives of the Saints*, among which is a biography of Edmund, King of East Anglia.

Aelred of Rievaulx (1109–67)

Aelred (or Ailred) was born at Hexham in Northumberland, England, in 1109. His father was a priest and he received a good education in the monastic school at Durham. He entered the infant Cistercian community at Rievaulx in about 1133, after spending some years in the court of King David of Scotland. He became Abbot of Revesby in 1143, but returned to Rievaulx only four years later to become abbot, there to spend the rest of his life. Aelred was a warm, gentle and humane man, and under his wise leadership the monastery consolidated and expanded, becoming one of the largest in England and in his own lifetime making five further foundations. He exercised a profound influence through his friendships and his spiritual writings, such as his treatise *On Spiritual Friendship* and *The Mirror of Charity*.

Aidan (d. 651)

According to Bede, Aidan was a monk of Iona, a gentle and moderate man who was sent to Northumbria at the request of King Oswald to re-establish the Church in his kingdom following the collapse of the earlier mission of Paulinus. Oswald became his loyal friend and interpreter, and the two worked together. Aidan was consecrated bishop in 635, and chose the island of Lindisfarne, near the royal palace at Bamburgh, as his base. From the island he was able to keep in easy communication with the king, combining a monastic lifestyle with missionary journeys to the mainland. Like all monks of the Celtic tradition, Aidan valued solitude and being close to the natural world. His concern for the poor and enthusiasm for preaching, won him wide popular support. It is sometimes said that it was Aidan, not Augustine, who was the true apostle of the English.

Alberic of Cîteaux (d. 1108)

Little is known of Alberic's early life. He, Robert of Molesme, Stephen Harding and their companions are honoured as the founders of the New Monastery in 1098 which came to be called the Abbey of Cîteaux. Their desire was to live the Rule of St Benedict more integrally, to rediscover the meaning of the monastic life and to translate this into structures adapted to their age. Robert was initially their leader, but following his return to Molesme, Alberic succeeded him as abbot. During the short time of his abbacy Alberic laid the foundations for what emerged as a huge reform movement across the face of monasticism.

Alcuin (c.735–804)

Alcuin was probably born in 735 in or near York. He entered the cathedral school there as a child, continued as a scholar and in 778 became its Master. In 781, at the invitation of Charlemagne, he went to Aachen to head up the new school that Charlemagne had founded, and became his chief religious adviser. As Master of the Palace School, he established an important library and promoted high standards of scholarship. He wrote poetry, revised the lectionary, compiled a sacramentary and was involved in significant liturgical reform. Charlemagne issued decrees that schools should be set up in every diocese and monastery in his kingdom modelled on that led by Alcuin. Although not a monk and only in deacon's orders, in 796 Alcuin retired to Tours where he became abbot of its monastery, and there in 804 he died. He is acknowledged as one of the great founders of mediaeval scholarship.

Aldhelm of Malmesbury (639–c.709)

Aldhelm was born of noble stock. He became a monk at Malmesbury, England, and was later elected its abbot. Under his leadership the community made other foundations, notably at Frome and Bradford-upon-Avon. He is reputed to have also been responsible for introducing the Rule of St Benedict into the area. Towards the end of his life, when in 705 the growing Wessex diocese was divided, he became the first Bishop of Sherborne, founding the abbey church. Aldhelm was a great scholar, writing in both Anglo-Saxon and Latin. He was also an acclaimed teacher and singer who, according to Bede, completed the conquest of Wessex by his preaching. Tradition has it that he would attract listeners by his singing and then preach the gospel to them.

Alphege (c.953–1012)

Alphege entered monastic life at Deerhurst near Gloucester, England, subsequently withdrawing to become a hermit in Somerset. He was appointed the first Abbot of Bath and, in 984, Bishop of Winchester. In 994 King Ethelred sent him to negotiate a peace with the Danes which brought him wide acclaim. In 1005 he was made Archbishop of Canterbury, where his holiness of life and generous almsgiving made him a revered and much-loved man. In 1011, however, the Danes resumed their raids and overran south-east England. They besieged Canterbury and took Alphege himself prisoner, placing an enormous ransom of £3,000 on his head. Alphege refused to pay it and forbade anyone from doing so, knowing that it would impoverish the populace. Outraged by his defiance, the Danes bludgeoned him to death with ox bones at Greenwich in 1012. Initially he was buried at St Paul's Cathedral in London, but subsequently his remains were translated to Canterbury.

Anselm (1033–1109)

Anselm was born in Aosta in northern Italy in 1033. As a young man, he left home and travelled north, visiting many monasteries and other centres of learning. Eventually, he arrived at the Benedictine Abbey of Le Bec Hellouin in Normandy where he met Lanfranc who advised him to embrace monastic life. He was to remain at Le Bec for the next thirty-four years, as monk, prior and finally in 1078, as abbot. Anselm had an outstanding and original mind which continues to secure for him an international reputation. During his lifetime, he sustained a vast correspondence, and wrote numerous theological, philosophical and devotional works, most notably the *Proslogion* and a treatise on the incarnation, *Cur Deus Homo*. His intellectual rigour was softened by his sensitivity and the generosity of his affection. Following the death of Lanfranc in 1093, Anselm succeeded him as Archbishop of Canterbury.

Antony of Egypt (*c.251–c.356*)

Antony may not have been the first Christian monk, but he stands pre-eminent among his contemporaries. Born in about 251, he heard the gospel message: 'If you would be perfect, go, sell your possessions, and give the money to the poor, and you will have treasure in heaven; then come, follow me.' According to his biographer Athanasius of Alexandria, Antony was twenty years old and rich, following the death of his parents. Obedient to the gospel he went to live in the desert, living an austere life of manual work, charity and prayer. The story of his life achieved a wide circulation and provided highly influential in promoting the monastic ideal. Along with the lives of the other Desert Fathers and Mothers, it was compulsory reading for Benedict and his disciples. Antony died peacefully in the desert in 356 reputedly at the great age of 105, asking that he be buried secretly, so that his person might be hidden in death as in life.

Augustine of Canterbury (d. 604/5)

Augustine was prior of the monastery of St Andrew in Rome. In 596, at the instigation of Pope Gregory the Great, he was dispatched as the leader of a group of forty monks to re-evangelize the English Church. It has been suggested that it was he who first brought Benedict's Rule to England. Augustine appears, however, to have been not a particularly confident person, and in Gaul he wanted to turn back, but Pope Gregory's firm resolution held the group to their mission. The monks finally landed in Kent in the summer of 597 where they were well received by King Ethelbert whose wife, Bertha, was a Christian. Once established, Augustine returned temporarily to Gaul to receive ordination as a bishop. Pope Gregory would have preferred London to have become the primatial see, but in the event Canterbury was chosen, and thus Augustine became the first Archbishop of Canterbury.

Baker, Augustine (1575–1641)

Born in the reign of Queen Elizabeth I, David Baker was educated at Christ's Hospital, London, before going up to Broadgates Hall (now Pembroke College), Oxford. He read law, becoming a member successively of Lincoln's Inn and of the Inner Temple in 1596. In 1605, however, he became a Catholic, quitted England for the continent, and entered the Benedictine monastery at Padua where he took the name Augustine. He was ordained priest around 1615. He became the spiritual director of the English Benedictine nuns at Cambrai, and later worked at Douai. He was a distinguished Benedictine writer on ascetical theology and history, who taught the way of an interior search for God based on the training of will, mind and heart. A collection of his writings was published posthumously under the title *Holy Wisdom* (two volumes in 1657). He also wrote a *Life of Dame Gertrude More*.

Baldwin of Canterbury (d. 1190)

A native of Exeter, Baldwin entered the Cistercian monastery at Ford in Devon, England. He became Bishop of Worcester in 1180, and in 1184, Archbishop of Canterbury. He took part in the Crusade of 1190, but returned to England very disillusioned at the poor discipline of the Christian troops. This experience had a profound effect on the rest of his ministry and preaching. A number of his sermons survive.

Basil the Great (c.329–79)

Basil, his brother Gregory of Nyssa, and his friend Gregory of Nazianzus are known collectively as the 'Cappadocian Fathers'. They were outstanding in their defence of the divinity of Christ, as set forth in the Council of Nicea, against the attacks of Arianism. Basil is sometimes known as the theologian of the Holy Spirit for his powerful treatise on the subject. But it is not for this that he is remembered by Benedictines, but for his formative role in establishing monastic life in the East. Near Caesarea Basil organized a complete city of social service run by monks. The people gave it the name 'Basiliad'. It contained a guest house, a hospice, an orphanage, a hospital, and there were free meals and lodging for the poor. In his own Rule, St Benedict commended 'the Rule of our holy father Basil' to his monks for reflection. Basil himself never enjoyed a robust constitution, and died prematurely in his fifties, worn out by hard work.

Bede (c.672–735)

Bede was born in Northumbria, England, around 672. When he was seven years old, his family sent him to the monastery of St Peter and St Paul at Wearmouth. From there he moved to Jarrow where he lived as a monk for the rest of his life. He became a deacon in his nineteenth year, and a priest in his thirtieth. Although it seems he never travelled further than York, his monastery under the leadership of first Abbot Benedict Biscop and then Abbot Ceolfrith was a major centre of learning, and Bede was at its heart. He was an able and astute scholar, writing numerous commentaries on the scriptures, and composing the most complete history of Christian England to date through which we gain considerable information on the growing influence of monastic culture in England. He died peacefully in 735 and is buried in Durham Cathedral.

Benedict of Aniane (c.750–821)

Benedict was a great reformer and rigorously ascetic. As a young man he abandoned the court of Charlemagne to enter monastic life, joining a monastery near Dijon in 773. In 779, however, he founded on his own property at Aniane in Languedoc a monastic community on very austere lines. The result was disappointing, and he adopted the Rule of St Benedict and established a larger monastery in the same place. This foundation flourished, and its influence and that of its founder spread throughout France. At length Benedict became virtually supreme abbot over all the monasteries of Charlemagne's empire. Under his presidency, a synod of abbots met an Aachen in 817 which issued a code of regulations which were binding on all their houses. Although this centralizing tendency was not to last much beyond his death, he gave impetus to monastic reform and the wider dissemination of the Rule.

Bernard of Clairvaux (1090–1153)

Bernard was one of the greatest minds and personalities of mediaeval Europe. He was born at Fontaines, near Dijon, in France in 1090. In 1112, he entered the Benedictine abbey at Cîteaux, taking with him many of his young companions, some of whom were his own brothers. He became the leader of the reform movement within monasticism at this time, and in 1115 was sent to establish a new monastery at a place he named Clairvaux, or 'Valley of Light', in Champagne. Though times were hard, he built up the community through his remarkable qualities of leadership. He preached widely and powerfully, and proved himself a theologian of renown. Literally hundreds of houses were founded on the Cîteaux or Cistercian system. It is difficult to over-estimate his influence on his own generation and beyond that, the life of the Church in Europe.

Bernard of Cluny (d. *c.*1140)

Bernard of Cluny (also known as Bernard of Morval or Morlass) was a monk of Cluny during the abbacy of Peter the Venerable. A distinguished preacher and poet, he is best remembered today as the author of several hymns, notably 'Jerusalem the Golden'.

Bernard Tolomei (1272–1348)

Giovanni Tolomei was a Sienese noble, born into one of the wealthiest merchant families of Tuscany. At around the age of forty, he felt called to a more austere lifestyle. With some friends who shared his ascetic ideal, he retired to property of his family to the south-east of Siena (then known as the desert of Accona) and founded the monastery of Monte Oliveto. He took the name Bernard in honour of the great abbot of Clairvaux. In 1319 the Benedictine Rule was formally adopted, and Bernard and his followers received the (white) habit and foundation charter from the Bishop Guido of Arezzo. The foundation flourished, and in 1344 Pope Clement VI canonically established the Benedictine Congregation of St Mary of Monte Oliveto to foster the monastic movement that had spontaneously developed around the monastery. Bernard himself died in 1348 ministering to victims of the plague.

Biscop, Benedict (628–89)

Biscop Baducing was born in Northumbria, England, in 628. As a young man he served at the court of King Oswy until he joined Wilfrid of York on his pilgrimage to Rome. He made a second trip accompanied by the King's son and on his way home was clothed a monk at the Benedictine house of Lérins where he took the name Benedict. On his third trip to Rome he met and returned to England with Theodore of Tarsus, the newly appointed Archbishop of Canterbury, who made him Abbot of St Augustine's in 669. Five years later, he was permitted to make his own foundation at Wearmouth, which he had built in the Roman style and endowed with a huge library. He also brought back the precentor of St Peter's to teach the monks to sing in the Roman fashion, and encouraged the development of the Uncial script. He is sometimes referred to as Bene't Biscop.

Boniface (c.675–754)

Boniface is honoured as 'the Apostle of Germany'. He was a great missionary preacher, an outstanding administrator, and a learned, gentle and holy man. Born Wynfrith at Crediton in Devon, England, in about 675, he took the name Boniface upon entering monastic life in Exeter. In 716 he became a missionary to Frisia, following in the steps of Willibrord, and was eventually commissioned by the Pope to work in Hesse and Bavaria where he went after being consecrated a bishop in 722. He courageously felled the oak of Thor at Geismar, an object of local superstition, and widespread conversion to Christianity followed. In 732 he was made Archbishop of Mainz. He founded several monasteries across southern Germany and made sure that they were places of learning for the systematic evangelization of the country. He also worked assiduously for the reform of the Church in France and promoted the extensive adoption of the Rule of St Benedict in monasteries. He was murdered by a band of pagans in 754.

Bosschaerts, Constantine (1889–1950)

Born in Antwerp, Arthur Bosschaerts is honoured as the founder of the Vita et Pax Foundation – a renewal movement of monks, nuns and lay people committed to the search for Christian unity. He entered monastic life at the Abbey of Afflinghem, of the Subiaco Congregation, taking the name Constantine. At the end of the First World War, he was appointed chaplain to a community of nuns at Eccleshall, Staffordshire, England. He instilled within the sisters a commitment to pray for Christian unity which became a hallmark of his life. Under his guidance, the majority of the community went with him to Schotenhof in Belgium. There, in association with Dom Lambert Beauduin, he established a dual-rite monastery of monks and nuns, with Byzantine and Latin rites celebrated in parallel. Tension between Flemish and French speakers in Belgium contributed to Dom Constantine's community being closed down, the monks transferring mainly to Dom Lambert's foundation at Amay-sur-Meuse (later Chevetogne). In 1933, Dom Constantine transferred to the Olivetan Congregation; and in 1936, at the suggestion of the Abbot General, returned to England with a group of monks, nuns and oblates to found a new venture at Cockfosters in north London. He pioneered a more contemporary expression of Benedictine life in which art, beauty and culture were honoured, and the liturgy celebrated contemplatively.

Buckley, Sigebert (1517–1610)

Dom Sigebert Buckley is an important figure in the history of the English Benedictine Congregation. Born Robert, he took the name Sigebert upon entering monastic life. He lived through the trauma of the dissolution of the English monasteries under Henry VIII, and was one of the surviving band of monks which Queen Mary I gathered for her project to restore monastic life in England at the reconstituted Abbey of St Peter, Westminster, on 21 November 1556. The revival was short-lived, the monastery being dissolved by her sister, Queen Elizabeth I. During 1560–1603 Dom Sigebert was imprisoned as a recusant, latterly at Framlingham. During the last five years of his life, he was imprisoned again, this time in London. By 1607, he was the only monk of the pre-Reformation Congregation to be still alive. On 21 November he aggregated two young English monks of the Cassinese Congregation to his own Congregation in order to maintain some sort of continuity with the first monks who had arrived with St Augustine at the end of the sixth century. He surrendered his authority for perpetuating the succession to Thomas Preston in 1609, the year before he died.

Butler, Cuthbert (1858–1934)

Edward Joseph Aloysius Butler was born in England in 1858. He was educated at Downside Abbey, Somerset, and in 1876 entered the monastery himself, taking the name Cuthbert. Shortly after his ordination as priest, he was appointed headmaster of the school. In 1906 he was elected abbot, a position which he held until 1922. He was a distinguished Benedictine abbot and scholar, and his two principal works *Benedictine Monachism* (1919) and *Western Mysticism* (1922) remain noteworthy.

Cabrol, Fernand (1855–1937)

Born in Marseilles in France, Fernand Cabrol entered monastic life at the Abbey of Solesmes, and was professed in 1877. In 1896, he was sent to England as prior of the projected new foundation at Farnborough in Hampshire. The abbey had been commissioned by the Empress Eugenie, and was built in the French Gothic and Romanesque styles to house the mausoleum of Napoleon III and his family. In 1903, he was elected abbot. Cabrol was a distinguished scholar, and under his leadership the monastery gained an international reputation for studies in liturgy, Gregorian Chant and church history. His own publications included *Le livre de la priere antique* (1900), and in collaboration with Dom Henri Leclercq, *Monumenta Ecclesiae Liturgica* (4 vols, Paris, 1903–13).

Carlyle, Aelred (1874–1955)

Benjamin Fearnley Carlyle began his professional life as a medical student at St Bartholomew's Hospital, London, in 1892. During that time he became an Anglican Benedictine oblate, and in 1896 gave up medicine. He took the name Aelred, and in 1902, founded the Benedictine community which eventually in 1906 settled on Caldey Island, off the south-west coast of Wales. In 1913 he was received into the Roman Catholic Church, and was professed and ordained a year later. In 1928 he and other members of the community who had converted with him, moved to Prinknash, near Gloucester, where he is honoured as the founder of the present Benedictine community. Aelred resigned the abbacy in 1921 to work in the Canadian mission fields, returning to the community in 1951.

Cassian, John (c.360–435)

As a young man John Cassian joined a monastery at Bethlehem, but left it soon after to study monasticism in Egypt. Eventually, he seems to have established himself permanently in the West.

He wrote two books on monastic life called the *Institutes* and the *Conferences* out of the material he had gathered during his stay in Egypt. These proved to be highly influential in disseminating the monastic ideal in the Western Church. In his Rule, Benedict commends these works to be read by his monks.

Chapman, John (1865–1933)

The son of an Anglican clergyman, Henry Palmer Chapman was educated at Christ Church, Oxford, before taking holy orders in the Church of England in 1889. In 1890, however, he was received into the Catholic Church, and two years later entered monastic life at Maredsous, Belgium, taking the name John. In 1895, he returned to England to live at Erdington Priory in Birmingham, a community founded by monks of Beuron in 1876. A distinguished, if conservative, biblical and patristic scholar, he was appointed a member of the Commission for the Revision of the Vulgate. In 1913, he was sent for a year as superior of the community on Caldey Island, off the south-west coast of Wales, which had recently become Catholic. With the outbreak of war, there was no possibility of returning to Belgium, so together with some other English monks of Maredsous, he transferred to Downside Abbey, near Bath in Somerset. In 1922, he was appointed prior, and in 1929, was elected abbot. He was a wise spiritual director, and a collection of his writings were published posthumously (1935) under the title *Spiritual Letters*.

Cuthbert (c.635–687)

Cuthbert was a man of great faith, gentleness and simplicity, one of the great heroes of Celtic monasticism. He was probably born in the Scottish lowlands. He entered monastic life at Melrose Abbey. It was from here that he began his missionary work, walking the countryside and talking of his faith to all whom he met. In 661, in the company of his abbot Eata, he visited Ripon to observe the Roman customs introduced by Wilfrid, and in

664 attended the Synod of Whitby. As Abbot of Lindisfarne he persuaded the monks to adopt the decrees of Whitby, and tried to weld the strengths of both traditions into the life of the Church. Later, he became a hermit on the island of Farne, but in 685 was elected Bishop of Lindisfarne. He remained an indefatigable traveller and preacher, walking all over his diocese. After two years, however, he became gravely ill and resigned his office, returning to Farne to die. He is buried in Durham Cathedral.

Delatte, Paul (1848–1937)

The closing decades of the nineteenth century were turbulent for monastic life in France. The decrees of the government of 29 March 1880 effectively led to the dissolution of practically all houses of religious men in France. In November 1880, the monks of Solesmes were expelled. Following the death of Abbot Couturier in 1890, Dom Paul Delatte (then prior) was elected third Abbot of Solesmes. He proved a wise and strong abbot, and under his leadership, the community regained its confidence, and was able to repossess its buildings, and to make foundations at Farnborough in England, and at Kergonan in Brittany. But the peace was short-lived. Following further legislation of the Third Republic in 1901, all religious congregations were shut down, and the monks of Solesmes went into exile in England, on the Isle of Wight. They purchased the site of the ancient Abbey of Quarr on the island, and began an ambitious programme of building. Dom Delatte himself was a natural contemplative with a brilliant intellect. His magisterial commentary on the Rule, first published in French in 1913, and then in English in 1921, remains a classic exposition of St Benedict's text.

Dix, Gregory (1901–52)

George Eglington Alston Dix, better known as Dom Gregory Dix, was educated at Westminster and Merton College, Oxford.

Following his ordination, he entered the Anglican Benedictine Monastery of Nashdom, England, in 1926, taking the name Gregory. He served the community with distinction as prior from 1948 until his premature death in 1952, but his greatest renown is as a historian and liturgical scholar. His magisterial survey of the development of the Eucharist, *The Shape of the Liturgy*, published in 1945, won him international acclaim, and remains a standard work of reference.

Dunstan (*c.*910–88)

Dunstan is credited with the distinction of restoring monastic life for men in England. He was born into a noble family near Glastonbury around 910. He received a good education and spent time at the court of the King of Wessex. He entered monastic life at Glastonbury, becoming abbot in 943. There he developed the first organized monastic community for men for several generations, and launched a great revival of monastic life in England. During a period of exile in Ghent, he learned much about Benedictine monasticism and the standards of scholarship it promoted. Upon his return he became the leader of a remarkable triumvirate with bishops Oswald and Ethelwold. In 960 he became Archbishop of Canterbury which enabled him and his followers to extend their reforms to the whole English Church. In around 970 he summoned a conference of bishops, abbots and abbesses which drew up a code of national monastic observance, known as the *Regularis Concordia*. It was in line with continental custom and the Rule of St Benedict, but had its own distinctive features; notably that English monasteries were more integrated into the life of the nation.

Ethelburga of Barking (d. *c.*675)

Ethelburga was a sister of Erconwald, Bishop of London, and was probably of royal blood. According to Bede, it seems she may well have owned, as well as been made abbess of, the monastery at Barking. It may have been her introduction to monastic life, for it is said that her brother appointed a French nun as prioress to teach his sister Benedictine observance. There was a tradition developing in Anglo-Saxon England of monks and nuns sharing monasteries, often with a woman superior, as for example Hilda at Whitby and Cuthburga at Wimborne; and Barking was such a double monastery. Though they lived quite separate lives, often divided by high walls, the monks and nuns would occasionally celebrate the Office or mass together. There was also probably an element of safety involved with the ever-present threat of marauding Danes.

Etheldreda of Ely (d. *c*.678)

Etheldreda (otherwise known as Audrey) was born in Suffolk, in the seventh century, a daughter of King Anna of East Anglia. She desired to commit her life to prayer and chastity and, after two arranged and unconsummated marriages, was given leave to found a religious house at Ely, then an island surrounded by swamps and marshes in east England. It was a double monastery for both men and women, over which she ruled as abbess. It is thought that she adopted the Rule of St Benedict. At her death in around 678, she was revered as a woman of austerity and prayer.

Ethelwold of Winchester (*c*.908–84)

Ethelwold was formed in the monastic life at Glastonbury under the direction of Abbot Dunstan, with whom he and Oswald of Worcester were to be associated in the great tenth-century revival of monastic life in England. In 954 he was entrusted with the re-establishment of Abingdon Abbey, and in 963 was made Bishop of Winchester. In the years that followed Ethelwold founded or refounded a number of monasteries, among them Peterborough, Ely and Thorney. With St Dunstan he drew up the *Regularis Concordia*, a directory of national monastic observance which sought to bring order to the anarchy and confusion following the Danish invasions. He also translated the Rule of St Benedict into English for the benefit of nuns who had no Latin.

Frances of Rome (1384–1440)

Born into the Roman aristocracy in 1384, Francesca married Lorenzo de' Ponziani by whom she had several children. A deeply religious woman, she had a natural sympathy for the sufferings of others, and during the plagues worked among the sick and destitute. After their home was pillaged by Neapolitan troops in 1409, her husband was forced into exile, returning a broken man some five years later. In 1425 she and a number of other Roman ladies given to charitable good works organized themselves into a society, and eight years later established a community, in association with the Benedictine monks of Monte Oliveto. Its members came to be known as the Oblates of Tor de' Specchi, after the house in which they lived. Following the death of her husband in 1436 and forty years of marriage, she withdrew to the community and directed its development for the remaining years of her life.

Gertrude of Helfta (1256–c.1302)

Gertrude was born in 1256. At the age of five she was given by her parents to be brought up by the Benedictine nuns of Helfta in Thuringia. She was a gifted child and received a good education at their hands. At the age of twenty-five she experienced a profound conversion in consequence of a vision of Christ, and for the rest of her life she led a life of contemplation. Of the so-called *Revelations of Gertrude*, only *The Herald of Divine Love* is genuinely hers, written partly from her notes or dictation, and partly by herself. She is sometimes called 'Gertrude the Great' to distinguish her from Gertrude of Hackeborn who was Abbess of Helfta when she was brought there as a child. Gertrude was one of the first exponents of devotion to the Sacred Heart.

Gilbert of Sempringham (1083–1189)

The Gilbertine Order was the only purely English monastic foundation before the dissolution of the monasteries in the sixteenth century, and was an extraordinary hybrid. Gilbert was born in 1083 in Sempringham, Lincolnshire, the son of the squire. He became the parish priest in 1131. He encouraged the vocation of seven local women, forming them into a company of lay sisters. A group of lay brothers also came into being and they all kept the Benedictine Rule. Gilbert was unsuccessful in his bid to obtain pastoral guidance from Cîteaux for the incipient communities and instead they came under the ambit of Augustinian canons, Gilbert himself becoming the master. At his death in 1189, aged 106, there were nine double monasteries in England and four of male canons only.

Gregory the Great (540–604)

As a young man Gregory pursued a governmental career, and in 573 was made Prefect of the city of Rome. Following the death of his father, he resigned his office, sold his inheritance, and became a monk. In 579 he was sent by the Pope to Constantinople to be his representative to the Patriarch. He returned to Rome in 586, and was himself elected pope in 590. At a time of political turmoil, Gregory proved an astute administrator and diplomat, securing peace with the Lombards. He initiated the mission to England, sending Augustine and forty monks to refound the English Church. His sermons and writings were pastorally oriented, as seen for example in his treatise on Christian leadership entitled *Pastoral Care*. His spirituality was animated by a dynamic of love and desire for God. It is from Gregory that we have the main source of information about Benedict. In the second book of his *Dialogues*, written some forty years after the saint's death, we get an account of his life and miracles.

Gregory VII (Hildebrand) (*c.*1021–85)

Hildebrand was born in Tuscany of poor parents. At an early age he travelled to Rome and received his education in a monastery on the Aventine, but may not himself have become a monk. He entered papal service as chaplain to Pope Gregory VI, and in 1073 was himself elected pope, taking the name Gregory. He initiated a systematic programme of reform and renewal throughout the Church, including issuing decrees against simony and lay investiture. The latter was the practice of investing bishops and abbots elect with the symbols of their offices by lay princes, a practice that had led to serious abuse. Papal protection defended reformed monasteries against the interference of hostile bishops or the depredations of lay proprietors. In return, the monasteries provided the papacy with a source of loyal monks who were instrumental in cleansing the Church from corruption and carrying forward papal reforms.

Griffiths, Bede (1906–93)

In his autobiography *The Golden String*, and in his other works, Bede Griffiths brought the conversation between Christianity and Hindu spirituality to a wide public. Born in England, the youngest of four children, Alan Griffiths was educated at Oxford. He became a catholic in his mid-twenties, and shortly afterwards in 1933, entered monastic life at Prinknash Abbey, Gloucestershire. He took the name Bede. In 1947, he was sent by the abbot as superior of Farnborough, then a dependent priory of Prinknash. In 1951, however, Bede was peremptorily dismissed and sent to Pluscarden, another dependent house in the far north of Scotland. There he remained for the next four years until in 1955, feeling a need to discover 'the other half of my soul', he sought leave to go to India. Initially, he lived at Kurisumala, but following Abhishaktananda's retirement to the Himalayas, he moved to lead the ashram at Shantivanam in Tamil Nadu where he built up a thriving spiritual community. He believed that Eastern and Western spirituality could enrich

248

each other, and was open to all paths by which people seek God.

Guéranger, Prosper (1805–75)

From childhood Louis Pascal Guéranger had the dream of restoring monastic life to France following the ravages of the French Revolution. In 1827 he was ordained to the priesthood, and five years later purchased the Priory of Solesmes with a view to re-establishing the Benedictine monastery. It was opened in 1833, and in 1837 Guéranger made monastic profession in Rome, taking the name Prosper. Pope Gregory XVI appointed him first Abbot of Solesmes, and it was there that he spent the rest of his life. Guéranger was a great inspiration to many, including J. P. Migne whom he launched on his project of compiling the writings of the Church Fathers, the collection known today as the *Patrologia Latina et Græca*. A keen liturgicologist and a voluminous writer himself, he also encouraged a renewal of interest in the chant and the reform of the Office. Under his dynamic leadership, the Abbey of Solesmes became the leading force of monastic renewal in France and beyond.

Guerric of Igny (*c.*1070–1157)

Little is known of Guerric's early life. He seems to have lived a life of prayer and study at or near the cathedral of Tournai in France. At some point he became a Cistercian novice, and in 1138 was made Abbot of Igny, near Rheims. A number of his sermons have survived.

Hilda of Whitby (614–80)

Hilda (or Hild) was born in 614 of the royal house of Northumbria, England. At the age of twelve she was baptized in York by St Paulinus. At the age of thirty-three, following the example of her sister and encouraged by Aidan of Lindisfarne, she become a nun. She established monasteries first at Hartlepool, and two years later in 657 at Whitby. This house became a great centre of learning and culture, and in 664 hosted the important Synod of Whitby at which it was decided to adopt Roman customs, including the dating of Easter, in preference to Celtic traditions. Although herself a Celt in religious formation, Hilda played a crucial role in reconciling others to the decision of the Synod.

Hildegard of Bingen (1098–1179)

Hildegard was born in 1098 at Böckelheim in Germany. From her earliest years she had a powerful, visionary life. At the age of fifteen she entered monastic life, much influenced by her foster-mother, Jutta, who had established a Benedictine community and whom she succeeded as abbess in 1136. Sometime between 1147 and 1152 Hildegard moved the community to Bingen. Her visions of light, which she described as 'the reflection of the Living Light', deepened her understanding of God and creation, sin and redemption. These she recorded in music and poetry, and in her letters. She sustained a huge correspondence, writing letters of advice to prominent people, including four popes and Emperor Frederick Barbarossa. In her sixties she even began to travel extensively throughout the Rhineland, founding a daughter house and lecturing monks and nuns. She wrote three visionary works, a natural history and a medical compendium. She was a pastor, a poet, a composer and teacher, seeing herself as a 'feather on the breath of God'.

Hugh the Great (1024–1109)

Hugh was born of a noble Burgundian family, and entered monastic life at Cluny under Abbot Odilo at the age of fourteen. As a novice his holiness of life was such that he was allowed to take vows barely a year later. By the age of twenty-one he was prior, and upon Odilo's death in 1049, was elected abbot unanimously. An intelligent and wise man, he became the personal adviser to no less than nine popes, and consequently exercised a huge influence upon the affairs of the Church. Although this resulted in him being absent from Cluny for considerable periods of time, the monastery appears not to have suffered. Indeed, during Hugh's abbacy Cluny reached a position it was never to surpass.

Hume, George Basil (1923–99)

Born in Newcastle-upon-Tyne, England, in 1923, Basil Hume was one of the outstanding churchmen of his generation. Educated at Ampleforth College, St Bene't's Hall, Oxford, and Fribourg University, he entered monastic life at Ampleforth Abbey. In 1963, he was elected abbot, a position he held with distinction until his appointment as (Cardinal) Archbishop of Westminster in 1976. A warm, but shy man, he brought to his work, both as abbot and archbishop, a humility and humanity which secured for him high regard, in and beyond England. His many publications on prayer and the spiritual life helped to make Benedictine spirituality accessible to a wider audience.

John of Salerno (dates unknown)

John was a monk of Cluny, and a disciple and eventually biographer of Abbot Odo. During his lifetime the great abbey church of St Peter and St Paul was completed, and the influence of Cluny greatly extended.

Julian of Vézelay (1080–1160)

Julian was a Benedictine monk who in later life became abbot of his community at Vézelay in France. Some twenty-seven of his sermons have survived. They reveal him to have been a man of wide learning, including knowledge of Plato and Greek philosophy.

Knowles, David (1896–1974)

Michael Clive Knowles was educated at Downside Abbey in Somerset, England, and subsequently at Christ's College, Cambridge. Barely eighteen years old, he joined the monastic community, taking the name David. Marked out from his early days as a supremely gifted scholar, he became the Classics master at the Abbey School, but found that his teaching clashed with the call to a life of prayer. The idea formed of founding a new community, but the plan was rejected by Rome in 1934, and he moved to Ealing Priory. Tensions continued, and eventually in 1939 he withdrew from the community. In 1944 he was elected to a fellowship at Peterhouse, Cambridge, becoming successively Dixie Professor of Mediaeval History, and in 1954, Regius Professor of Modern History. His magisterial volumes *The Monastic Order in England 940–1216*, and *The Religious Orders in England* (3 vols) remain standard texts, unsurpassed in scholarship and analysis.

Lanfranc (*c*.1005–89)

Lanfranc was born in Pavia, Italy, around 1005. He was educated in Italy and Paris, and gained a reputation as a scholar and a teacher. In 1042 he entered the monastery of Le Bec in Normandy, where he founded the school which rose rapidly to renown throughout Europe. He was a brilliant administrator, and in 1063 Duke William of Normandy appointed him first Abbot of Caen and, following the conquest, in 1070 Archbishop of Canterbury. Lanfranc was a great statesman, overseeing administrative, judicial and ecclesiastical reforms with the same energy and rigour that the Conqueror displayed in his new kingdom. He appointed many Norman abbots and bishops to implement his vision in what he considered a rather unsophisticated English Church. New dioceses were formed and new cathedrals built. Nor did Lanfranc forget his monastic formation: he wrote new Constitutions for Christ Church, Canterbury, based on the customs of Le Bec.

Leclercq, Henri (1869–1945)

Henri Leclercq was a distinguished Benedictine scholar. Born in Tournai in Belgium, he entered monastic life at the Abbey of Solesmes in France. Following profession, he was sent to England as part of a contingent of French monks making a foundation at Farnborough Abbey, Hampshire. It was there that he was ordained, and also entered into his scholarly collaboration with Dom Fernand Cabrol (later abbot) in liturgical research. Together they edited the four volumes of *Monumenta Ecclesiae Liturgica* (1903–13), and the *Dictionnaire d'archéologie chrétienne et de liturgie* (15 vols, 1907–53). The latter work was completed after his death, and has since been criticized for its inaccuracies. Leclercq's own interest lay chiefly in the formation of Latin Christianity.

Leclercq, Jean (1911–93)

Dom Jean Leclercq stands out as one of the great monastic scholars of the twentieth century. He entered monastic life at the Abbey of Clervaux, Luxembourg, a foundation of Solesmes, but in the tradition of monastic *peregrinatio* became an inveterate traveller, researching in the archives and libraries of monasteries across the length and breadth of Europe. Essentially a mediaevalist, he had a deep sense of the monastic tradition, and became an authority on the history of Christian spirituality. For Leclercq, monastic life was above all contemplative, nourished by listening, and therefore fundamental to the Benedictine way is the practice of *lectio divina*. Of his numerous publications, his highly acclaimed study of monastic culture, *The Love of Learning and the Desire for God* (1982) remains an authoritative text.

Mabillon, Jean (1632–1707)

Jean Mabillon was a leading member of a group of seventeenth-century monastic scholars in the Congregation of Saint-Maur.

The Maurists spearheaded reform and renewal of the Benedictine life following the ravages of the reformation. He entered monastic life at the Benedictine Abbey of Saint-Rémy at Rheims in 1653, but in 1654 was sent to Saint-Germain-des-Prés, the powerhouse of the congregation. Perhaps the most influential of the group, his historical and literary output was prodigious. He produced some twenty folio works, including an edition of the writings of St Bernard, and collated the annals of the Benedictine order.

Maieul of Cluny (d. 994)

Maieul was the third Abbot of Cluny, succeeding Abbot Odo in 942. Cluny stood for the supreme development of the liturgical life: a sense of adoration and intercession for the whole of society. It had begun as simply a new and fervent monastery, but it had the good fortune to be ruled by a succession of exceptionally able, holy and, in the case of Maieul, long-lived abbots. This brought a strong sense of stability and continuity to the new foundation. He proved a wise and prudent abbot.

Main, John (1926–82)

Douglas William Victor Main was born in north London of Irish parentage. After the war, he briefly tested his vocation with the Canons Regular of the Lateran, but withdrew, moving to Ireland (where his family were then living) to read law at Trinity College, Dublin. Following graduation, he joined the British Commonwealth Service, and was assigned to Malaya where he met a Hindu monk, Swami Satyananda, who taught him to meditate using a mantra as the way of deepening his Christian discipleship. In 1956, he returned to Dublin to teach international law. Following the tragic death of a nephew, he entered monastic life at Ealing Abbey in 1959, taking the name John. The last seven years of his life were spent in Canada where he had been invited to establish a new and radically contemplative community in Montreal. His writings, particularly *The Present*

Christ (published posthumously in 1985), bear testimony to the integrity of his monastic journey, to his commitment to meditation and the community that silence creates.

Marmion, Columba (1858–1923)

Joseph Marmion was born in Dublin in 1858. Following ordination and a period as Professor of Philosophy at Holy Cross College, Dublin, he entered monastic life at the Benedictine Abbey of Maredsous in Belgium where he took the name Columba. In 1909 he was elected abbot. During his lifetime he was recognized as a wise, holy and gifted spiritual director. Collections of his spiritual conferences were published and widely circulated in many languages, notably *Christ the Ideal of the Monk* and *Christ the Life of the Soul*.

Maurus and Placid (*c*.580)

According to the *Dialogues* of Gregory the Great, written shortly after the death of St Benedict, Maurus and Placid were two boys entrusted to the care of Benedict at his monastery in Subiaco. The custom of giving children to monasteries in this way was already established by the sixth century: that they were children of the nobility indicates the level of the acceptance and influence of monasticism in the Christian West. Pope Gregory tells us that on one occasion Maurus saved the young Placid from drowning. Maurus later gave his name to the French Benedictine Congregation of St Maur (1621–1818) which became famous for its learning and scholarship.

McLachlan, Laurentia (1866–1953)

Margaret McLachlan was born in Lanarkshire, Scotland, into a large old-Catholic family. She entered monastic life at Stanbrook Abbey, Worcestershire, England, in 1884 at the age of eighteen, and took the name Laurentia. The community had been formed from nine English exiles in 1625 in Cambrai, Flanders. In 1795, following imprisonment and destitution during the French Revolution, the community of nuns came to England, but did not move to Stanbrook until 1838. Dame Laurentia was a gifted musician who made a particular study of the Chant. She had an attractive and engaging personality, with a great capacity for friendship, both within and beyond the cloister. Her friendship and extensive correspondence with George Bernard Shaw and Sir Sydney Cockerell is a case in point. In 1931 she was elected abbess, and under her wise leadership the community prospered.

Mechtild of Magdeburg (c.1210–80)

Mechtild was born in about 1210. The mystical writings for which she is known speak of her experience of the love of God as it was revealed to her. This experience began when she was twelve years old. She responded to it by joining a community of Béguines at the age of about eighteen. After forty years, she moved to the Cistercian convent of Helfta and in about 1270 completed her writings there. Helfta was a remarkable centre of learning at that time with other outstanding personalities in the community. She wrote with poetic sensitivity in direct and simple language of the exchange of love with God.

Mellitus of London (d. 624)

Mellitus was a Roman abbot who was sent to England by Pope Gregory the Great in 601 at the head of a second band of missionaries to undergird the work of St Augustine and his party. Augustine consecrated him Bishop of the East Saxons, with his see at London. He dedicated his first church to St Paul. After some local setbacks and having to reside in northern France, he and his fellow bishops were recalled to England, but Mellitus was unable to return to London. He was made Archbishop of Canterbury in 619 and died five years later.

Merton, Thomas (1915–68)

Born in France in 1915, Thomas Merton's childhood was marred by the death of his mother from cancer. He was brought up partly in England, partly in the United States, but educated in England. He dropped out of Cambridge and returned to the States where he eventually entered monastic life at the Abbey of Our Lady of Gethsemani, Kentucky – a monastery of the Cistercians of the Strict Observance, commonly known as Trappists. He took the name Louis. His autobiography, *The Seven Storey Mountain*, excited much public interest, and in the years that followed his extensive publications on monastic life and spirituality secured an ever-widening audience. Towards the end of his life he became extremely interested in the eremitical ideal and monastic inter-faith dialogue. Tragically, he died in 1968 at the age of only fifty-three, accidentally electrocuted while attending a monastic conference in Bangkok.

More, Gertrude (1606–33)

A direct descendant of Sir Thomas More, Gertrude entered the house of the English Benedictine Congregation of nuns at Cambrai in France in 1623. She was seventeen, and one of nine young English exiles who formed the nucleus of the new community. During her novitiate she was much troubled by temptations and scruples, until she came under the direction of Dom Augustine Baker who encouraged her to pursue the way of an interior search for God based on the training of will, heart and mind. A holy and devout young woman, Gertrude made monastic profession in 1625, and in 1629 at the age of twenty-three, became abbess. Tragically, she died of smallpox only four years later. Several of her meditations and writings survived and were published posthumously.

Odilo of Cluny (c.962–1049)

Odilo was the fifth Abbot of Cluny. He entered the monastery in 991, and was elected abbot barely three years later. He was a man of learning, holiness and integrity, but above all he was an outstanding administrator. During his abbacy the number of Cluniac houses increased from thirty-seven to sixty-five, Cluny becoming the mother-house of a vast network of dependent monasteries. The order was further consolidated by his strategy of centralization, whereby most of the reformed houses were made directly dependent on Cluny. It was Odilo who introduced the commemoration of the faithful departed on All Souls' Day: initially a purely local observance at Cluny, it gradually spread and was adopted by the whole Church.

Odo of Cluny (879–942)

The son of a Frankish knight, Odo was brought up in the family of William, Duke of Aquitaine, who in 909 founded the Abbey of Cluny near Dijon in Burgundy. To protect it from lay or episcopal usurpation William subjected it to the Church of St Peter in Rome, i.e. the papacy. In a climate of general decadence when the papacy itself was passing through a degrading and impotent phase, this meant little; but it did leave the new foundation free to grow and evolve. In due time its link with a reformed papacy became the axis of its greatness. Odo was initially a canon of St Martin's in Tours, and studied in Paris under Remigius of Auxerre. Upon returning to Tours he read the Rule of St Benedict and was deeply affected by it. Three years later in 909 he resigned his canonry, and entered monastic life at Baume. The following year when his abbot Berno became abbot of the new foundation, Odo was put in charge of the monastery school at Baume. Upon his death in 927, Odo succeeded him, and was largely responsible for the huge expansion and development of Cluny in the years that followed. During his abbacy the great monastic church of St Peter and St Paul was completed, and was the largest church in Europe until the sixteenth century.

Oswald of Worcester (*c*.925–92)

Oswald, Ethelwold and Dunstan are the names associated with the great tenth-century revival of monastic life in England. A Dane by birth, Oswald studied in the household of his uncle, Archbishop Odo of Canterbury, and later at the Benedictine Abbey of Fleury in France. He was ordained there, not returning to England until 959. In 962 he became Bishop of Worcester, and began to assist Archbishop Dunstan in his project of reforming the monastic life in England. In 972 he became Archbishop of York, though he continued to be Bishop of Worcester as well in order to promote monastic reform.

Pachomius (d. 346)

Pachomius is honoured as the first Christian monk who not simply tried to bring hermits together in groups, but actually organized them with a written Rule and structures of a communal life (*cenobium*). He is said to have been born in Upper Egypt, of pagan parents, and to have been a conscript in the imperial army. Upon discharge he was converted and baptized. He became a disciple of a hermit, and then in about 320, founded a monastery at Tabennisi near the Nile. He used his military experience to organize his growing number of followers, and by the time of his death in 346 he was ruling as abbot-general over nine monasteries for men and two for women. He is honoured, therefore, as the founder of cenobitic monasticism.

Paris, Matthew (*c*.1199–1259)

Matthew Paris was a Benedictine monk of St Alban's Abbey, England, and an expert scribe and illuminator. His chief claim to fame is his *Chronica Maiora*, a history of the world from

creation to 1259. He was also the biographer of St Edmund of
Abingdon.

Paulinus of York (d. 644)

Paulinus was born in the latter part of the sixth century, probably in Italy. He was among the second group of monks sent
by Pope Gregory the Great to England to assist Augustine in
his work of renewing the Church in England. Augustine was
established in Canterbury, but had not extended his work outside Kent. It was Paulinus who went with the party that accompanied Ethelburga (sister of the King of Kent) to Northumbria,
where she was to marry King Edwin, who subsequently took
his wife's Christian faith as his own. According to Bede, Paulinus
built the first church in York in about the year 627 and was its
first bishop (not yet archbishop). He travelled much north and
south of the Humber, building churches and baptizing new
Christians.

Peter Damian (1007–72)

Born of poor parents in Ravenna in Italy, Peter proved to be a
highly intelligent child. He was orphaned when young, and it
is said that he adopted the name Damian in gratitude to his
brother of that name who ensured that he received a good education. In 1035 he entered the Benedictine hermitage at Fonte
Avellana founded by St Romuald. In about 1043 he became
prior, and spent the next few years reforming monasteries and
founding new ones. In his ideas about monastic living, he always
looked to the example of the Desert Fathers, and praised their
austerity and simplicity. In 1057 he was made Cardinal Bishop
of Ostia, and set about the task of ecclesiastical reform with
equal vigour. He was a great preacher and was highly influential
in the Church of his day. He was essentially a reformer in an
age of reform.

Peter the Venerable (*c.*1092–1156)

Peter the Venerable was the eighth Abbot of Cluny. Educated at the Cluniac monastery of Sauxillanges, he made profession at the age of seventeen under Abbot Hugh. After periods as Prior of Vézelay and Domène, in 1122 he was elected Abbot of Cluny. Cluny in Burgundy was the mother-house of a vast network of dependent monasteries. It stood for the supreme development of the liturgical life: a sense of adoration and intercession for the whole of society. Against much opposition he successively carried through a series of reforms, particularly in regard to finance and education. His interest in the pursuit of studies, however, brought him into conflict with his friend and contemporary, Bernard of Clairvaux, who preferred the monastic life to be focused on prayer and manual work. Peter had the Koran translated into Latin (completed in 1143) and he himself engaged in disputation with Moslems. Famously, it was Peter who in 1140 gave shelter to Abelard. His moderation and gentleness earned him the title 'Venerable' in his own lifetime.

Polding, John Bede (1794–1877)

Born in Liverpool, John Polding was educated by English Benedictine monks of St Gregory's College, then near Shrewsbury. In 1811, he entered monastic life, taking the name Bede. Three years later, the monastic community moved to Downside, near Bath in Somerset. In 1834 he was consecrated first Vicar Apostolic of New Holland and Van Diemen's Land in Australia, and reached Sydney in 1835. Following a successful petition to Rome for the establishment of an Australian hierarchy, he was named Archbishop of Sydney in 1842. Polding's aim was to establish a Benedictine form of Catholicism in Australia, with the Church administered from a monastery in Sydney. The Catholic population he encountered, however, was substantially Irish, and he found it difficult to persuade Benedictines from England to join him in the venture. Tensions increased and, in 1853, he was forced temporarily to resign. His vision of a Benedictine Catholicism was not to be. Nevertheless, he was highly successful in representing the Catholic Church to a largely Protestant nation. He had a tremendous vitality, and under his leadership, the infant Church was consolidated, new dioceses and parishes were formed, and the foundation of a Catholic educational system established. He is also remembered for helping to secure the fundamental rights of Aborigines.

Rabanus Maurus (776 or 784–856)

Rabanus Maurus was one of the greatest theologians of his age, and known as the 'Teacher of Germany'. He was educated at the monastery of Fulda and later at Tours under the direction of Alcuin. He was ordained priest in 814, and elected abbot in 822. He resigned the abbacy in 842 to lead a life of prayer and study, but in 847 was made Archbishop of Mainz. He carried forward the evangelization of Germany and wrote many commentaries on Scripture, often with a mystical interpretation.

Rancé, Armand-Jean le Bouthillier de (1626–1700)

The godson of Cardinal Richelieu, by the age of ten de Rancé already held no less than five commendatory abbacies, including that of the Cistercian monastery of La Trappe, and from which he derived a considerable income. A distinguished classical scholar, he was ordained priest in 1651, but led a dissolute life. It is said that his conversion and ensuing reforming zeal began in 1657 when, returning home late from an evening in the Parisian salons, in the dark he tripped over the severed head of his dead mistress Mme de Monbazon which had been abandoned on the floor, her corpse being too big for the coffin. In 1664, after a period of intense spiritual reflection and a year's novitiate at Perseigne, he moved to La Trappe, and was blessed as its regular abbot. The impetus for monastic reform had already begun before his arrival, and to this movement he gave his authority, adding his own austerities and observances. Eventually these were codified as the *Constitutions de la Trappe*. They were intended for domestic use, but their success in reinvigorating monastic life meant that they were adopted by other houses of the Strict Observance, hence the popular name of 'Trappists' for this branch of the Cistercian Order.

Robert of Molesme (c.1027–1111)

Robert was born of a noble family near Troyes in France. He first became a monk at the age of fifteen, and over many years lived in various monasteries, trying with varying degrees of success to encourage a more rigorous observance of the Rule of St Benedict. Eventually, in 1075 he established a monastery at Molesme in Burgundy, but it did not develop as he had hoped. In 1098 he, Alberic, Stephen Harding and their companions moved to a forest outside Dijon to try again, and are honoured as the founders of the New Monastery which soon came to be called the Abbey of Cîteaux. Their desire was to live the Rule of St Benedict more integrally, to rediscover the meaning of the monastic life and to translate this into structures adapted to their age. After only eighteen months, however, the monks of Molesme asked Robert to return. He did so, remaining abbot until his death at the age of eighty-four.

Romuald (c.950–1027)

A nobleman of Ravenna, Romuald entered monastic life at the Abbey of Sant' Apollinare in Classe in reaction to the horror of his father having killed a man in a duel. In 998 he was appointed abbot, but resigned a year later, retiring to the neighbouring marshes at Camaldoli (Campus Maldoli) near Arezzo in order to pursue a more ascetic lifestyle. In later life he travelled throughout Italy, founding hermitages and monasteries, and encouraging a more ascetic and eremitical expression of the monastic ideal. The monastery at Campus Maldoli remains the centre of the Camaldolese Order.

Samson (1135–1211)

Samson was one of the great Benedictine abbots of mediaeval England. Born at Tottington, and educated in Paris, he entered the monastery of St Edmundsbury, Suffolk, and was professed in 1166. He became mitred abbot in 1182, and in the same year was appointed by Pope Lucius III judge-delegate in ecclesiastical causes. In 1188 he secured exemption with his successors from metropolitical jurisdiction. His high European profile also enabled him to visit Richard I when held captive in Germany. He wrote several treatises, and added extensively to the abbey.

Scholastica (c.480–c.543)

Scholastica is a more shadowy figure than her famous brother, Benedict. It is assumed that she too was born at Nursia in central Italy, probably around 480. At an early age she chose to consecrate herself to God, but only after Benedict moved to Monte Cassino did she settle at Plombariola, some five miles away, joining or maybe founding a religious community for women under his direction. According to the *Dialogues* of Pope Gregory the Great, which is the only source of information about her life, Scholastica met her brother once a year at a house near his monastery where they would praise God together and discuss spiritual matters. She died in about 543. Benedict had a vision of her soul rising up to heaven and, collecting her body, he had her buried in the tomb prepared for himself in the monastery. Scholastica is the patron saint of all Benedictine nuns.

Stephen Harding (?–1134)

Stephen Harding, Alberic and Robert of Molesme, along with their companions, are honoured as the founders of the New Monastery which came to be called the Abbey of Cîteaux. Born probably in Dorset, England, Stephen became a monk at Molesme in Burgundy. In 1098, however, he and his companions left Molesme for Cîteaux. Their desire was to live the Rule of St Benedict more integrally, to rediscover the meaning of the monastic life and to translate this into structures adapted to their age. In 1101 he was elected abbot and remained so until his death in 1134. If the title of 'founder' of the Cistercian Order can be ascribed to anyone that person would be Stephen Harding. Today, however, the charism of the founder of the Order is more usually located in the group of twenty abbots who assembled for the General Chapter of 1123, among whom most significantly was Bernard of Clairvaux. But it was from Abbot Stephen that Bernard received his monastic formation, and if nothing else, Stephen Harding is honoured for discernment in recognizing and fostering the outstanding gifts of this young monk.

Sylvester Gozzolini (1177–1267)

Sylvester was born of a noble family in Osimo, Italy, and studied law at Bologna and Padua. Following ordination, he became a canon of Osimo Cathedral and remained so until the age of fifty, when a combination of factors (including a disagreement with the bishop) led him to resign his canonry. He moved some thirty miles away and pursued a rigorously ascetic existence. Following a subsequent move to Monte Fano, near Fabriano, in 1231, Sylvester established a monastery for the disciples who now surrounded him. The Benedictine Rule was embraced, but giving particular emphasis to poverty in the expression of the monastic endeavour. By the time of his death in 1267 at the age of ninety, eleven such monasteries had been founded. The houses of the order, known as the Sylvestrine Benedictines, are technically independent of the Confederation of Benedictine Congregations. The monks wear a dark blue habit.

Ullathorne, William Bernard (1806–89)

A direct descendant of Thomas More, William Ullathorne entered monastic life at the Benedictine monastery of Downside,

Somerset, in 1824. In 1832, the year following his ordination to the priesthood, he volunteered for the mission in Australia, of which he was appointed Vicar General. In Australia, he established the life of the Catholic Church on firmer foundations, and in the face of considerable opposition championed the cause of the convicts. Following his return to England in 1840, he was put in charge of the Benedictine mission at Coventry. In 1846, he was appointed Vicar Apostolic for the Western District of England; and two years later of the Central District. He was instrumental with Cardinal Wiseman in securing the restoration of the Catholic hierarchy to England, and became in 1850, Bishop of Birmingham.

Werburgh (d. *c*.699)

Werburgh is honoured as one of the great early English royal abbesses. The daughter of Wulfhere, King of Mercia, she entered monastic life at the Abbey of Ely where she became abbess. At the instigation of King Ethelred, she was commissioned to reform the monasteries of nuns throughout his kingdom. She travelled widely, establishing several new monasteries in Staffordshire and Northamptonshire. She was renowned for the holiness of her life, and died around 699 at Threekingham in Lincolnshire. In 875, however, for fear of the Danes, her body was translated to Chester where remains of her shrine (dismantled at the Reformation) can still be seen in the cathedral.

Wilfrid of Ripon (*c*.633–709)

Wilfrid, or Wilfrith, was born in Northumbria and educated at the monastery on Lindisfarne. He disapproved of what he judged to be their Celtic insularity, and travelled first to Canterbury where he met Benedict Biscop, and thence to Rome. He entered monastic life at Lyons in France where he remained for three years. Following his ordination, he returned to Northumbria and was appointed Abbot of Ripon where he immediately introduced the Roman monastic system and the Benedictine Rule. At the Synod of Whitby in 664, he was largely responsible for the victory of the Roman party over the Celts. When elected Bishop of York, he went to Compiègne to be consecrated by twelve Frankish bishops rather than risk any doubt of schism by being ordained by Celtic bishops. He was not a sympathetic man, but his energy and vision ensured that the English Church became more integrated into the life of the wider Church. He died in 709, and was buried at Ripon.

William of Malmesbury (c.1090–c.1143)

William was the chief English historian of his generation. He was a monk of Malmesbury where he was offered, but declined, the abbacy in 1140. His two most important works were the *Annals of the English Kings* (1120) and the *Annals of the English Prelates* (1125), which dealt with respectively secular and ecclesiastical English history. He also wrote a *Life of St Dunstan* and a *Life of St Wulfstan*.

William of St Thierry (c.1085–1148)

William was born at Liège. He entered the Benedictine Abbey of Rheims in 1113, and in 1119 or 1120 was elected Abbot of St Thierry nearby. Before his election as abbot, however, he had already made the acquaintance of Bernard of Clairvaux, and in 1135 he resigned his abbacy and went to join a group of Cistercian monks from Igny. He wrote a number of influential treatises, including several expositions of the Song of Songs. His last years were devoted to a synthesis of his doctrine and experience, known as *The Golden Epistle*.

Wulfstan of Worcester (c.1009–95)

Born in about the year 1009, Wulfstan's first twenty-five years after his ordination were spent in the Benedictine monastery at Worcester. Against his will, he was elected Bishop of Worcester in 1062/3, and went on to prove an able administrator and pastor. Following the Norman Conquest in 1066, he was one of the first of the bishops to make his submission to William the Conqueror. Despite his Saxon heritage, he already enjoyed strong links with Benedictine houses on the Continent, and carefully and gently nurtured both church and state through the transition from Saxon to Norman rule. In his later years, he rebuilt Worcester Cathedral which had been largely destroyed in the Danish invasion of 1041, and was buried there when he died at the remarkable age of eighty-six.

Compiled by Robert Atwell

Bibliography

Butler, Cuthbert, *Benedictine Monachism*, Longman, London/New York, 1924.

Butler, Cuthbert, *Western Mysticism*, Longman, London/New York, 1924.

Chapman, John, *Spiritual Letters*, Sheed & Ward, Winsconsin, 2000.

Dix, Gregory, *The Shape of the Liturgy*, A & C Black, London, 1945, reprinted 1997.

Gregory the Great, *Dialogues*, II, U. Moricca, ed., Rome 1924; translated by O. Zimmerman and Benedict Avery in *The Life and Miracles of Saint Benedict*, The Liturgical Press, Collegeville, Minnesota, 1981.

Griffiths, Bede, *The Golden String*, HarperCollins, London, 1994.

Knowles, David, *The Monastic Order in England 940–1216*, Cambridge University Press, Cambridge, Second Edition, 1963.

Knowles, David, *The Religious Orders in England*, 3 vols, Cambridge University Press, Cambridge, 1979.

Leclercq, Henri and Fernand Cabrol, eds., *Dictionnaire d'archéologie chrétienne et de liturgie*, 15 vols, 1907–53.

Leclercq, Henri and Fernand Cabrol, eds., *Monumenta Ecclesiae Liturgica*, 4 vols, 1903–13.

Leclercq, Jean, *The Love of Learning and the Desire for God*, Third Edition, Forham University Press, New York, 1982.

Marmion, Columba, *Christ the Ideal of the Monk*, Sands, 1952.

Marmion, Columba, *Christ the Life of the Soul*, Sands, 1963.

Merton, Thomas, *The Seven Storey Mountain*, SPCK, London, 1999.

Benedictine Holy Places

For over fifteen centuries St Benedict's 'little rule for beginners' has provided countless men and women with a framework for Christian living. Marked by moderation and sanity, this short document of seventy-three chapters is regarded by many as the most influential text in Western society after the scriptures. Whether or not one agrees with this, it cannot be denied that monasteries have played, and continue to play, a major role in the preservation of culture and the development of art and learning throughout the world. These considerations, however, are secondary to the fundamental purpose for which the monastery exists: in the words of Vatican II's decree, *On the appropriate renewal of religious life*, 'A monastic's first duty is the humble, devout service of God's majesty within the bounds of the monastery.' It is the rhythmic cycle of prayer, day after day, season after season, which gives monasteries their distinctive atmosphere, establishing them as places apart to which men and women are drawn for refreshment, renewal and worship.

Like their occupants, Benedictine monasteries come in a variety of shapes and sizes. These range from masterpieces of European mediaeval and Baroque architecture to the simple structures of new foundations in the developing world. All have in common their commitment to the search for God. The manner in which Benedictine life is lived varies widely as well, ranging from entirely enclosed contemplative communities to congregations heavily involved in education and social work. The following gazetteer makes no claims to being either comprehensive or politically correct but focuses on European monasteries significant for their symbolic and historic status as well as those that demonstrate the diversity of contemporary monasticism.

Italy

The Monastery of St Scholastica and the Sacro Speco (holy cave) at Subiaco are perhaps the most evocative and moving of the early Benedictine foundations. Situated in an area of great natural beauty, south-east of Rome, it was here that Benedict began his life as a hermit before founding thirteen monasteries in the surrounding Aniene valley. Of these only the monastery of St Scholastica survives. Among the frescoes in the Sacro Speco is one of Francis of Assisi, claimed to be a life portrait of the saint. St Scholastica's was the site of the first printing press in Italy and the monastery is a fascinating mix of every conceivable architectural style.

The motto of Monte Cassino, *Succisa virescit* – cut down, it springs up anew – summarizes the vicissitudes of St Benedict's principal foundation. Established on the site of an ancient Roman fort and sanctuary, it was completely destroyed on four occasions: once by earthquake in 1349, and three times by armies: the Lombards in 590, the Saracens in 883 and the Allies in 1945 (the first to destroy it from the South). The monastery was rebuilt in the Baroque style after the Second World War and is the principal shrine of St Benedict and St Scholastica. The monastery's library and archives, saved by the German army, are among the most important in Europe.

A number of important reforms of Benedictine life began in Italy. In the eleventh century, St Romuald, a native of Ravenna, founded the monastery of Camaldoli in Tuscany. This reform combined elements of eremitical and community living and the monastery at Camaldoli continues to flourish. St Bernard Tolomei and a small group of companions founded the Archabbey of Monte Olivetto Maggiore near Siena in 1313. It is the motherhouse of the Olivetan Benedictine congregation and houses a particularly fine cycle of Renaissance frescoes depicting the life of St Benedict by Sodoma and Signorelli. The monastery of

St Justina in Padua appears as a Benedictine foundation in 734 but was at its most influential during the abbacy of Luigi Barbo at the beginning of the fifteenth century. He instituted an important reform that led to the foundation of the congregation of St Justina whose constitutions were adopted by many other fifteenth and sixteenth-century reformers. The Cassinese congregation later sprang from this reform. The Benedictine monastery attached to the Basilica of St Paul outside the walls in Rome is first mentioned in the eighth century and played an important role in promoting the reforms of Cluny and St Justina in Italy. In the nineteenth century it provided the springboard for the revival of monasticism in France, Germany and Belgium as Prosper Guéranger, founder of Solesmes, and the brothers Maurus and Placid Wolter, founders of Beuron and Maredsous, received their initial monastic formation there. In 1687 Pope Innocent XI founded the College of Sant' Anselmo at St Paul's as a centre for advanced studies. This was re-established in 1887 by Pope Leo XIII. Now situated on the Aventine hill in Rome, it is also the seat of the Abbot Primate of the Benedictine confederation. Other important Italian monasteries include Praglia near Padua, Noci in Puglia and Vallombrosa near Florence. The mixed, ecumenical community at Bosé near Turin draws on the Benedictine tradition for its inspiration and spirituality and is an inspiring example of the vitality of contemporary monasticism.

France and Belgium

Monasticism in France has an ancient and venerable tradition and numbers St Martin of Tours (d. 397) and John Cassian of Marseilles (d. *c*.430) among its luminaries. The Rule of Benedict was followed in many early French monasteries, often in conjunction with the monastic legislation of the Irishman St Columbanus (d. 615) while the monastery of Saint-Benoît-sur-Loire at Fleury, a seventh-century foundation, claims the relics of St Benedict and is a major centre of pilgrimage. A number of influential mediaeval reforms, most notably those of Cluny and Cîteaux, sprang from French houses and in the seventeenth and eighteenth centuries the Congregation of St Maur made important and enduring contributions to the world of learning. The French revolution, the Napoleonic era and the anti-religious legislation of the modern period all but destroyed this monastic tradition and such monasteries as survive emerged from the monastic revival of the nineteenth century, even if they occasionally occupy mediaeval buildings. Of these the monastery of Solesmes near Le Mans is the most famous. Revived on an eleventh-century foundation in 1833 by Dom Prosper Guéranger, its emphasis on a strict form of monastic observance, worthy celebration of the liturgy and scholarly research has had a defining influence on modern monasticism with communities modelling themselves on (or reacting against) the Solesmes formula. Its promotion of Gregorian Chant has also been influential in the Church, though this has waned somewhat since Vatican II.

Another distinctive version of French Benedictine life finds expression in the monastery of La Pierre-qui-Vire in eastern France. Founded by Jean-Baptiste Muard in 1850, it attempted to combine elements of Benedictine and Trappist observance with a missionary charism. It is still noted for an austere and simple observance of the Rule. The Abbey of Le Bec in Normandy, though revived only in 1948, draws on the reputation of its former members Lanfranc (d. 1089) and St Anselm (d. 1109), both Archbishops of Canterbury, to foster close ecumenical relations with the Anglican Church. In recent years a number of French houses such as Fontgombault and Flavigny have promoted what some describe as a 'traditionalist' observance. The liturgy there is celebrated according to the norms obtaining before the Second Vatican Council.

In Belgium Dom Placid Wolter established the Abbey of Maredsous from Beuron in 1872. From 1909 to 1923 it was governed by the Irish abbot, Blessed Columba Marmion, whose writings enjoyed widespread popularity among religious. In 1925, with the encouragement of Pope Pius XI, the monastery of Chevetogne was established as a bi-ritual monastery by Dom Lambert Beuaduin with the intention of furthering the cause of unity between the Roman Catholic and Orthodox Churches. This goal is furthered through scholarly work, hospitality and the celebration of the liturgy in the Byzantine and Latin rites.

England

The Rule of St Benedict has been followed in England since the seventh century and the Benedictines were both prominent and influential in the pre-Reformation Church. An interesting feature of the mediaeval English tradition was the practice of monks forming the chapters of some of the English cathedrals. The consequent emphasis on the noble celebration of the Divine Office survived the upheavals of the sixteenth century and choral office remains one of the glories of Anglican worship.

The genius of English Benedictine observance lies in its moderation, urbanity and adaptability. Forced abroad after the accession of Elizabeth I the monks reinvented themselves as a missionary congregation while the nuns pursued a more contemplative, scholarly existence. Many were martyred for their missionary activity. The monasteries of St Gregory, now at Downside in Somerset, St Laurence, now at Ampleforth in Yorkshire and St Edmund, now at Douai in Berkshire returned to England in the nineteenth century and continued their traditional apostolates of parish work and education. The abbey churches at Downside and Buckfast are among the most beautiful in England while that of Douai has recently been completed in an exciting contemporary idiom. The Benedictine nuns of Stanbrook have announced their intention of moving to a new monastery.

Other important Benedictine houses in the United Kingdom include Quarr on the Isle of Wight, Ealing Abbey and Tyburn in London and Pluscarden in Scotland.

In Ireland the Benedictine monks are represented by the communities of Glenstal in Co. Limerick and Rostrevor in Co. Down. The oldest Irish foundation, however, is that of the Nuns of Kylemore, which began at Ypres in Belgium in the seventeenth century. Their current location at Kylemore in Connemara is one of the most beautifully situated of all monasteries and is a popular tourist destination. A small community of Benedictine nuns from Tyburn has recently been established at Cobh, Co. Cork.

Switzerland, Germany and Austria

The Abbey of Einsiedeln in Switzerland was founded in the tenth century on the site of the hermitage of St Meinrad (d. 861). It is one of the oldest continuously occupied monasteries in the world and its image of the Black Madonna is the principal Marian shrine in Switzerland and a major pilgrimage centre. The Baroque monastery was constructed between 1704 and 1735. The monks are involved in education and parochial work and have made a number of missionary foundations in North and South America.

The Abbey of Melk in Austria, founded by the Babenberg family in 1089, occupies an imposing site overlooking the Danube and is one of the most astounding pieces of gilded Baroque architecture in Europe. The monastery of Gottweig (founded in 1094) occupies a similar location but here the architecture is less overpowering. Owing to the persecution of the Church by Emperor Joseph II at the end of the eighteenth century the Austrian Benedictine monasteries are heavily involved in education and parish work with less emphasis on elaborate choral offices or public liturgical worship.

In Germany the revival of Benedictine life began with the re-establishment of the monastery of St Martin at Beuron in 1863. Founded originally as a house of Augustinian canons in 1077, the monastery passed through various secular and religious incarnations before being presented to the Wolter brothers by the princely Hohenzollern family. After a period of rapid expansion Beuron became the mother-house of a revivalist congregation establishing houses in Germany, Belgium, Austria and England. Of these the Abbey of Maria Laach, a magnificent twelfth-century Romanesque complex revived in 1892, was significant as a centre of liturgical renewal in the first half of the twentieth century. Through its art school established in 1894 Beuron exercised a tremendous influence on ecclesiastical art. The Archabbey of Sankt Ottilien near Munich, founded in 1884 by a monk of Beuron, is the mother-house of a large missionary congregation working chiefly in East Africa.

Spain

The Abbey of Montserrat near Barcelona in Catalonia is the ethnic and religious centre of the Catalan people. Occupying a dramatic site on the side of a steep, serrated mountain, the monastery is one of the most important pilgrimage centres in Spain after Santiago di Compostella. The focus of the pilgrimage is a twelfth-century polychromed image of the Black Madonna and Child Jesus. The community is also home to a world-famous boys' choir, an important library and art collection and a major publishing house. The community of Santo Domingo di Silos in Burgos has also enjoyed a reputation for musical endeavour with a number of their recordings of Gregorian Chant topping the charts in several European countries.

Colmán Ó Clabaigh OSB

Part Four

Living the Rule

Living the Rule in Community

One of the fundamental dynamics of cenobitic monastic life is the interplay of individual and community. The Rule itself reflects a certain tension between the two as Benedict speaks to both the spiritual development of the individual and the workings of a community, which though based upon a shared Rule is composed of diverse members.

Much of the first part of the Rule seems to be focused on the individual. The opening lines of the Prologue speak tenderly to a single listener (*tu*, 'thou'), and the chapters on the Tools for Good Works, Obedience, Silence, and Humility (Chapters 4–7) seem to have individual spiritual perfection in view. But Benedict can never repress his cenobitic reflexes. Even in the Prologue the focus broadens quickly to 'we' and a plural 'you' (*vos*) as it becomes clear that someone who responds to this invitation is drawn immediately into something larger than the individual self. The logic of Benedict's teaching inexorably leads to the establishment of the 'school for the Lord's service' (Prologue, eighth paragraph) to provide both the environment and the necessary means for the individual's search for God. For Benedict, community is not simply functional, a matter of providing necessary material or even spiritual resources to sustain each individual's monastic journey. The common life becomes the very language and texture of growth into Christ, as the call is tested and refocused in the myriad interactions, formal and informal, that create monastic community.

Benedict defines the cenobitic form of monastic life very succinctly: this kind 'belongs to a monastery, serving under a rule

and an abbot' (Chapter 1, first paragraph). The brevity is decep-
tive, for each element (monastery – rule – abbot) requires further
explanation. The remaining 72 chapters of the Rule flesh them
out. Cenobites are not just 'monastic', they 'belong to a monastery', and are fundamentally oriented to life in monastic community. This orientation is expressed by the Benedictine vow of
stability. Hermits can be monastic, living the monastic vocation
wherever they settle. Cenobites are not so free, as the rest of
Benedict's definition makes clear. The relationships of accountability established by the Rule and tended by the abbot create
cenobitic life, distinguishing it from other ways to follow the
Gospel. Every Christian prays, serves others, and has interper-
sonal relationships that demand accountability. Cenobites do
all of these things within a community energized by obedience
to rule, abbot, and one another. These overlapping relationships
and the flow of attentiveness from one member to another create
the cenobitic path to God.

Benedict is perceptive enough to know that healthy community requires accountability. He also knew that true accountability is possible only when the participants are stakeholders
in the common enterprise. He writes of accountability in his
teaching on obedience, and of stakeholding in his descriptions
of how each member is given a place and a voice in the community's life. Finally, service emerges as the intersection of
accountability and stakeholding, as the members of the community recognize Christ in one another.

Accountability

Benedict writes more about obedience than about any other
monastic virtue. Although the longest chapter of the Rule is on
humility (Chapter 7), even that chapter is fundamentally about
the surrender of self-will that is the essence of monastic obedience. Benedict shared the biblical view that unless we are in
honest relationships with God and other human beings we will
inevitably prefer our own desires to the demands of the Christian
life. The first step toward freedom from such false self-sufficiency

is to recognize the problem. The Prologue to the Rule speaks directly to one's dawning realization that moving through life on auto-pilot goes nowhere. When Benedict invites his hearer into the 'school for the Lord's service' (Prologue, eighth paragraph), the primary entrance requirement is willingness to open the tightly-closed fist of self-will to the guidance of Gospel, Rule, abbot, and the members of the community. Everyone, including the abbot, is accountable to the Gospel and the Rule (Chapter 3, second paragraph; Chapter 64, fourth paragraph).

Although his judgement on self-will seems very negative, Benedict's call for trust in God and other people speaks of a very positive sense of the human capacity for life-giving relationships. The starting point may be a need to rely largely on another's judgement rather than on one's own, but Benedict expected his monks to grow in their capacity to discern what was expected of them in community life and in their dealings with one another. The 'good zeal' he praises at the end of the Rule presumes the ability to make appropriate judgements about the needs of others (Chapter 72). To hone this skill Benedict devotes much of the Rule to structuring opportunities for loving service of others. He knew that such altruism rescues us from our narrow self-interest through a deeper sense of our dependence on God's mercy and on the love of our brothers and sisters.

Benedict was realistic about the challenges of building community. He knew that his ideal of a common life motivated by Christian charity depended on human beings who were at various stages of spiritual and emotional development. He was willing to admit the possibility of failure and he provided ways to deal with it. Daily at Lauds and Vespers the monks heard their abbot pray the Our Father 'because of the thorns of contention that are bound to arise' (Chapter 13, second paragraph). They needed to hear that mutual pledge of forgiveness on a regular basis. He expected his monks to acknowledge their transgressions against the common good promptly and honestly (Chapters 45–46). Those who would not do so were to be warned privately and then in the presence of the rest of the community.

Benedict knew that a viable community has limits on what it can tolerate, and that it is important for everyone's sake to mark those bounds clearly. If inappropriate behaviour continued, Benedict recommended some degree of separation from the common life according to the seriousness of the offence (Chapters 23–25). The process was therapeutic rather than juridical. Being excluded from the table or the liturgy was meant to bring the offender to better understanding of how his actions had violated the common good. The abbot was to be ever-attentive to the situation, using every spiritual and pastoral resource to ensure that the one being punished was not sliding toward despair or resentment (Chapters 27–28). The rest of the community, who had probably been quite aware of their brother's misconduct, saw the values of the common life being upheld in response to their breach. At the same time, Benedict knew that it was just as important to be clear about forgiveness. Rather than let troubled monks live under a cloud of communal suspicion indefinitely, he brought them back into the heart of the community in visible stages (Chapter 44). As necessary as distance can sometimes be, the goal must be reintegration.

Keeping communication open and honest, noting inappropriate behaviour, identifying needed help, and knowing when a situation has become impossible in community life are important and often delicate tasks. Benedict took pains to ensure that such vital processes took their course in the best possible manner. He knew that the abbot could not fix every problem and would need to use helpers (*senpectae*, Chapter 27, first paragraph). He was wary of involving those who did not fully understand a particular situation, and explicitly forbade his monks to interfere by arguing someone else's case out of turn (Chapter 69) or by taking upon themselves the task of punishing a wrongdoer (Chapter 70). For accountability to work properly, the lines of communication and author must be clear.

Benedict's forms of accountability reflected his own age and culture, but the values are important ones today. From both a monastic and a psychological standpoint, human growth requires challenge from relationships with other people. For cenobites, the primary relationships are those with other members of the community. A healthy community needs a clear understanding of what it can tolerate lest the fabric of the common life be stretched so thin that it disintegrates. Individuals need to know that they do not operate in isolation, and that their behaviour affects everyone else in the group.

Stakeholding

Accountability works only if the members of the community are genuine stakeholders in the common project of monastic living. For cenobites, the commitment made in monastic profession is concretized most vividly in the renunciation of any claim to private property. Benedict insisted vigorously on this cenobitic imperative. Indeed, in the Rule he sets aside his usually moderate tone only when addressing two issues, private property and murmuring, for both erode community. He knew that having access to one's own financial resources inhibits and even precludes wholehearted embrace of the community's fortunes. If the members of the community do not depend on one another for their material needs, then any kind of dependence is equally undermined, whether for guidance, encouragement, or correction. A half-hearted commitment means that there is always an escape hatch, whether to the outside or the internal exile of a self-contained life in the midst of the community.

In return for their radical commitment to the common enterprise, Benedict gave each member of his community a place in the common order (rank) and a voice in key deliberations. By ordering his community according to the date of each member's entry into monastic life, he established that the conventional marks of social status in his sixth-century context would no longer have currency. He also uses this ordering to establish a protocol for relations in the monastery, asking his monks to call their seniors *nonnus*, 'reverend father', and their juniors *frater*, 'brother' (Chapter 63, second paragraph). Everyone has a title, regardless of his previous social class. Everyone is *nonnus* to some and *frater* to others.

This relative system of order, quite revolutionary in its day, was also designed to lubricate daily interactions. In any situation the junior was to show respect to the senior, the senior to show tender concern for the junior (Chapter 63, second paragraph). The junior requested a blessing or begged forgiveness; the senior blessed and forgave (Chapter 63, third paragraph; Chapter 71, second paragraph). One sees Benedict attentive to the dangers of vainglory and stand-offs in the common life, and providing a mechanism to facilitate communal charity. At the same time, he did not bind his monks to a purely ritualized manner of relating. Chapter 72, on 'The Good Zeal of Monks', points beyond good order to the Christian ideal of selfless charity, where everyone, heedless of even relative rank, looks out for the good of the other in love.

The second way Benedict encourages his monks to become true stakeholders in the community is by allowing every member a voice in important matters. Benedict demonstrates a confidence in God's ability to work through the group and each of its members. He asks the abbot to call the community together to discuss major issues, and foresees that the Lord may sometimes choose the most junior in the community to offer the wisest counsel (Chapter 3, first paragraph). Similarly, the community is to be involved in the selection of their abbot, and again the most junior may be the one who would serve best (Chapter 64, first paragraph).

Benedict's openness to counsel, even from unexpected quarters, reminds us that he understands authority in terms of charism rather than privilege. Leadership in the community derives not from seniority, but from evidence of God's gifts of discernment, teaching and stewardship. Because these qualities can be found in many people within a community, the contribution of each member is necessary for building up the whole. The interplay of both charismatic authority and community counsel modelled in the Rule is a challenge to exaggerated forms of either one of them.

Service

One of Benedict's simplest imperatives is 'let the brothers serve one another' (Chapter 35, first paragraph). The daily connections forged through serving food to one another, caring for the sick, reading in church or refectory form the web of community and provide much of its strength. No one in Benedict's monastery was to think himself above the obligation to serve even if some might be excused from one form of service or another because of infirmity or other duties. St Basil the Great had one of the richest insights into the theological value of the common life, and Benedict is his heir: life in common provides the best possible opportunity for fulfilling the commandments by serving Christ in one another (cf. Matt. 25:35–40).

Benedict's teaching on service is theologically profound, for he recognized Christ in both one who serves (e.g. the abbot, Chapter 2, first paragraph; Chapter 63, second paragraph), and those who are served (the sick, Chapter 36, first paragraph; the visitor, Chapter 53). He hopes that his monks will develop altruistic reflexes, naturally placing the needs of others before their own (Chapter 72, first paragraph). Such a reflexive consideration for others requires training at every stage of monastic development. Therefore many of Benedict's 'Tools for Good Works' (Chapter 4) are directed toward service of those in need. These are not ideals, but exercises for building up virtue. Benedict also recognized that the members of the community would provide spiritual care for one another as *senpectae* or as trusted guides (Chapter 4, eighth paragraph; Chapter 27, first paragraph; Chapter 46, second paragraph); he did not reserve all pastoral work to the abbot.

Benedict concludes his famous chapter on 'Good Zeal' with the hope that Christ 'may bring us all together (*pariter*) to everlasting life' (Chapter 72, first paragraph). The adverb he uses, *pariter*, can mean either 'together' or 'equally'. A few sentences later, at the very end of the Rule, he reverts to the intimate form of address with which the Prologue began, speaking directly to the individual (Chapter 73, second paragraph). Benedict maintains his dual focus on individual vocation and communal life right to the end.

Columba Stewart OSB

Living the Rule in Solitude

'Clearly,' says St Benedict, 'there are four kinds of monks', and in the Rule, Chapter 1, he looks at the way of life of each. For present purposes we can omit the two kinds he disapproves of, and consider only the ones he takes seriously. One of these is the race of anchorites, or hermits, of whom he says,

> Their vocation is not the result of the first fervour so often experienced by those who give themselves to a monastic way of life. On the contrary they have learnt well from everyday experience, with the support of many others in a community, how to fight against the devil. Thus they are well trained in the ranks of their brethren before they have the confidence to do without that support, and venture into single combat in the desert relying only on their own arms and the help of God in their battle against the evil temptations of body and mind.

No hermit would think that his or her vocation is a mark of any kind of holiness achieved. The call itself, and the ability to sustain a life of solitude, are pure gifts from God. What is striking about these few lines is the correlation they suggest between community and hermitage. Long experience in the community has prepared Benedictines called to solitude; they have received a great deal from the 'many others'. The Rule cannot mean that a hermit turns his back on his experience in, or his commitment to, the community that has nurtured him. He depends on it, and hopes somehow to give something back.

The spirituality of the desert

'Single combat in the desert', says the Rule, and certainly the desert, or the wilderness, is an essential dimension of Christian life, indeed of every fully human life. The desert is the place into which, like Jesus, you are led for God's loving purposes. God had formed his people long ago through the experience of the wilderness, where they were forced to believe in him and depend on his providential care, where they confronted their sin and unfaithfulness, where God tested them that he – and more especially they – might 'know what was in their hearts'. Israel failed God, for the most part. They grumbled, worshipped idols, rebelled, and many a time almost abandoned the whole enterprise: even slavery in Egypt had included the comforts a highly-developed civilization could provide. Anything was better than the covenant-God of the desert.

But Christ came to relive his people's vocation. After the overwhelming experience of himself as the beloved Son at his baptism, he was 'driven' by the Spirit to the desert to be alone with his Father and grapple with his vocation. What was it like? Hardship, temptation, assuredly; the gospels are explicit. But surely there was joy in it too, the pure joy of his Father's presence, and of depending wholly on him:

O God, you are my God, I long for you,
for you my soul is thirsting.
My body aches for you
Like a dry, weary land where there is no water.[1]

John the Baptist, the saint of the desert, knew this joy too, the joy of being alone with God. Austere he certainly was, but the motif of joy rings through the gospel stories about him.

It is no facile joy, nor is it in the least romantic. It is not the relief of escaping from complications or annoyances or noise or multiplicity. It is the joy on the further side of emptiness. The real desert is inside you, and you must 'look steadfastly towards the wilderness'[2] if you are to know there the glory of the Lord.

Our desert may be weariness, tedium, emotional confusion, the stifling sense of failure, the feeling that we have nothing to give. Paradoxically, a sense of being trapped in material comforts and in a consumer lifestyle can itself have a desert-like quality. Another very common desert experience in the modern world is the felt absence of God from society, with the fear that faith is losing ground all the time, and that the young will have even less sense of God's presence than their parents had. The conviction that you constantly fail God in prayer is another aspect of the desert. You have to accept your radical poverty, your inner confusion and squalor, and your inability to pray. All our ideas about God fall infinitely short of his reality, and if we cling to them too tightly we can be trying to make God in our own image. But God wants us for himself, and so he gently takes away anything that impedes him. Then you begin to know the joy of the desert: the joy that God is God, and that you can do nothing but let him be God for you, and for all the others with whom you know yourself to be deeply united.

This is one of the strange things about being alone with God: you have never been so close to all the others. When you pray, you are part of a great crowd of praying people. The psalms in particular come alive. As you pray them you articulate in Christ, with Christ, the shouts and groans of all the poor in every century and every place, their joy, their sorrow, their delight and their ordinary reactions to their ordinary lives. God is in this ordinariness. The psalms have always been a school of prayer in Benedictine life, a keynote, a pervasive atmosphere. This is true in community life as in the hermitage, though the hermit may have more time to listen.

Some rocks in the wilderness: the provisions of the Rule

To listen: the first word of the Prologue: 'Listen'. Modern society is inebriated with words. Noble words, beautiful words, poetic words, inspiring words, wise words – but also endless chatter, the manipulative words, the euphemisms that deceive, hiding the unaccepted, unacceptable truth. You will not automatically achieve inner silence by being physically alone, for the chatter is inside you. The silence in which you can listen to God's word is the fruit of a long inner asceticism, but it is above all a gift from God, an awareness of his presence. Benedict's spirituality is marked by an awed awareness of God's presence; it is spelled out especially in his first step in humility in Chapter 7 of the Rule, and in his teaching on prayer in Chapters 19 and 20. Inner silence, said a Russian hermit, is never to judge anyone.

You listen, because your silent waiting on God is an openness to his word. The word sounds through many channels, but one of the most vital for you when you are alone is Scripture. When you read it with open heart and mind, reading in God's presence and expecting to meet him there, the same Spirit who spoke through prophets, psalmists, evangelists, who spoke and speaks still in the mighty river of tradition which is the Church's life – this same Spirit is shaping you, attuning you to the word, leading you deeper into the central mystery of Christ. 'Today, if you should hear his voice,' says the Rule, quoting a psalm, 'do not harden your hearts'; and the monastic fathers loved to repeat the scriptural promise, 'The word is very near to you; it is in your mouth and in your heart.'[3] Sometimes as you read you will be inspired, helped, filled with the joy of discovery; often you will be challenged, sometimes baffled, or bored, or acutely uncomfortable. As with prayer, you cannot altogether direct the business. You can only make yourself available. Whatever your particular experience, this practice of *lectio divina* is at the very heart of monastic spirituality. Like prayer to which it is so closely related, it is never entirely a solitary activity, even though the solitude is reader-friendly. You read within the river of tradition, and your reading is part of the Church's age-long search into the mystery.

St Benedict's Rule provides for a rhythm of lectio, prayer and work. The same harmony and balance are realized in the Rule's sensitivity to the changing seasons of the year, the pivotal place of Easter, the alternation of nights and days. Living alone, you may be more intensely aware of these rhythms. The solitary life is no honeymoon. Most hermits work hard. The rural hermit struggles with weather, weeds, slugs and damp firewood, but there is a simplicity of lifestyle and a closeness to nature denied to many who live in towns and cities, and there is the very special joy of friendship with birds and other animals. Some of the legends about hermit-saints abound with stories about the hermit's affinity with animals, like that of Cuthbert with his otters. The stories affirm something about the harmony with nature which is regained by humans who live in filial harmony with God; they hint at paradise regained. But we need not take too pious a view. Animals react to a solitary human in a different way, as though they feel her or his equal; it is a different situation from that where humans converse with each other and animals feel excluded. And you, the privileged human, feel an intense joy at being trusted. This may seem to have little directly to do with the Rule, but Benedict was reverently aware of creation, and if the legends about him in St Gregory's Dialogues are to be taken as factual, he was on good terms with a raven.[4]

The solitary life in relation to common human hardships

Monastic asceticism, lived with discernment, does not isolate monks and nuns from common human experience; rather it is an acknowledgement of the human condition as fallen, redeemed, and loved by God. This point is important in the consideration of the solitary life, but before we look at that directly, a few examples taken from other monastic practices may help to make it clear.

Fasting is an ancient ascetical discipline; but in the modern world it cannot seem irrelevant to the involuntary and life-long fasting of millions of our brothers and sisters. Celibacy is undertaken voluntarily as part of the monastic vocation; but an unsought celibacy is the lot of many people, something they would never have thought of as their vocation, though it now seems required by their fidelity to Christ. Many of the separated or divorced who believe their former marriage to have been valid, the spouses of the seriously ill, the people who hoped to marry but somehow never found the right person – all these may be driven to find God in a painful aloneness. Keeping vigil at night is another ancient Christian and monastic practice. Since apostolic times the Church has watched and waited for the Lord, and we keep solemn vigil in the night of Easter. Certain gospel parables speak of Christian life as a vigil: we are servants waiting for the master's return, or bridesmaids who need to keep the lamps alight. It is a spiritual attitude, a watchfulness; but to embody it literally sometimes by getting up in the night to pray can be a kind of sacrament. This habit is common among hermits, and here again they know themselves to be spiritually united with very many who are awake at night for less positive reasons, with the sick and people in pain, those kept awake by fear or worry, the homeless, even the parents of crying babies.

Fasting, celibacy, night vigils: all traditional monastic disciplines that have their counterpart in the lives of many for whom the experience was neither freely chosen nor laden with any obvious spiritual significance. Within the unthinkably close union of us all in Christ's body, there must be a communion of life and grace here, and in some cases perhaps a hope and encouragement, when those who struggle can use the monastic parallel as a sign to help them find God in their own situation.

A similar parallel is valid for the solitary life itself. A few Benedictines are called by God to go out 'well trained in the ranks of their brethren to single combat in the desert'. It seems at first sight an extraordinary vocation, but their free response may unite them in a communion of spirit with great numbers of people who do not feel called to solitude, but are forced by circumstances to live alone or to experience long periods of loneliness: the elderly, the widowed, prisoners, and many who in the conditions of urban life feel alone in a crowd. Like Jesus, these have been 'driven into the desert', and there is the place where God will be God for them. Loneliness can be transformed into aloneness with God, and made whole.

No one can live entirely without the support of others, and 'solitude' is therefore a relative term. Some measure of it may be present in most people's lives, and only a few are called to embrace it as a vocation (or, in the case of Benedictines, a vocation-within-a-vocation). But for the few who are so called, it has a place within the diversity of ways in which men and women are drawn into the Easter mystery of Christ. In them the Church lives out one aspect of its work in this world, and one aspect of the monastic life that has been part of that work since its early days.

Benedict himself sought the wilderness in his youth, and there, according to St Gregory, tried to 'live alone with himself in the sight of his Creator'.[5] After a time he turned his back on the solitary life and found his vocation in community. Gregory would hardly have said so, but perhaps Benedict's attempt was untimely. In any case it may have been an indication that monastic life in the West would for the most part develop on cenobitic lines. Since the Rule's declared intention is to legislate not for hermits but for monks or nuns living in community, an attempt to apply all its practical provisions to life in solitude would obviously be unreal. Yet the great spiritual foundations of the Rule can be realized as truly in a hermitage as in a community: the presence of God and obedience to his will, prayer, self-emptying, lectio, frugality, hard work, silence. A monastic father sums it up. Commenting on some words of Jesus to Peter, he says, 'These are the words that have filled the cloisters with monks, and the lonely places with hermits.'[6]

Maria Boulding OSB

Notes

1 Psalm 63:1.
2 Exodus 16:10.
3 Romans 10:8.
4 Dialogues II,8.
5 Dialogues II,3.
6 Sermon on the gospel, 'Lo, we have left all', sometimes attributed to St Bernard.

Living the Rule as an Oblate

I was a young theological student at an Anglican college when I first visited a Benedictine monastery. Coming from a conservative Evangelical background, a visit to a Catholic monastery was about as strange as it might be for a good Irish Catholic boy to be invited to a Pentecostal praise service.

My visit happened to be during Lent, so my retreat was suitably austere. I was given what I later learned was a typical Benedictine welcome, which both made me feel at home while it also respected my privacy. As I found my way around the liturgy and the monastery I was immediately captivated by the monastic life. The monks exhibited a sense of solemn self-mockery. It was clear that, while they took their religion very seriously, they did not take themselves seriously. My next visit took place on the eve of the feast of St Benedict himself, 10 July, and I shall never forget a fat monk with gleaming eyes saying, 'You've come at a good time!' I had. The ensuing feast was as suitably sumptuous as the Lenten fare had been severe. Coming from a background that was uneasy with both fasting and feasting, the Benedictines introduced me to a new way of seeing.

That first visit about twenty years ago. I have been going back ever since. In the summer of 1987 I hitch-hiked to Jerusalem from England and stayed in Benedictine monasteries across France and Italy before travelling down through Greece to hop on a boat from Athens to the Holy Land. During that journey I not only walked across Europe, but I walked back in time to experience the rich Benedictine tradition, and to get a glimpse of its great influence on Western religious history. I also got a closer look at the lives of the monks themselves, and was impressed by the practicality of the Benedictine principles.

Eventually I married and we were blessed with four children. It then became clear to me how well Benedict's 'little rule for beginners' applies to family life. I studied the rule and produced *Listen My Son – St Benedict for Fathers*,[1] which is a daily commentary on the Rule for parents. I also asked to become an oblate at Downside Abbey. Convinced that the Rule offers much wisdom for lay people, I compared it to the 'little way' of St Thérèse of Lisieux. *St Benedict and St Thérèse – The Little Rule and the Little Way*[2] was the product of this study.

As a Benedictine oblate, as well as a husband and father, the Benedictine Rule comes alive in my life in many ways. But there are four simple applications that surge with fresh meaning each day. These principles spring from Benedict's instructions for a good abbot. As I studied the Rule I could see that all the basic requirements for the abbot are also necessary for Christian fathers. Of course, the word 'abbot' comes from the same root as 'Abba – Father' and I am touched by the idea that this tender word 'Papa' is the same word that Jesus used for his heavenly father, and which St Paul instructs us to use for God as well.

Benedict's abbot understands human psychology. He expects his monks to be obedient, but Benedict insists that he must practise what he preaches. This is the first lesson I must always remember. I cannot expect my children to listen and obey if I am not prepared first to listen and obey God. Furthermore, towards the end of the Rule Benedict establishes the principle of mutual obedience in the monastery. In Latin the word 'obedience' is linked with the verb 'to listen' and in the Prologue Benedict instructs us to listen 'with the ears of our heart'. If we are expected to follow mutual obedience, and if obedience is linked with listening, then it is up to me to first listen to the needs of my children. This listening not only means taking the time to really listen when they are being fractious or boring. It also means listening to what they *don't* say; listening to their actions and listening to their innermost, unspoken needs. If I can take the time to do this, then what I expect of my children will be for their own good and not just for my own convenience.

The second Benedictine principle that helps me as a father is Benedict's instruction to the abbot to treat each monk equally. But Benedict's equality, like that found in the gospel, is not the crude form of equality in which each person receives an equal share of everything. Instead each person receives everything according to his or her own particular needs. One child may need firm handling. Others may need gentle encouragement. Each one of my children, indeed each person I deal with day by day, is a unique individual with a unique blend of needs, gifts and insights. Benedict teaches me that my role as father is not to force conformity to my own expectations, but to see their particular needs and to work with them to discover the most complete fulfilment of God's will in their lives.

I am also touched by Benedict's attention to the daily details. The monks are expected to find God in the difficulty of rising for the early office, serving in the refectory and infirmary and in the daily struggles of self-will, discipline and community life. He does so in a beautifully subtle way. Some commentators have noticed that in Chapter 22, in his instructions on how the monks should sleep, Benedict's language echoes the gospel parable of the wise and foolish virgins who have to keep watch. Therefore when Benedict tells the monks to keep a lamp burning, and to encourage each other as they hasten to meet their Lord, he is revealing his incarnational principle that the gospel is lived out in our lives in the most profound and simple way. Likewise, in his instructions for monks in the refectory in Chapter 35, Benedict gives instructions for the serving monks that echo in words and action the Divine Office and the Maundy Thursday liturgy. So in the daily routine of serving a meal the beautiful mystery of the incarnation is unlocked.

Through this Benedict teaches me about Emmanuel – the God who is with us. Some people say the devil is in the details. Benedict thinks the divine is in the details. This is nowhere more true than in the rough and tumble of modern family life. The Jews refer to the family as 'the domestic church'. Benedict reminds me that it is in the religious community of my family that I will learn the difficult lessons of love. Tertullian once wrote that 'marriage is the seminary of the human race'. His saying may well be amended to say that 'the family is the monastery of the human race'. Just as Benedict's monks were to find God in the nitty-gritty of sixth-century domestic life, I am called to find God in the daily sacrifices, pressures and uncertainties of family life at the beginning of the twenty-first century. These are the pressures of love, but if I can find love then I will find God for, as St John teaches, 'those who live in love live in God and God lives in them'.

This is not to equate Christian family life with the life of the monastery or convent. I do not believe either way is superior, but if they are equal they are not interchangeable. I could not attempt the Benedictine life as an oblate if there were no monks, and the monasteries would soon tumble if there were no faithful families to foster monastic and priestly vocations. Instead, in the wider context of the whole body of Christ, the Benedictine way in Christian families and in the monastery complement one another.

Finally, in the midst of a busy family life, I am immensely reassured by Benedict's teaching on prayer. In the Rule we do not find a lofty treatise on prayer. There are no purple passages of mystical love for God. Instead we find a rather lengthy and full treatise on how to pray the psalms at particular times of the year.

Interspersed with this rather mundane approach to prayer are delightful details. The oratory is to be kept open so anyone may go in at any time for a quick time of private prayer. With great relief I find that prayer is to be kept short, to the point and full of simple trust and child-like passion. This combination of liturgical prayer and spontaneous prayer works perfectly in the family life. Children thrive on routine and set prayers. They love to memorize and respond with passages of Scripture and the psalms. So as a family we do establish set times of formal prayer. Before we set out for school and work, before we sit down to a meal, before we go to bed at night there are short recitations of prayer. Weekly Mass and daily devotions are set times for short 'liturgies' that combine prayer, praise and Scripture. At the same time we teach the children that God is with us always and that we can turn to him at any time with a request or a brief word of thanks. Many families follow the Benedictine example and establish a little *poustinia* or quiet place so that the home actually has an oratory so anyone can pop in to pray briefly or just sit still.

I am also striving to establish and maintain this balance in my own personal life. As an oblate I have a rule of daily devotions, *lectio divina*, and formal prayer. But I also have time to simply refer back to God and offer him thanks, speak to him about the daily problems and needs and moments of reflection in which I am simply made aware of his presence and love.

Undergirding these practical points are the three Benedictine vows of stability, obedience and conversion of life. As a married man I have not made these religious vows. But within the sacrament of my marriage I believe these three vows are there just as surely as they are for a monk or nun. When my wife and I promised to love and honour one another 'until death do us part', we were taking our form of Benedictine vows of stability and obedience. Stability because we had taken a life-long vow. Obedience because within Christian marriage my wife promised to obey me, but I also promised to love her 'as Christ loved the church and gave himself for her'. This form of mutual obedience is built into the sacrament of marriage, and thus we try to fulfil this most difficult Benedictine vow together.

The final vow is to conversion of life. The three vows are intertwined so that the vow of stability provides the environment for conversion of life while the vow of obedience provides the method. Whether we are monks, nuns or lay people, conversion of life is the final aim of the whole enterprise. Like the desert monk, Abbot Joseph, we want to rise up and be converted into a living flame. Conversion of life means that we have got to the point where we are stable and obedient to one another not because we think we ought to, but because we want to. As Benedict says in Chapter 7,

Thus when all these steps of humility have been climbed, the monk will soon reach that love of God which, being perfect drives out all fear. Through this love all the practices which before he kept somewhat fearfully, he now begins to keep effortlessly and naturally and habitually, influenced not now by any fear of hell, but the force of long practice and the very delight he experiences in virtue.

If we can finally get to that place where what we want is also what God wants, then without even realizing it we will have reached the point where we are running 'on the path of God's commandments, our hearts overflowing with an inexpressible delight of love'.

Dwight Longenecker

Notes

1 Dwight Longenecker, *Listen My Son – St Benedict for Fathers*, Gracewing/Morehouse, 2000.
2 Dwight Longenecker, *St Benedict and St Thérèse – The Little Rule and the Little Way*, Gracewing/Our Sunday Visitor, 2002.

Living the Rule in the World

When I first picked up the Rule my immediate reaction was gratitude that it was short. I was expecting it to be largely irrelevant to my life, but I had been trained as a historian and so it seemed natural when I found myself living in a house that had originally been the prior's lodging in the cathedral precincts at Canterbury to look at the text ultimately responsible for these mediaeval buildings which now surrounded me. I enjoyed the visual reminders of past greatness, not only the glorious cloisters and the magnificent monastic church, its crypt dating from the years in which St Anselm was abbot and archbishop here, but equally the less splendid, the remains of the infirmary, the brewhouse and the bakehouse, the water tower. I asked myself questions about the monastic way of life: What was the inspiration that led men to create this place? What practical skills could construct underground tunnels for the water supply, and artistic skills could create the fantastic images of the Romanesque capitals in the crypt or the lyrical beauty of stained glass windows?

And so it was by an irony, or God's sense of timing, that I as a married woman, with four young sons, should first encounter the man and his writing that would change my life. It was the more unexpected since I had been brought up, as had so many Anglicans of my age and background, with a profound love for Britain's heritage in monastic buildings and works of art but had always considered anything to do with the life itself as something of an aberration, an escape from the world of men and women, for those who chose the enclosure with a rule and vows that were clearly life-denying.

But reading the text of the Rule itself was a revelation. I had only the briefest contact with any existing Benedictine community and so I read the words as though they were addressed to me personally. The opening words of the Prologue immediately caught my attention. They were warm and loving, showing a personal concern for me and for my way to God. As I moved on I found that in the main body of the Rule Benedict's concern was with relationships, with the living out of community life, and that he knew all about the demands of living at close quarters with others and trying to accept and love them without wanting to control. As these were people who had to earn their living he knew about manual work, the tools of daily life, and the importance of handling material objects with respect and reverence, and above all imposing structure on one's work schedule. The open door of the monastery meant that he understood the importance of hospitality but also the necessity of preserving boundaries for the sake of one's self and the family. He recognized the vital role of good order, and an underlying structure with regard to both place and time. I could extend the list – what was clear was that Benedict spoke to my heart and my condition. The world of this man living in rural Italy in the sixth century was totally different from mine and yet such was his grasp of the human psyche that he touched what was most authentic to my own experience. It was as though my own questions and struggles, often only half articulated, were here being clarified and addressed.[1]

It was like the start of a conversation with a friend, a conversation in which I would explore new issues and discover new depths, always finding myself revived, encouraged and also challenged. Benedict became friend and guide.[2] When I first read the Rule it was as the wife of busy husband and the mother of four teenage sons. It spoke to my situation then, and that has remained true through all subsequent change, and not least in my present situation where I find myself living on my own. For the Rule is like the Gospel itself, a spring or source, to which one returns all the time, for it possesses a dynamism capable of inspiring the lives of those in every age who approach it prayerfully with openness and receptivity. The following words are taken from the introduction of St Benedict's Rule for Monks, a recent translation by the Anglican Benedictine community of West Malling. I love their opening:

> My son, listen carefully to your master's teaching.
> Treasure it in your heart. Be open to receive and generous to respond to the counsel of a loving father.[3]

This of course should hardly surprise us since essentially Benedict's aim is to make the demands of the Gospel relevant and accessible in daily living – and therefore of course unavoidable. His intention is never that I should think of myself as a follower of his way but as a follower of Christ. He wants my whole life to become permeated with Christ so that I come to love Christ, to live Christ. This will not be easy. The road is hard and narrow, and Benedict never patronizes with easy promises. But he tells me that change will come, it will come in me, in a heart that grows larger and expands 'overflowing with the inexpressible delight of love'.[4] This is to be expressed in active compassion, since Benedict is looking to us not for words but deeds. So while at one level this is manageable, since the values of the Gospel are radical values it becomes demanding and disturbing. Yet in the depths of my heart I believe that this is what I most truly and deeply desire and ultimately Benedict is asking me to live from my truest and deepest self.

One of the biggest threats (and one that Henri Nouwen recognized and which led in his case to his significant stay in a Trappist abbey)[5] is that of becoming over-busy. It is easy in a society which applauds the workaholic to find oneself pulled in many directions and to lose a sense of balance and order. Yet I know that what I most desire is to live with an awareness of the presence of God, trying to carry a heart of stillness wherever I am and whatever I may be doing.

Benedict shows me a life in which there is no separation between praying and living, for everything is undergirded by prayer. Of course I would like to say the daily offices but I find that impossible. I do, however, begin each morning with prayer and reading, a commitment which lays the foundation for the rest of the day. Often in the psalms there will be a small phrase to which I pay particular attention, listening with the 'ear of the heart' and making it my very simple daily *lectio*. 'If you hear his voice today do not harden your hearts'.[6]

I return time and time again in my mind to the image of the cloisters which said so much to me in those early Canterbury days and which I have now internalized. What other complex of buildings would have the audacity to put emptiness at its centre? What does that tell me about myself? Round the cloisters are ranged the places which serve the daily needs of body, mind and spirit: dormitory and refectory, for Benedict tells us to respect the needs of the physical self; library (scriptorium) and chapter house, for Benedict wants us to use the mind, whether in administration and practical affairs or in study and artistic expression; and then the church itself, the base-line as it were, from which everything flows, and to which everything returns. I find that I constantly think of this image for it gives me the ideal of the flow and rhythm of a life of unity and harmony, in which all things are interrelated and connected. Of course I fail time and again. But I never give up trying to impose this pattern of wholeness and balance, and I know that this has made a real difference to how I live. So now when I notice how much attention the media and popular writing pay to the subject of stress, and all the problems which are the result of pressure, overwork and anxiety, and also the popularity of the remedies on offer in a consumer society (therapy and self-help manuals, popular spirituality, 'working-out' at the gym, meditating and dieting), I realize with gratitude that this is what Benedict knew all along.

Far from being narrow and restrictive, as I had once imagined it to be, the monastic life on the contrary encourages me to rejoice in the riches of my God-given humanity and helps me to live fully and openly, alive, alert, mindful. I often say to myself those words from the Prologue which give me particular delight: *apertis oculis . . . attentis auirbus*.[7]

But at the same time I am also aware of the danger that

this could easily become a comfortable spirituality emphasizing balance and moderation and holistic values to the neglect of the extent to which it is also counter-cultural. It is important to remind myself that Benedict is also passionate and prophetic, bringing me a message of discomfort. It would be dangerous if the Rule were to become something safe and attractive. I need to keep myself open to what is new. This is the openness of hospitality not only to the stranger at the door but also to new questions, circumstances, ideas which I welcome with the cry of the porter: 'Deo Gratis. Thanks be to God. I have been waiting for you!'[8]

Benedict wants us to be people of open mind. When he wrote the Rule he drew on different streams of the previous monastic experience, and then expected his followers to read further from sources that were, strictly speaking, incompatible. In effect he is saying that truth can be expressed in divergent ways. He stands opposed to all forms of fundamentalism or polarization. He reminds me that I must be *discipulus*, a disciple who will go on learning for the rest of my life.

When I first read the Rule I immediately responded to what Benedict said about handling material goods with respect and reverence, and this has been a huge consolation when I am at work in the kitchen and garden, although more demanding when I am at my desk. Applying this to the earth itself, to my own cottage and the land around, and then recognizing the implications for wider environmental concerns, was much more difficult. However, when I realized that everything matters, even a cracked or broken pot, and that everything is on loan, then I see myself as steward and I handle God's gifts with gratitude and responsibility.[9] It is of course also a responsibility to share them with the wider human family so there is now the further implication for social and racial justice, to work for those deprived of the right to live with full human dignity and self-respect. When I try to make this apply in my own situation I know that, in Britain at least, we have a society which quickly judges, categorizing and labelling, by accent, education or work. With Benedict there can be no class or status or privilege since it is Christ himself whom he sees in all who come. When that seems almost impossible I remind myself of that scene in the cave at Subiaco. God has sent a priest so that he should not be alone on Easter day, the first person that he has seen during his time of solitude, and Benedict exclaims: 'Easter it is indeed since I have the joy of seeing you.' In the face of this man he sees the first fruits of the resurrection, the resurrected self, the true self in Christ.[10]

I have come to think of the vows as something essential to my Christian discipleship and although of course I cannot begin to pretend that they mean the same to me as they do to the professed monastics or to oblates, I find that they prevent my following of Benedict from becoming abstract or theoretical. They are like a touchstone or a point of reference on which I continually focus and refocus. They remind me of what is central in my commitment to Christ; they support me and keep me on the path when I seem to be losing my way and I turn to them for guidance in times of decision. Stability ensures that I remain earthed, grounded, in my own deepest interior self, not beguiled by fantasy or dreams into escaping from reality. But in order not to stand still and firm in the wrong way and thus become static, I am also committed to continual and ongoing conversion, ready to leave the past behind and look ahead, even when what seems risky and frightening. And then obedience is like the key-stone of the arch for it puts the will of God firmly at the centre of my life. Every day I am asked to listen intently (*ob-audiens*) with 'the ear of the heart'. If I am carrying that heart of stillness and emptiness then I have more chance of being available, able to hear the Word and thus discern whether it is God's will that I am trying to follow and not my own self-centred fulfilment.

Since I am not an oblate, I try instead to draw up my own contract or covenant. I revise it every year so that it will reflect my changing circumstances and situation. I put it in the form of questions, generally six or eight, so that it is like a check-list helping me to see whether I am drifting or straying from the path. I love the underlying image of the Rule, which is given to us in the opening words, of being the prodigal, having lost the way, strayed from the path. Benedict promises to bring us home.

That is why I and so many others like me today are turning to this gentle and compassionate man, who is also passionate and urgent, to help us on our way to God.

Esther de Waal

Notes

1 In 1983 when I wrote *Seeking God*, I explained this in the introduction: Sometimes one finds a place, a landscape, which is new and yet the forms, the shapes, the shadows seem already familiar. So it was for me with the Rule. It was not remote or past or cerebral, but immediate and relevant, speaking of things that I already half knew or was struggling to make sense of.

2 Many years later I was to find myself teaching a young African who wanted to become a Benedictine in South Africa and we looked together at the *Dialogues* of St Gregory which in the way it presented Benedict's life had so much in common with the oral tradition of story-telling of his own country. 'This man is my friend – he will walk with me on my journey', he exclaimed, a young black man and an older white woman sharing the same sense of identifying with this *vir Dei*, this man of God.

3 St Mary's Abbey, West Malling, Kent ME19 6JX, UK.

4 Prologue, eighth paragraph: love is the key idea in these amazingly warm and beautiful verses which show us the mystical and poetic side of this down to earth man Benedict. The Latin carries a delicacy with its deliberate alliteration to which no translation can do justice: *dilatato . . . dilectionis dulcedine*.

5 *The Genesee Diary: Report from a Trappist Monastery*, 1976, in successive editions in America with Image, Doubleday, New York and in England with Darton, Longman and Todd. Told with humility and humour, we see how the structure of the day and the rhythm of the life brings to Nouwen that focus which his earlier life so much lacked.

6 Prologue, first paragraph; and Chapter 10; Ps. 94 (95):8. There is now a vast amount of interest in *lectio* reflected in the number of recent studies on the subject.

7 In his commentary, Terence Kardong sees here a possible allusion to the Transfiguration which I have found very illuminating. I think of myself as one of the drowsy disciples startled by the shining forth of Christ in sight and sound. It encourages me to keep awake with open eyes and alert ears. *Benedict's Rule: A Translation and Commentary*, Liturgical Press, 1996, p. 11.

Living the Rule

8 The Rule, Chapter 66, first paragraph.
9 Chapter 32 on the goods and tools of the monastery loaned to the
 brothers expresses profound truths in the context of dealing with utensils and clothing, which is so typical of the Rule. Its full significance
 was pointed out to me by Sr Judith Sutera OSB in her article 'Stewardship and the Kingdom in the Rule, Chapters 31–33' in *American
 Benedictine Review* 41 (4), 1990, pp. 348–57.
10 This point was made by Dom Andre Louf, for many years the abbot
 of the Cistercian community of Mont des Cats in France, in an article,
 'A Man of God for all Time'.

Books on Benedictine spirituality by Esther de Waal

Seeking God: The Way of St Benedict, Collins Fount, London, 1984. New
 edition, Canterbury Press, Norwich, 1999.

Living with Contradiction: Reflections of the Rule of St Benedict, Collins
 Fount, London, 1987. New edition, subtitled *An Introduction to Bene-
 dictine Spirituality*, Canterbury Press, Norwich, 1997. HarperCollins,
 San Francisco, 1988. New edition, Morehouse Publishing, 1998.

A Life-Giving Way: A Commentary on the Rule of St Benedict, Geoffrey
 Chapman, 1995. Reissued, Mowbray, Continuum, 1999. New edition
 containing the text, The Liturgical Press, Collegeville, 2000.

The Wisdom of St Benedict, Lion Publishing, Oxford, 1999.

Part Five

The Benedictine Family

A Short History

Although the Benedictine charism can be traced to the earliest record of Christian monasticism in Egypt and the Mediterranean world in the fourth and fifth centuries, it was only with the life of Benedict of Nursia (480–547) and the Rule he wrote that one can speak of a discernible line of historical development.

One can argue that Benedict himself never intended to establish a 'Benedictine' Order. His Rule, written at Monte Cassino in the last stages of his life, was designed as nothing more than a modest and practical norm for his own monastic foundations in Italy. It was also one of a considerable number of other monastic rules for men (Rule of the Master, Rule of Columban, Rule of Isidore) and women (Rule of Augustine, Rule of Caesarius of Arles) that were observed in and around the time of Benedict.

It was only at the end of the eighth century that the Rule of St Benedict began to be upheld as a standard of cenobitic life in wider monastic circles. During the rule of Charlemagne there was a policy of centralization initiated for affairs of the Church. In conformity with this tendency, the synods of Aachen in 802, 816, 817 and 818 enjoined all monasteries in the Carolingian Empire to adopt uniform observance (e.g. a common habit) and follow the Rule. A major impetus in implementing the Carolingian policy was Benedict of Aniane, who compiled a *Codex Regularum* and *Concordia Regularum*, a collection of existing monastic rules and a commentary on other rules as they corresponded to the Rule. Another means for the spread of the Rule was the missionary work done by individual monks. The mission of Augustine of Canterbury and others to England and the subsequent efforts of monks such as Boniface, Willibrord and Columba to the European continent, carried both a monastic culture and observance of the Rule to a broader arc of Western civilization. This was also a time when monks in Europe preserved priceless manuscripts and became innovators of agricultural techniques and architectural design.

It was this same Rule that constituted the basis of reform for monasteries in the early middle ages. The founding of the abbey of Cluny in Burgundy, France (910), set in motion a highly centralized movement of reform for monastic life and for the Church. The renewal of monastic life in France, Italy and Spain in succeeding years was due largely to the activity of Cluniac monks. In England in the tenth century there was also a monastic reform that introduced a uniform system of observance according to principles derived from the Rule. The monastic reforms of Cluny in turn helped to produce the wider Gregorian reform of the Catholic Church in the eleventh century.

Elements that characterized the reformed monasticism of the eleventh and twelfth centuries were administrative centralization (as seen in the system of the general chapter and regular visitation), uniformity of observance (detailed in the community customaries that emerged in this period), an emphasis on intense study of Sacred Scripture and Patristic texts (articulated by Jean Leclercq as 'The Love of Learning and the Desire for God'), expanded economic investment (in land and buildings) and a development of more elaborate liturgical ritual. This culminated in the reform of the Cistercian Order, a development treated separately in this handbook, in the chapter, The Cistercian Tradition.

There is some irony in the historical movement, that just as the general public began to use the term Benedictine to refer to the network of monasticism that dominated mediaeval Europe, the cenobitic life carried out in these monasteries had become different from that outlined in the Rule. There was a growing clericalization of the monastic order, with a substantial increase in ordained members. At the same time, there arose a distinct class of monks called *conversi*, laymen who were admitted to

monasteries, but were exempt from the regular round of liturgical and private prayer. Instead they devoted themselves to the
manual work of the monastery.

The middle ages also witnessed vibrant expressions of Byzantine monasticism. The Studite reform centred at Constantinople
and Mount Athos and the spirituality associated with John
Climacus at Mount Sinai were noteworthy examples of this. So
too were the expressions of idiorhythmic monasticism and the
Jesus Prayer, as well as the modes of monastic life brought by
Russian monks to the Slavic world.

The Benedictine Order began a decline in influence and
numbers in the thirteenth century. One of the reasons for this
was the parallel rise of the mendicant orders, especially the
Franciscans and Dominicans, and the canons regular in the city
cathedrals. As European culture became less dependent on a
land-based, rural economy, the largely rural monastic centres
lost their influence. There was a corresponding decline in
religious observance, along with the devastation brought by the
Black Death in the 1300s, that decimated numbers in many
monastic houses.

The rise and fall of Benedictine fortunes in this period witnessed a number of extremely capable leaders and spiritual
guides. Among women monastics, the names of Hildegard of
Bingen, Elizabeth of Schönau, Mechtild of Magdeburg, and
Gertrude the Great are only a few who rose to prominence
at this time. Among Benedictine founders and leaders of the
mediaeval era, one can include Cluniac abbots such as Hugh,
Odo, Odilo and Peter the Venerable. Monk churchmen such as
Peter Damian and Pope Gregory VII forged Church reform
through zealous and confrontational preaching. There were also
the vanguard of Cistercian abbots and writers in the company
of Bernard of Clairvaux, Aelred of Rievaulx, Isaac of Stella and
William of St Thierry.

By the fifteenth century, there was a general consensus that
monastic life needed reform. There were efforts to bring that
about introduced by a number of new Benedictine reform movements. One came from Kastl in Bavaria and restored Cluniac

customs to a number of Bavarian abbeys. Another was associated with the Austrian Abbey of Melk (1419), and carried the reform of Subiaco to abbeys of Austria and Germany. Still another effort at reform that originated in German-speaking lands was that of Bursfeld, a reform that was given congregational status by the Council of Basle (1431–37). Perhaps the most successful of the fifteenth-century reforms, however, was that of the Abbey of Santa Giustina in Italy. Under the abbot, Ludovico Barbo, Santa Giustina exercised an influence that eventually extended to Spain and the Congregation of Valladolid. Influential Benedictine figures were not lacking in this period either. Garcia de Cisnernos and Louis de Blois both wrote works that received a wide dissemination.

The Protestant Reformation that represented so crucial a landmark for the Catholic Church's identity also left its mark on the Benedictine family. The reform of religious life enunciated by the Council of Trent included a number of measures that earlier reform movements had advocated. They included the elimination of *commendam* abbots (those who were not required to take up residence in their monastery), obligatory affiliation of monasteries with congregations, minimum age of entry and profession, and requirements of general chapters and visitations.

At the same time, the Reformation had witnessed the dissolution of the monasteries of England, Scotland and Ireland. The Lutheran Church in Scandinavia and many German-speaking territories suppressed monastic houses as well. The northern half of Germany lost most of its Benedictine houses. Some of the more decadent communities in the rest of Germany and Switzerland closed of their own accord, while other houses in Catholic areas of Europe were tested by the religious wars of the period after the Reformation. Only the Benedictines of Spain, Portugal and Italy were relatively unscathed by the religious upheaval of the Reformation.

The Catholic Reformation, however, also brought clear evidence of new reforms in Benedictine life. This was especially the case in France, where the Congregations of St Vanne and

St Maur (commonly known as the Vannists and Maurists) were founded at the start of the seventeenth century. Their contributions to scholarship and their highly centralized structure were models for other congregations. The number of Benedictine women in France grew as well in the seventeenth century. New congregations included the Cistercian Feuillantines, Our Lady of Calvary, and the Perpetual Adoration of the Blessed Sacrament. In the period of the 1600s the English Benedictine Congregation also found refuge in France, inspired by such spiritual writers as Augustine Baker and Gertrude More. It was at France's Abbey of La Trappe that the famous reform of Armand de Rancé began in the seventeenth century.

Just as the seventeenth century witnessed a resurgence of numbers and new congregations in France, so it did in the rest of Europe. The Swiss Congregation, spearheaded by the Abbey of Einsiedeln, was established in 1602. The Austrian Congregation began in 1625. The Hungarian Congregation, centred at the royal Abbey of Pannonhalma, was restored in 1639. The Bavarian Congregation began its existence in 1684.

The period of the Enlightenment was another challenge for Benedictine communities. Many new governments, imbued with secularist and rationalist sympathies, identified monastic life with the monarchies and religious 'superstition'. A number of monasteries were forced to take on tasks of teaching and parish supply work if they did not want to be suppressed. As the level of observance dropped in some houses, so did the numbers of men and women. This was especially the case in France. It was in France that monastic life was to receive its greatest test with the coming of the Revolution at the end of the eighteenth century. Shortly after the French Revolution had begun, all the monastic houses of France were suppressed and many of the bloody reprisals of the revolutionary government included Benedictines as their victims. In the last decades of the eighteenth century, Emperor Joseph II of Austria also suppressed monasteries in Austria, Bohemia, Hungary and areas of Poland. In the wake of the Napoleonic wars, Benedictine monasteries in Switzerland, Spain, the Netherlands and Italy were forced to close. By 1810, it was said there were fewer monasteries in existence than at any time since the age of St Augustine.

Even while the monastic order in Europe was in severe decline at the beginning of the nineteenth century, indicators of rebirth and renewal were evident. In 1802 the suppressed abbeys of Hungary formed a new congregation from the royal monastery of Pannonhalma. English monks who had fled from oppression while in exile in France now returned to England where they formed monasteries at Ampleforth and Downside. English Benedictine women did the same, going from Cambrai in France to Colwich and Stanbrook. In Bavaria the Abbey of Metten and convent of Eichstätt were restored and they in turn were to promote the revival of monastic life in other German abbeys.

The real nucleus of the nineteenth-century revival was found in France. There, in 1833, a young diocesan priest, Prosper Guéranger, founded the Abbey of Solesmes. Driven by a desire to return to ancient monastic sources, Solesmes became a centre for liturgical life and scholarship. It marked the beginning of the French (now known as the Solesmes) Congregation and gave birth to other monasteries at Ligu/ and Marseilles. Solesmes also assisted in the foundation of the Sisters of St Cecilia under Abbess Cécile Bruyère, a companion reform of the monks. Other new congregations of Benedictine women in France included the Nuns of the Heart of Mary (Pradines), the Adorers of the Heart of Jesus (Montmartre) and the Congregation of Missionary Benedictines (Liguge).

In Italy, Pietro Casaretto transformed Benedict's Abbey of Subiaco into a reform centre (1851) and then went on to form the Subiaco Congregation, an entity that absorbed abbeys across the European continent and was known for its missionary thrust. It was this congregation that, through the labours of Spanish Benedictines Joseph Serra and Rosendo Salvado, brought, along with the work of the English Benedictines, a Benedictine presence to the Australian continent.

Another branch of the nineteenth-century revival came from the foundation made in 1863 at Beuron by two German brothers, Maurus and Placid Wolter. Taking Solesmes as their model, the Beuronese Congregation became influential in stimulating a return to the sources of monastic life and a concentration on liturgical life. This emphasis on the liturgy is seen in the abbeys of Maredsous and Mont-César in Belgium and Maria Laach in Germany, all of which became centres for the Liturgical Movement. Another Beuronese monk, Andreas Amrheim, founded still another new congregation in Bavaria that was missionary in orientation, that of St Ottilien (1884). This congregation had its female counterpart in the Benedictine missionary sisters of Tützing.

It was from Bavaria and Germany that the first pronounced Benedictine presence in North America was to come. Under the leadership of a monk of Metten Abbey, Boniface Wimmer, the Abbey of St Vincent in Latrobe, Pennsylvania, was founded (1846). It provided the impetus for the American Cassinese Congregation. Monks from the Swiss abbeys of Einsiedeln and Engelberg soon followed, establishing communities at St Meinrad, Indiana (1854), and Conception, Missouri (1871), as well as the new Swiss-American Congregation. Coterminous with the foundations of monks, Benedictine women from a variety of houses in Germany and Switzerland were established. These houses of Benedictine women eventually took shape in the Federation of St Scholastica, the Federation of St Gertrude, the Federation of St Benedict and the Benedictine Sisters of Perpetual Adoration.

The end of the nineteenth century witnessed an increasing centralization of the Benedictine Order. Under the impetus of Pope Leo XIII, there was a revival of the monastery of Sant'Anselmo in Rome. It became a central house of studies for the Order. It was at Sant'Anselmo that the first Congress of Abbots was held in 1893 and the position of abbot primate created as part of the effort to organize a Benedictine Confederation and highlight a unified Benedictine Order.

Many Church leaders, along with an impressive list of liturgical and spiritual writers, reflected the revitalized monasticism of the early twentieth century. Cardinals Gasquet, Dusmet and Pitra exhibited the fruits of scholarship from the Benedictine revival. Writers such as Beauduin and Botte, Butler and Chapman, Marmion and Morin, exemplified the efforts of the return to Scriptural and Patristic sources.

New monastic congregations were added in the first part of the twentieth century. These included the Belgian Congregation (1920), the Austrian Congregation (1930) and the Bohemian Congregation of St Adalbert (1945). Particularly in Europe and North America, there was a marked growth in both individual members and new monastic houses.

The twentieth century was not without its challenges to monasticism. The punitive legislation passed by governments in Germany, France and Italy at the close of the nineteenth century slowed the progress of monasticism in these countries. Even more harmful to monasticism were the two world wars that marked the first half of the century. The devastation that so marked the monastic patrimony of Europe in these wars was epitomized in the destruction of the Abbey of Monte Cassino by Allied bombers and the wholesale loss of priceless manuscripts and books contained in monastic libraries throughout Europe. Nonetheless, the period of reconstruction after the Second World War witnessed another resurgence of the monastic order. Noteworthy in this period was a strong contemplative movement. It was influenced in part in the English-speaking world by the popularity of the works of Thomas Merton and was reflected in the growing numbers flocking, not only to Cistercian monasteries, but also to new communities of Benedictine men and women that had turned away from traditional apostolates of education and pastoral work and become centres of prayer and liturgical life.

Political persecution was a part of the experience of many twentieth-century Benedictines. Spanish monks of Silos Abbey were expelled from Mexico in 1913. In the Spanish Civil War in 1936 monks of the Abbey of Pueyo suffered a collective martyrdom. Benedictines were driven from the China mainland after the Second World War. Another post-war phenomenon was the suppression of large numbers of monastic houses in Eastern Europe behind the Iron Curtain. But there was also a strong missionary thrust, this time directed to Latin America, Asia and Africa. By the 1950s there were thriving Benedictine communities in Argentina and Mexico, India and Vietnam, Madagascar and Morocco.

The decade of the 1960s marked not only the decisive event of Vatican Council II (1962–65) but also another period of renewal of monastic life. This was accomplished through a variety of changes: structural changes in the constitutions of Benedictine congregations, the introduction of the vernacular in the liturgical prayer of monasteries, new patterns of ministry taken on by many communities, and a comprehensive re-evaluation of monastic spirituality as it came to terms with the challenges posed by the contemporary world. At the same time, this period initiated a time of demographic change, with a pattern of decreasing numbers from Benedictine houses in Europe and North America and correspondingly increased numbers from the sub-continents of Africa, Asia and South America.

The conciliar call for all religious to return to the sources of their charism led to a flowering of monastic scholarship. A new wave of Benedictine scholars appeared, intent on distilling the best of the Benedictine tradition of intellectual work and extending it to a wider audience. The Benedictine Pontifical University of Sant'Anselmo in Rome offered an international venue for this to take place, particularly with its Liturgical and Monastic Institutes. There were also flourishing centres for study and publishing in other parts of the monastic world.

Benedictines exercised considerable leadership in renewal efforts of religious life in the period after the council. American Benedictine Rembert Weakland, elected as abbot primate in 1967, did much to promote the renewal of liturgical life. He also broadened contacts with houses of Benedictine women and supported the growing influence of monasticism in Third World countries. American Benedictine Sister Joan Chittister became a prominent voice in the renewal efforts of women Benedictines and religious. In the Roman Curia, Cardinal Augustine Mayer played a significant role under Pope John Paul II in expediting the religious renewal of communities of consecrated life and later served as a liaison with the Society of St Peter. Cardinal Basil Hume, a monk and abbot of Ampleforth Abbey before being named Archbishop of Westminster, was widely recognized as a spokesman and spiritual figure of influence in the European Church in the last decades of the twentieth century.

The end of the twentieth century witnessed the return of a more vibrant monastic life to countries that had long suffered from political oppression under Communist rule. This was the case in Vietnam after the difficult period of war and internal discord. It was especially the case in the countries of Eastern Europe after the fall of Communism in 1989. Many of the restrictions formerly imposed on monastic houses in Soviet satellites such as Poland, Hungary and Czechoslovakia were lifted. The 1990s witnessed an entirely revitalized form of monastic life in countries such as Lithuania, Slovakia and the Czech Republic, nurtured with material and human resources from monasteries of the free world.

As the twentieth century came to its close, Benedictine monasticism was distinguished by its international character and its pluralism. Technology expedited an ease of communication among far-flung monasteries. This was buttressed by frequent encounters and personal exchanges among monastics of different houses. Another notable feature was the surge in growth of lay associate or oblate programmes, in which many lay people, Catholic and non-Catholic, affiliated themselves with monastic life. Benedictine practices such as *lectio divina* also became accessible to a wider public, as did the interest generated in monastic spirituality by a new generation of Catholics.

In 2000 there were just over 8,400 monks and over 17,000 Benedictine women throughout the world. Although this represented a decline from the membership at the time of Vatican Council II, it was less than that experienced by other religious orders in that same period. The numbers also reflected a growing diversity and vitality, especially in countries of the Third World.

Joel Rippinger OSB

Benedictines Worldwide

This chapter does not provide a detailed and comprehensive account of the Benedictine presence in the modern world. The relevant statistics can be found in each year's edition of *The Benedictine Yearbook*,[1] published by the English Benedictine Congregation. The purpose here is, rather, to offer a more impressionistic account of the *shape* of this presence, to suggest some of its historical roots and to comment on its relation to modern cultures.

The Benedictine story is full of anomalies and contradictions, and is characterized by a wide variety of styles and initiatives. The reason for this is very simple. St Benedict's Rule, written in the sixth century, was written for one monastery at one time, not for all monasteries of all times, and it has an inbuilt flexibility: 'Let the Abbot decide ... according to local circumstances.' It was not until three centuries later, in the time of Charlemagne, that a certain uniformity of practice and custom was imposed, and this was as much for political as for monastic reasons.

There has been, throughout monastic history, a tension between two fidelities – fidelity to the letter of the Rule, and fidelity to the call of immediate and localized charisms. This tension has produced, on the one hand, intermittent and strong moments of Reform (e.g. the twelfth-century Cistercian movement, the seventeenth-century Trappist Reform, the nineteenth-century 'Gothic revival' in Germany and France) and, on the other hand, a series of powerful and original initiatives (e.g. the sixth-century mission of Augustine to Britain, the tenth-century

Cluniac movement in France, the nineteenth-century foundations in the USA, the development of the inter-continental Congregation of Subiaco).

St Benedict did not found an 'Order'. The concept of an Order,
with its centralized and pyramidic structures, is a later invention.
He founded, rather, a tradition, out of which grew what remains
essentially a loose, though strong, federation of autonomous
monasteries. These have come in recent centuries to be grouped
into 'congregations', which provide an element of centralization
but in a variety of ways. Some of these congregations have a
national base (e.g. the English, the Bavarian, the Dutch, etc.),
but others do not (the congregations of Subiaco, St Ottilien and
the Annunciation are, in practice, international). Some congregations are more centralized than others, but the principle of
autonomy remains strong.

The Benedictine Confederation

Towards the end of the nineteenth century, Pope Leo XIII
founded the international college of St Anselmo on the Aventine
Hill in Rome, to be presided over by an abbot primate. The
centralizing intention was clear, and it coincided with a revival
of monasticism in Europe, primarily in France (Solesmes) and
Germany (Beuron). In the event, St Anselmo became a focus
and a symbol rather than a centre. The abbot primate (elected
by his peers every eight years) has no subjects and little power.
His role is to represent the Confederation in Rome, to be a
unifying influence in the Confederation, and to preside over a
theological college in which the teachers and the students are
monks, whose commitment is to their own monasteries, and
whose residence in Rome is, as it were, provisional. This distinguishes it from the mother-houses of other Orders.

St Anselmo embodies the central paradox of the world's Benedictine family. Its unity is one of tradition rather than of structure, and this unity co-exists with great diversity of style, custom
and work. Those who come to live, for a time, in St Anselmo
bring with them their own special traditions, and it is the task

of the college not to impose a 'model' uniformity, but to identify and to emphasize the deeper aspects of monastic custom which are common to all monasteries. It is a fact, experienced by all travelling monks, that the Benedictine style has a profound common core, rooted not only in conventual life and prayer, but also in certain shared courtesies. For this reason, the unfamiliar experience of living with monks of other traditions can be both an encounter with diversity and a reaffirmation of what is essential.

The diversity of Benedictine monasteries is much greater than many think. Monks in habits look much the same wherever they live, but the impression is misleading. There are large monasteries (of one hundred or more) and small ones (of five or fewer). Some monasteries have extensive pastoral or educational work (including parishes or chaplaincies), others have no work outside that of the monastery itself. There are urban monasteries (like the Brazilian ones in the heart of Rio de Janeiro and Sao Paulo) and remote rural ones. Down the centuries, monasteries have specialized in agriculture, academic study, education, or missionary work, according to local need or their traditional charisms. A new foundation may, therefore, take up work and a lifestyle which are quite different from those of its mother-house. To use the terms 'contemplative' and 'active' is not wholly appropriate (the distinction comes from a terminology later than that used by St Benedict), as most Benedictine monasteries cultivate a spirituality in which prayer and work are blended in varying proportions.

For Benedictine women, however, the distinction might be (for historical reasons) more appropriate. The Canon Law of the Roman Catholic Church makes no distinction, in the case of men, between monks who live strictly within the monastic enclosure and those whose work takes them outside it. In the case of women, however, it does. This is not the place to comment on the reason for this gender differentiation. What it means is that, in the eyes of the Church, there are two classes of women dedicated to living according to the Rule of St Benedict. Those who live an enclosed life are the nuns, those who are active, in missionary and other work, outside the cloister are the sisters. The women are, like the men, present in all the continents, and it is worthy of comment that their number (about 17,000) is more than double that of monks. These are Roman Catholic figures; the proportion is even higher when Benedictines of other communions are added. The differentiation between men and women, together with the fact that there is no necessary link between monasticism and priesthood, also leads to the comment that the Benedictine tradition is, essentially, not a clerical one. St Benedict was a layman, and it was only by an accident of history (the monastic tradition of learning) that it became normal for many monks to become priests. The Rule represents an attitude to the search for God which is, in all its basic features, lay rather than clerical. This fact has had the effect, in recent years, of encouraging increased lay involvement in the Benedictine life. On the more negative side, monasteries with extensive pastoral or educational commitments are being compelled by circumstance to 'educate' lay collaborators into their Benedictine tradition. On the positive side, lay movements inspired by the Rule are starting to have significant influence. Some of these represent a new flowering of the Oblates (or Third Order) tradition – lay people associated with a particular monastery. Others are less traditional. The Manquehue Apostolic Movement in Chile (which runs four schools, as well as having a significant involvement in diocesan activity) is an entirely lay body (affiliated, in an unlikely way, with the English Benedictine Congregation), whose aim is to live and teach the Benedictine way without the aid of 'qualified monks'. They are, as it were, 'reclaiming' the Rule for those for whom it was originally written – groups of ordinary lay people seeking God through prayer, community, work and shared study of the Word of God. The significance of this 'declericalization' of the monastic tradition has yet to be measured.

Benedictine culture and world cultures – Europe

When St Benedict was 'promoted' in 1980 to be the first Patron of Europe, non-European Benedictines were slightly disconcerted. Did this mean that St Benedict was, in some way, specifically a European saint? The answer is, of course, Yes and No. Yes, in the sense that he was the Father of Western monasticism, which was, for a thousand years, one of the most formative elements of European culture. No, in the sense that Benedictine culture is one of the many European elements that has been exported to several New Worlds, where it has taken on new forms.

The influence of monasticism on the development of Europe, as we know it, was both profound and paradoxical. The life and the achievement of St Benedict himself were paradoxical: on the basis of an ideal of solitude he built a philosophy of community; he began by seeking the desert and ended by civilizing it. The same paradox runs through the history of all monasteries which have drawn their primary inspiration from his Rule: so-called 'Western monasticism', which appears at first sight to aim at establishing an alternative society, set over against the structures and aspirations of ordinary worldly society, turns out constantly to achieve something rather different, by becoming a transforming agent *within* human society rather than a revolutionary one acting *outside* it. Many monks down the ages have started by being anarchic drop-outs and ended by being experts on agrarian reform or builders of cities; many others, who wished to be hermits or gardeners, have ended as missionaries, librarians or bishops. This is no less true today than it was at the time of Charlemagne or Cluny.

This contradiction was, repeatedly, profoundly influential in the slow emergence of European civilization. In England we are fortunate in possessing, in Bede's Ecclesiastical History,[2] a rich account of the cultural consequences of St Augustine's mission to England in 597. The monks went to England to bring the faith, but ended up by creating a culture. The map of Europe became strewn with monasteries, which were animating centres of learning, agriculture, education and civic life, as well as of prayer and liturgy.

The extensive and centralized network of Cluniac houses gave for a time great uniformity to the monastic culture of Western Europe, but this came to be replaced and overshadowed later by the explosive Cistercian Reform of the twelfth century. Many Cistercian houses were situated in the wildest corners of the country. The desert bloomed, as it had in the time of St Benedict himself.

The most striking cultural feature of the monastic movement was the way in which monasteries came to be centres of aesthetic creativity. Monks made things in a beautiful way. Buildings, books, gardens and music became the natural language of monastic celebration. In the period of highest creativity, the monastery became a kind of paradigm of cultural wholeness and excellence. The doors of the cloister led to oratory, refectory, workshops, orchard, library and recreation rooms, pointing to the holistic relationship between sacred and human activities. Gregorian Chant, in which popular and sacred styles had grown together, was a melodic tapestry linking together all the monasteries of Christendom. The prosperity which had made possible this proliferation of creative activity was also one of the causes of decline. Others were the growing influence of the newer religious orders, and the period of intense political and religious unrest which accompanied the Reformation and the Enlightenment. The ruins of Cluny, Rievaulx and countless smaller monasteries have an ironic beauty. They also played their part in creating the mood of the nineteenth-century Gothic revival, which was the backdrop for a remarkable period of monastic revival, first in France, Germany and Switzerland, and subsequently in the New World and elsewhere.

The nineteenth century – new horizons

While the great monasteries of the Austro-Hungarian Empire had remained largely untouched by the divisions and persecutions which decimated other European monasteries, elsewhere the nostalgia for the newly perceived romance of mediaevalism, combined with the charisms of several great monastic figures, led to a burst of monastic fervour in Western Europe. The monasteries of Beuron (Germany) and Solesmes (France) were the main centres, but the impact of the new movement came to be felt throughout Europe and, not long afterwards, far further afield.

The waves of emigration and exploration which carried nineteenth-century Europeans into the Americas, Africa and the East were accompanied by Benedictines, especially from France, Germany and Switzerland. These founders were, once again, inspired by contradictory ideals. On the one hand, their style was deeply coloured by their neo-Gothic enthusiasm (their clothes, architecture and music were largely mediaeval). On the other hand, they were missionary pioneers involved in the creation of new societies and new cultures. The result was the 'invention' of a new kind of Benedictine presence, at once deeply rooted in ancient styles and open to new kinds of Apostolate. The Congregations of Subiaco, St Ottilien and the Annunciation gradually became inter-continental in character. These groups, together with the two North American Congregations, now include more than half the number of monks worldwide.

The story of the monks is echoed by that of the nuns and sisters, who are also active in all the continents, whether as enclosed contemplative communities or as active missionary sisters.

Benedictines and modernity

From its earliest days, the Benedictine movement has been characterized by tensions and contradictions – between the search for solitude and the building of community, between the desert and the city, between the cloister and the mission, between a rootedness in tradition and a desire to break new ground, between the love of ancient forms and a commitment to creativity. In Latin America, some of the monasteries are built in severely neo-Gothic style, others in dazzlingly white concrete

The Benedictine Handbook

blocks. In a sense, Benedictines suffer from a chronic identity crisis. Their deep sense of tradition makes them reluctant to change, other than slowly. Their commitment to offering a style of life which is both a refuge from excessive modernity and a way of evangelizing it means that they are in a permanent crisis of adaptation and inculturation. St Benedict's young community at Monte Cassino found itself in a similar situation. They had no obvious future. All over the world, Benedictine communities of men and women, and the lay people who are increasingly involved with them, are facing new pressures of alienation, discouragement, challenge and hope, in a world which seems often to offer little purchase to those who simply wish to communicate the peace of a life lived according to the values of the Gospel. There is nothing new in the challenge, and the Benedictine response to it is, broadly speaking, the same as it has always been – puzzlingly contradictory, open to both past and future, and quietly trusting in a mission planned by God.

As I write, a group of about thirty Benedictines, who have responsibility for the formation of their candidates, is assembled in Rome for a three-month course. They are men and women, and they represent all six continents (the sixth being Oceania). Their task is to examine the interface between old treasures and new ones, and to celebrate the special Benedictine formula of unity in diversity.

Dominic Milroy OSB

Notes

1 *The Benedictine Yearbook*, Ampleforth Abbey, York YO62 4EN, UK.
2 Bede, *The Ecclesiastical History of the English People*, Oxford University Press, Oxford, 1994.

The Cistercian Tradition

The Cistercians were founded in 1098 by a group of Benedictine monks from the Abbey of Molesme in Burgundy. The land on which they settled was given to them by Hugh, Duke of Burgundy. The group was led by the abbot, Robert, whose two principal companions were Alberic, a Burgundian and Stephen Harding from England. They left Molesme in order to seek the literal observance of the Rule of St Benedict. Robert was eventually ordered back to Molesme by the Papal Legate, and Alberic succeeded him as abbot of 'The New Monastery'. After the death of Alberic Stephen became abbot. Stephen was the principal organizer who wrote 'The Charter of Charity'. This was the first 'law' of the Order, stressing that the link between the monasteries would be the Gospel, and not merely law and regulation. The Charter also provided for regular general Chapters.

Beginnings

For some years The New Monastery (as it was known) barely survived, with hardly anyone joining the community. Then in 1113, Bernard of Fontaines, son of a minor Burgundian noble family, joined the community. He is often regarded as the second founder and there is some truth in this. He brought thirty companions with him, and the Cistercian Reform took off. Many of the thirty were members of his family, brothers, cousins and other relatives, with some friends. Within a few years, the first foundations were made and Bernard was appointed Abbot of

Clairvaux. He became one of the most powerful men in Europe and was for many years the confidant and adviser of those in authority in the Church. He left a huge spiritual legacy in the form of sermons and treatises. His sermons on the Song of Songs are among the finest products of the mediaeval mystical tradition. Bernard was far from being the only Cistercian who wrote about the spiritual life in the twelfth century, and there is an enormous wealth of Cistercian spirituality, which continues to inspire monks and nuns today.

Cistercian nuns

Cistercian nuns existed from the beginning. When St Bernard entered Clairvaux, his only sister Humbelina was already married. When her husband died some time afterwards, she entered a community of nuns at Tart in Burgundy, and they adopted the customs and way of life of the Cistercian monks. This house is regarded as the first Cistercian monastery for women. The riches of the writings of the Cistercian Fathers and of the mystical tradition among the Cistercian nuns, such as St Mechtild and the two St Gertrudes (of Helfta and of Magdeburg) are a permanent legacy to the Church.

Lay brothers

The Order soon became wealthy and this was in large part due to the creation of the lay brothers. The monks had no difficulty in acquiring land – mostly in the form of donations from wealthy landowners. Donations of land were often given with the stipulation that the monks pray for the donor and his family. The monks soon discovered that if they were to observe the Rule of St Benedict literally in its recommendations about the Divine Office, they needed help. So they admitted men to the monasteries who were not monks, and who worked the land. They were full members of the monastic community, and lived under the particular care of the Master of the lay brothers. They attended very few of the Offices in choir and often lived in the out-farms, known in these countries as granges. The lay brothers were instituted in order to leave the choir monks free for the daily recitation of the Divine Office. Agriculture was the main support of the monks, and many monasteries had more lay brothers than monks. This large labour force produced increasing wealth and possessions. The greatest monument to the lay brothers is the monasteries themselves – over 700, some still in use and some in ruins – many the finest examples of mediaeval buildings, worthy to stand beside the great mediaeval cathedrals.

While the Cistercians took the Rule as their prime inspiration, it is not easy to see how the creation of lay brothers and the centralizing tendency (regular general Chapters and the primacy of the Abbot of Cîteaux) can be reconciled with this. Perhaps what we have here is a wise approach to a human situation where extreme emphasis on an ideal will simply overturn the whole project.

Decline and reform

By the time of the Reformation, which more or less wiped out the Order across Northern Europe, many monasteries had only a few monks and their future was uncertain. Observance had deteriorated and inevitably there was a reaction to this in a reform movement, at about the beginning of the seventeenth century. This eventually became known as The Strict Observance, as once again the monks set out to return to the literal interpretation of the Rule. Eventually a strong leader of this reform emerged in the person of Abbot Armand-Jean de Rancé of La Grande Trappe in France. The reform became so widespread that the monks soon became known as Trappists. The name has endured to this day and is now legally registered for a variety of products from cheese and beer to fruitcakes and candies, produced by the monasteries for their livelihood.

The two most outstanding characteristics of the Trappist Reform were total abstinence from meat, and silence. Indeed the rule of silence was so strict that it gave rise to a general belief among the public that the monks took a vow of perpetual silence, which was never the case. But the monks did not in fact talk to each other without the permission of the abbot. Instead of speaking they had a sign language which covered every eventuality and need in community life. The Trappist Reform was also characterized by strict fasting and a considerable austerity of life, such as sleeping in a common dormitory, and rising at 2 am for the first prayers of the day.

Regrouping

By the nineteenth century the Order had divided into a number of congregations, often along national lines, each with its own observance. In 1892 under the urging of Pope Leo XIII the abbots met and formed what amount to two separate Orders – the Cistercians of the Strict Observance (OCSO) and the Sacred Order of Cistercians (SOC). Both Orders included nuns as well as monks. Both branches spread into the New World and into the developing countries. At present the Cistercians of both observances number about 160 monasteries of men and 153 monasteries of women. These are major houses, alongside of which are some smaller houses which do not have the status of abbeys, and others associated with the Orders.

The twentieth century

The Order of the Strict Observance (the Trappists) was governed by constitutions published in the early part of the twentieth century. The very first article stated: 'The nature of our Order demands uniformity of observance.' No one ever explained why this was so. Nor did it seem that anyone ever asked why! As a result there was a stress on observance even in minutiae which was not invariably a contribution to either holiness or human development. As was generally the case at the time, Trappist monks did not foresee any changes ahead. It took the Vatican Council II to shake us out of this complacency, and out of the happy assumption that nothing would, or indeed should, ever change. The other events of the century, the two world wars, the anti-authority demonstrations of the 1960s, the emerging individualism of society, the shrinking world as travel became easier and more widespread, all contributed to a re-examination of where the Order stood.

Following the call of the Vatican Council, the Trappists held their Renewal Chapter in 1969. Two documents of enormous importance were published by this Chapter. One was The Declaration on the Cistercian Life, the other The Statute on Unity and Pluralism. The former set out to 'interpret for our own times the traditions which our Fathers have handed down to us ... we shall do this by recognising all that unites us in the Holy Spirit rather than by trying to impose a unity through legislation.'

All following quotations are from the 1969 Declaration on Cistercian Life.

It is now up to each community to work out the details of its own observance, within certain limits. A good example of the change is that while the former Book of Usages fixed the hour of rising, the present constitutions simply state that the first hour of the Divine Office (which we call Vigils) must be 'truly nocturnal prayer'. So the hour of rising is fixed according to the location of the monastery on the world time map. 'Individual communities can look after such details according to local needs ... so long as our wholly contemplative orientation is maintained.' 'The best laws are those which follow and interpret life, and it is therefore in the experience of the Cistercian vocation that we first of all recognise this life.'

Spirituality

Cistercian monks claim the 'Rule of Benedict as the practical interpretation of the Gospel for themselves'. They look back beyond St Benedict to the desert fathers, but more particularly to the rich tradition which they have inherited from the Cistercians of the twelfth century. 'The life of the monk is totally orientated to the experience of the living God.' How much one finds this is for himself. Liberty of spirit is essential to the monastic life and the monk must constantly remind himself that the whole of the Law is summed up in the two commandments, love of God and love of the neighbour. He lives these out 'in a community of love, where all are responsible, under a Rule and an Abbot'. The community is central to his life, and he is committed to it by a vow of stability. 'God calls and we respond by truly seeking him as we follow Christ in humility and obedience. With hearts cleansed by the Word of God, by vigils, by fasting and by an increasing conversion of life, we aim to become ever more disposed to receive from the Holy Spirit, the gift of pure and continual prayer.'

St Benedict says that the first question to be asked of anyone coming to join a monastic community (which he calls 'coming to conversion') is 'Does he truly seek God?' The monk's day is taken up with the chanting of the Divine Office, *lectio divina*, and manual work. It is in these that the 'conversion' of the monk is to be found and in his fidelity to these is his search for God.

Cistercians believe 'that the Church has entrusted a mission to us . . . to give clear witness to that heavenly home for which every person longs, and to keep alive in the human family the desire of this home . . . through the warmth of their welcome and hospitality our communities share the fruit of their contemplation and their work with others.'

Writers

The Trappists have produced a number of important writers on spirituality and the monastic life during the past century. The best known is Thomas Merton, the American monk, who wrote about fifty books and innumerable articles and letters, all of which have been published. Abbot Eugene Boylan, Andre Louf and Godfrey Belorgey have all made notable contributions to spirituality with their books. Likewise several others, men and women, are still writing for monks and laity. The two Orders have combined to form Cistercian Publications which hosts an annual congress on monastic spirituality and history in the

United States. Critical editions and translations of St Bernard and other Cistercian Fathers have been published. A number of journals are published in the Order. Finally a movement of lay associates has emerged whereby interested lay people meet in free association with an abbey, and share in the prayer and work of the monks. The past fifty years have been a time not only of renewal, but of increasing interest in and access to the Cistercian tradition.

Nivard Kinsella O CSO

Author's note

Since I am a Trappist, the main emphasis of the above is Trappist. To deal adequately with both Cistercian Orders would take me far beyond the space available in this book.

Part Six

A Glossary of Benedictine Terms

A Glossary of Benedictine Terms

Abbot/abbess goes back to the Aramaic *abba*, meaning 'father', as Jesus addressed God. Although he warned his disciples 'call no man your father on earth' (Matt. 23:9), that did not prevent the monks of the Egyptian desert from calling their elders *abba* or *amma*. The earliest monastic communities seem to have called their superior 'prior' (first), but by the time of Benedict, the leader is called abbot. The Rule, Chapter 2, first paragraph explains that the superior is called *abba* because he represents Christ, who is our father. The monastic superior must strive to engender sons and daughters through Christ for the Kingdom of God.

Cellarer comes from the Latin *cellarius* (storeroom). The qualities of the cellarer are outlined in the Rule, Chapter 31. The cellarer might be seen as the purchasing agent, or procurator, in charge of distributing the communal goods. In some circumstances this role could be likened to that of treasurer as well. Chapter 31, first paragraph highlights the role as steward, 'regarding all utensils and goods of the monastery as sacred vessels of the altar'. The gentle, humble attitude one is to employ in this role is described clearly in Chapter 31, second paragraph.

Cenobite derives from the Greek *koinos bios* (common life) and ultimately from *koinônia*, which in Acts 2:42 means shared life in Christ. When Pachomius called his extended community in southern Egypt 'the holy koinônia', he intended the full Christian implications of the term. The Rule, Chapter 2, first paragraph points to the same reality when it says that 'cenobites live in monasteries and serve under a rule and an abbot'. This is aimed at 'private monks', but in fact most monks before the time of Benedict, including anchorites, could be placed in that category.

Chapter. The Rule, Chapter 3 speaks of summoning the community for council. When all the professed members of a community are brought together, especially to vote, it is called a chapter. The purpose of such a meeting is to discern the spirit of God in whatever decision is being made. In his wisdom, St Benedict realized that God might reveal His will through any member of the community, regardless of the member's age.

Community of goods. St Benedict speaks out strongly against private ownership in the Rule, Chapter 33, and uses Acts 4:35 in Chapter 34 as a model for distributing goods according to need. All is to be held in common, but individuals should have the proper tools or supplies to do the job they are assigned to. This concept also appears in Chapters 54, 55 and 57. As with evangelical poverty, community of goods does not imply that the community as such is without possessions.

Compline comes from *completorium* (completion), the final Office of the day. According to the Rule, Chapter 42, there was public reading before this service, with the monks gradually assembling after their day of work. Chapter 18, fourth paragraph specifies that the same three psalms, namely 4, 90 and 133, are to be sung each night at Compline. These psalms were chosen because of their reference to evening, but also because they could be easily memorized and recited in the dark. The same custom prevails in Trappist monasteries today. Chapter 42 demands the strictest silence after Compline.

Congregation. Benedict often calls his community *congregatio* (con + grex = gathered flock), but nowadays this term refers to a union of monasteries as mandated by the Fourth Lateran

Council of 1215. According to that legislation, which was grudgingly implemented by the decentralized Benedictines, monasteries are to join together in regional associations for the purpose of mutual encouragement and discipline. The congregation must elect a president and council, who arrange for periodic chapter meetings and the visitation of individual monasteries. It is the general consensus of church historians that the congregational system has been helpful to the Benedictines.

Conversatio morum is one of three promises made at monastic profession (the Rule, Chapter 58, fourth paragraph). *Conversatio* literally means 'lifestyle'. Scholars have debated the meaning of this phrase for the last century, but the general consensus is that it refers to entering into monastic life and living it out as fully as possible.

Council. Although Benedict never uses this term, the Rule, Chapter 3, third paragraph does speak of calling a few elders together for advice on minor matters. Modern councils, however, do a great deal of important business in the monastery. They are elected and appointed according to precise rules, and their function is governed by church and monastic law. Yet the basic dynamics of the council are still the same as laid down by Chapter 3: the abbot convenes the council and asks for its advice, which is to be given with honesty and modesty.

Cuculla is a formal choir robe, which may be worn over the habit or other clothes at liturgical solemnities. The Latin *cuculus* (hood) originally referred to a Roman hooded outer garment or cowl. Benedict mentions it in the Rule, Chapter 55, first paragraph. In recent tradition, it is black with 72 pleats (one for each chapter of the Rule). It is also the traditional death-shroud in many Benedictine communities.

Customary. The Rule is the primary spiritual heritage of all Benedictine monasteries, but its great age makes it difficult to implement in detailed fashion. Since the early middle ages, monasteries have found it useful to draw up 'house-rules' (*consuetudines*) to be literally observed. These customaries are less abstract and easier to amend than congregational constitutions. Customaries such as those published in *Corpus Consuetudinum Monasticarum* constitute one of our most important sources for monastic history, for they tell us how monastic life was actually lived in past ages.

Dean derives from the Latin *decanus* or *decani* (plural) and refers to one who is put in charge of a group of ten. The Rule, Chapter 21 offers the dean as an assistant to the abbot/abbess, especially in larger communities. These are to be people chosen for their skills and example, not by rank. Pachomius and John Cassian spoke of deans long before Benedict. In some larger Benedictine communities today (especially women's) the concept of living in small groups or deaneries still prevails.

Dialogues of Gregory. In AD 595, Pope Gregory I (the Great) wrote four books on Italian saints, meant to hearten the beleaguered Catholics of Italy. Dialogue II is entirely given over to the life of St Benedict, Abbot of Subiaco and Monte Cassino. This account, which is full of miracles and portents, is the only written record we have of the saint. Gregory claims to have got its details from eye-witnesses, and from reading the Rule. Despite its charm and vivacity, Dialogue II has come in for increasing criticism by modern historians.

Divine Office. The Divine Office, or Liturgy of the Hours, is the principle work of Benedictines. Early Christians prayed at morning and at evening. The concept of praying at the third, sixth and ninth hours (9 am, 12 pm, 3 pm) was slowly added, and eventually there were seven hours of prayer in the cathedral tradition: Vigils, Lauds, Prime, Terce, Sext, None, and Vespers. St Benedict introduced an eighth and final hour of Compline. The Rule, Chapters 8–20 all focus on this communal prayer, and suggest an arrangement of psalms to be used, but Benedict also recognizes in Chapter 18, sixth paragraph that there might be a better arrangement of the psalms for different circumstances. Today some communities continue to pray the seven or eight hours, but many more communities have a modified format consisting of Morning Praise, Noon Prayer, Vespers and Compline.

Enclosure. From earliest monastic times (*Life of Pachomius*), parts of the house and grounds have been off-limits to visitors. Conversely, the Rule, Chapter 66 requires that all the necessities of life be contained in the same enclosure so that the monks need not go out, 'for that is certainly not beneficial to their souls'. Bishop Caesarius of Arles (*c.*535) drew up strict rules of enclosure for a convent of nuns, to protect them from the increasingly turbulent public life of the Late Roman Empire. Historically, the Church has required nuns to be more fully 'enclosed' than monks.

Fuga mundi literally means 'flight from the world' and was especially emphasized by the early hermits. In an effort to purify themselves from things of this world, these hermits largely shut out the world. This mentality carried into cenobitic monasticism for many years as well. But gradually, monks came to see that while they may be separated from the world by monastic enclosure, they can never be totally separate from the world, which must be embraced and prayed for.

General chapter. Every three or so years the president of a monastic congregation (with council) convenes a plenary meeting, which usually includes the superior of each member house, plus elected delegates. The general chapter is a decision-making body which alone can lay down the juridic constitution of the congregation. In addition to this, the general chapter deals with important questions involving the whole group as well as the individual houses.

Gregorian Chant, or plainchant, is the name given to the homophonic music that is often associated with monasteries.

Originally, these compositions were passed on aurally, but much of the music was collected, transcribed and placed in its final arrangement under the auspices of Pope St Gregory the Great (590–604). Most church music of the middle ages was written in this style, though some was lost in later years, and it fell out of use. In 1831, Dom Prosper Guéranger and the monks of Solesmes Abbey in France began a serious revival of plainchant. They clarified rules of performance, re-educated much of the monastic world in the manner of chant, and still constitute one of the world's great centres for chant. The importance of chant was reaffirmed in the 1967 Vatican II document, *Musicam Sacram*.

Habit. Monastic men and women have always worn a uniform of some kind to symbolize their status in the Church. The ancient monks did not dress too differently from their fellow citizens, since the Rule, Chapter 55, second paragraph directs that worn items be given to the poor. With the passing centuries, the monastic habit became more symbolic and less practical until in our own day it cannot be worn for many kinds of work. The great advantage of the habit is to increase the visibility and awareness of monastic values, both for the wearers and others.

Junior. After religious complete their novitiate, Canon Law decrees they must be temporarily professed for a period of at least three years. During this time they are usually referred to as junior members. Some women's houses use the term scholastic for this stage of formation.

Lectio divina. Literally 'godly reading', lectio divina meant biblical prayer for the early monks. According to the Rule, Chapter 48, lectio is to occupy about three hours of the day and usually the times when the mind would be most alert. Benedict says the monks should be 'free for' such pursuits, but to judge from Chapter 48, fifth paragraph, many of them found it burdensome. Lectio divina requires a contemplative spirit, something difficult to maintain in activist cultures. Lectio divina lies at the very heart of Benedict's spirituality, and without it there is no meaningful monastic life.

Monk derives from the Greek *monachos*, and has had several different meanings in different times. In the very early Church, monk may have referred to a religious hermit or anchorite; one who was alone (monos = one). But by the fourth century, the meaning had broadened, so that a monk might be a celibate religious, albeit living in community. While there is no exact feminine equivalent in English, nun is the closest term. Contemporary monastic writers sometimes use the term 'monastic' as an inclusive expression for monk or nun.

Novice. Before Benedict the formation of novices was intense but fairly brief; the Rule, Chapter 58 requires that it go on for a full year. Further, Benedict presents the novitiate as a well-developed institution, with a specially designated elder at its head. Throughout Benedictine history, novices were usually segregated from the rest of the community so as to inculcate monastic ideals while shielding them from some of the harsher aspects of reality. Today there is more concern to equip the novices with a spirituality that will nourish them in life as it is actually lived in the local community.

Nun. From the earliest days of desert monasticism, women have been seeking God in the same fashion as monks. Pachomius built an enclosure for women, and Paula founded a women's monastery in Bethlehem. 'Nun' has obscure Egyptian roots, but may be found in second-century Greek *nonna* and fourth-century Latin *nonna* as a term of respect, meaning elder or grandmother. The Rule, Chapter 63, second paragraph uses the male form *nonnus* in referring to the elders of the community as 'venerable father'. In strictest terms, 'nun' is a religious professing solemn vows and living within an enclosed monastery.

Obedience. From its very first lines (Prologue, first paragraph), the Rule insists that obedience is the way for sinners to return to God. For Benedict's monks, that largely means obedience to the abbot as interpreter of the Rule (Chapter 1, first paragraph). Following the Rule of the Master, Chapter 5 lays great emphasis on instant obedience as symbolic of a willing spirit. Yet Benedict goes beyond the Master in allowing a certain amount of dialogue in response to hard commands (Chapter 68). In addition, Chapters 71–72 speak of the 'mutual obedience' that cenobites owe one another, a thing that many monks find harder than 'vertical' obedience.

Oblate. People who believe that the Rule has value for them as they live out their daily lives become connected to a monastery as oblates, associates, or third order members. They may reside at the monastery (tertiary or claustral oblates), or they may live out and work away from the monastery (lay oblates). Individuals make a temporary commitment to live out the Rule as their state in life permits. The only oblation Benedict refers to is that of children presented to the monastery in Chapter 59.

Ora et labora. 'Pray and work' is often put forward as the Benedictine motto, but this word-combination is found nowhere in the Rule. Still, the two-word motto is useful as an expression of the Benedictine instinct for a balanced life that gives both the active and contemplative dimensions their proper place. If one were to base *ora et labora* loosely on Chapter 48, then it would have to be expanded to 'Pray, read and work', for Benedict's stress on lectio divina is more challenging to modern Western culture than his parallel emphasis on work.

Ordo. The Rule, Chapter 63, on community rank, states, 'The monks keep their rank in the monastery according to the date of their entry, the virtue of their lives, and the decision of the abbot.' Using this system of rank, communal members ate in order, sat in order, communicated in order, so that they never lost sight of their rank. The Rule insists that the juniors pay respect and reverence to the elders. A second usage of ordo refers to a liturgical directory of all the daily readings for mass and divine office.

Postulant is not an ancient term, but the reality is present in all the old Rules with people who first show up at the door. Invariably, they are to be tested for a few days in their resolve to endure the rigours of the monastic life (the Rule, Chapter 58, first paragraph) and then admitted to the novitiate. In our time, postulancy is more protracted but also gentler, with more stress on the discernment to be exercised by the individual as well as by the community.

Prior/prioress. One would think that prior and prioress would have parallel meanings, but this has not been the case through-out most of monastic history. In the Rule, Chapter 65, the prior is a monk appointed by the abbot to help him lead and govern the community. When Benedictine women came to the United States and formed new communities, they lost the right to be called abbeys, because they did not conform to the strict rules of enclosure enforced in Europe. Hence, the elected head of these communities is not called abbess but prioress. The second has become the first.

Profession. Benedict speaks of 'promises' in the Rule, Chapter 58, yet if a vow is an irrevocable promise made to God, then Chapter 58, fourth paragraph suggests that is what has taken place. Contemporary Benedictines actually make vows *twice*, the first time after the novitiate and in temporary form. After another period of formation (at least three years), monastics may petition the community for final profession as life-members of the community. The present-day profession ceremony still resembles that described in the fourth paragraph.

Rule of St Benedict is one of the two dozen or so monastic Rules that have come down to us from ancient times, and it is also the most famous and influential. Consisting of 73 chapters and in total length comparable to one of the gospels, the Rule was probably written for Monte Cassino in about AD 540. We have no evidence of any other monastery following this Rule before about AD 700, but when Charlemagne wished to reform and standardize the monasteries of his Empire in the early ninth century, he chose the Rule as the standard. He probably did so in order to capitalize on its Roman cachet, but subsequent monastic history has deemed it one of the best balanced and most evangelical of Christian monastic Rules.

Senior carries a multitude of meanings in the Rule. The title for one who has been a member of community and lived the monastic life for some time, and should be respected, is referred to in Chapter 63; Chapter 3, third paragraph; Chapter 21, first paragraph; Chapter 48, fifth paragraph; Chapter 58, second paragraph. It may also refer to the elderly and infirm members of the community, or to the wise *senpectae* (Chapter 27) who may be sent to help a troubled monk.

Sister. For most of their history, Benedictine women have been 'nuns', that is, enclosed religious living a contemplative life. With the coming of the Enlightenment in Europe, and especially in the pioneer Church of the United States, some Benedictine nuns were virtually forced to engage in work outside the cloister. This prompted the Vatican to deny them the right to make solemn vows, and even to use the term 'nun'. In recent years, however, the Benedictine nuns and sisters have rediscovered their common vision, calling the terminology itself into question.

Stability is the first of three promises that a Benedictine makes at profession (the Rule, Chapter 58). It is a commitment to live out life as a Benedictine within a particular monastery. This is both a spiritual and geographical commitment, calling the monk to continue the daily living of monastic life (Prologue, eighth paragraph). This promise is very different from the lifestyle of a wandering monk of Benedict's day, or that of many contemporary religious congregations, where a person may be assigned to any number of religious houses throughout their lifetime.

Stability is the 'till death do us part' aspect of monastic profession.

Statio. This traditional term meaning 'order' is not found as such in the Rule, but in Chapter 63 Benedict creates a hierarchical community based largely on date of entry. He stresses that this order, which has nothing to do with age or parentage, is to be maintained in daily life. Thus monks are to observe statio during the liturgy, giving the kiss of peace and receiving communion in seniority. Modern Benedictines tend to place less importance on statio, although the term is still used to refer to the order of processing into choir.

Suscipe. *Suscipe me domine* is the Latin translation of Psalm 119:116, 'Uphold me according to your promise, that I may live, and let me not be put to shame in my hope.' After a monk reads and signs his or her monastic profession formula, this versicle is repeated three times, by the individual making final vows, and the community echoes back in response. The procedure is described in the Rule, Chapter 58, fourth paragraph.

Table reading. The Rule, Chapter 38 is entirely devoted to table reading, a practice found in most monasteries throughout history. Table reading originally seems to have been an extension of the liturgy of the word at Mass, centred on the Bible. In the Rule of the Master, the brothers are encouraged to ask questions about the reading, and the abbot discourses freely on it. In contrast, Benedict wants general silence and laconic remarks at most from the abbot. Modern table reading often goes beyond Scripture to secular works of interest to the community.

Vespers. This term for evening prayer derives from the Latin, *vespertina synaxis*. Morning prayer and vespers are the two hours of prayer most commonly prayed within Benedictine houses as well as the broader Church. In the cathedral style of Office, vespers used psalms with night images, but Benedict had another approach. He assigned the psalms in consecutive order, disregarding their content. The Rule, Chapter 18, fourth paragraph suggests the use of Psalms 109–47 at this time of prayer. The proposed structure for vespers is given in Chapter 17, third paragraph, consisting of four psalms, a lesson, response, hymn, Magnificat, and a litany.

Visitation. Since Benedictine monasteries are largely autonomous, some form of outside reference seems necessary to prevent them from becoming decadent or myopic. The congregational system mandated by Lateran IV (1215) includes periodic inspection of monasteries by designated outside monastic observers to check on the quality of monastic life. Modern visitations include oversight of local finances. Special visitations are sometimes called for monasteries that find themselves in serious difficulties.

Vows. While the evangelical counsels of poverty, chastity and obedience are implied in monastic profession, in the Rule, Chapter 58, fourth paragraph the monk actually promises stability, *conversatio morum* and obedience. Benedict uses 'promise', but the word most now commonly associated with profession is 'vow'. Currently American Benedictine women are re-examining the complex etymology of 'promise' and 'vow' to determine which will be used in their future.

Compiled by Jill Maria Murdy and Terrence Kardong OSB